The Ant's Gift

Middle East Literature in Translation

Michael Beard and Adnan Haydar, *Series Editors*

Select Titles in Middle East Literature in Translation

The Book of Disappearance: A Novel
Ibtisam Azem; Sinan Antoon, trans.

A Cloudy Day on the Western Shore
Mohamed Mansi Qandil; Barbara Romaine, trans.

Gaia, Queen of Ants
Hamid Ismailov; Shelley Fairweather-Vega, trans.

In the Alley of the Friend: On the Poetry of Hafez
Shahrokh Meskoob; M. R. Ghanoonparvar, trans.

Jerusalem Stands Alone
Mahmoud Shukair; Nicole Fares, trans.

The Slave Yards: A Novel
Najwa Bin Shatwan; Nancy Roberts, trans.

Tenants and Cobwebs
Samir Naqqash; Sadok Masliyah, trans.

Turkey, Egypt, and Syria: A Travelogue
Shiblī Nu'mānī; Gregory Maxwell Bruce, trans.

For a full list of titles in this series, visit https://press.syr.edu/supressbook-series/middle-east-literature-in-translation/.

The Ant's Gift

A STUDY OF THE Shahnameh

Shahrokh Meskoob

Translated from the Persian by Dick Davis

Syracuse University Press

Translation of "Armaghan-e Mur: Jostari dar Shahnameh" (Tehran, 1384/2005, 275 pages, unpublished) from Persian to English sponsored by the Persian Heritage Foundation.

Syracuse, New York 13244-5290

First Edition 2021

21 22 23 24 25 26   6 5 4 3 2 1

∞ The paper used in this publication meets the minimum requirements of the American National Standard for Information Sciences—Permanence of Paper for Printed Library Materials, ANSI Z39.48-1992.

For a listing of books published and distributed by Syracuse University Press, visit https://press.syr.edu.

ISBN: 978-0-8156-3701-1 (hardcover) 978-0-8156-3708-0 (paperback)
978-0-8156-5510-7 (e-book)

Library of Congress Cataloging-in-Publication Data

Names: Miskūb, Shāhrukh, author. | Davis, Dick, translator.

Title: The ant's gift : a study of the Shahnameh / Shahrokh Meskoob ; translated from the Persian by Dick Davis.

Other titles: Armaghān-i mūr. English

Description: Syracuse : Syracuse University Press, 2021. | Series: Middle East literature in translation | Summary: ""The Ant's Gift" is a study of the major themes of the Shahnameh (the national epic of Iran completed in 1010 by the poet Ferdowsi)"— Provided by publisher.

Identifiers: LCCN 2020037535 (print) | LCCN 2020037536 (ebook) | ISBN 9780815637011 (hardcover) | ISBN 9780815637080 (paperback) | ISBN 9780815655107 (ebook)

Subjects: LCSH: Firdawsī. Shāhnāmah.

Classification: LCC PK6458 .M58213 2020 (print) | LCC PK6458 (ebook) | DDC 891/.5511—dc23

LC record available at https://lccn.loc.gov/2020037535

LC ebook record available at https://lccn.loc.gov/2020037536

Manufactured in the United States of America

Contents

Preface to Persian Text

HASAN KAMSHAD

SHAHROKH MESKOOB died on Tuesday 23rd of Farvardin (12th of April, 2005) in a hospital in Paris, and was buried the following week in the Behesht Zahra cemetery, in the area reserved for artists. When I reached him on his deathbed his first words were about this book, and he asked me to reread the manuscript and correct any errors.

More than any of his other works, writing this book, with its unadorned and incomparable language, wore Shahrokh out and exhausted his soul. He revised and rewrote its chapters in his effort to have "his language do justice to its subject"; his pen moved with difficulty and his thoughts came confusedly and thick and fast. He had loved Ferdowsi and the Shahnameh all his life; this was his farewell to both of them, and he didn't want his last words to be spoken carelessly. He considered speech to be "the life-giving elixir, the antidote to death." May this book be a fitting and lasting memorial to him.

Any faults or printing errors in this book are clearly my responsibility.

Ordibehesht 1384 (April–May 2005).

Translator's Note

DICK DAVIS

AS HASAN KAMSHAD, the editor of the Persian text of *The Ant's Gift*, has noted, this was Shahrokh Meskoob's last book, and he was still working on it at the time of his death. Had he been able to give the book a final revision Meskoob would certainly have corrected the few small slips that were still present in the text as he left it. I have silently corrected a very small number of obvious and trivial factual errors within the text; more ambiguous statements (for example that Jamshid is the first man in Iranian mythology, something that is not confirmed by the Shahnameh itself) I have left as Meskoob wrote them since he may have meant them in a way that he would have explained had he had time to give the text a final revision.

The reader should be aware that by "we" and "our" Meskoob is of course referring to Iranians and Iranian culture specifically, and not to any potentially more international audience, even though the reader may well feel that such remarks are frequently valid beyond the specifics of Iran and its literary and cultural history.

In the opening chapters of this book the names Hormozd and Ahura Mazda refer to the same mythological entity. In the book's last chapter Hormozd is usually used in the same mythological sense, but a few uses of the name refer to the historical king Hormozd IV (ruled 531–579); the context indicates which usage is correct.

Author's Introduction

THE ANT'S GIFT is an inquiry into a few of the concepts essential to the Shahnameh, divided into five chapters: Time, Creation, History, Sovereignty, and Speech.

Time is first and last, it is the bringer and bearer away of things and the hidden thread which links these chapters together. In some mythologies time existed even before Creation, and in others it is the first thing to be created.

History is the story of man's past in time.

Sovereignty is the management of the wheel of time in the world, according to the way of heaven.

And finally Speech is the means by which the poet is able to escape from the destructive trap of time, the way in which he dies without dying. Why is it that Ferdowsi says that after death "I shall not die, since I am alive"?

The Shahnameh is a historical work that is both an account of Iran's history in the world, and has itself been, from its first appearance, a strong pillar in the history of the Iranian people. Above and beyond this, the Shahnameh is a work that arises from history and is a product of tradition, one that as well as giving us insight into the preconceptions and religious and intellectual beliefs of its creator contains the source of many narratives from the distant past; for example:

The mythology and worldview of the Avesta.

The practical and ethical wisdom of the Pahlavi "Mirror for Princes" genre.

Royal chronicles, the political and social culture of the Sasanids.

The written and oral culture of the population of Khorasan during the first centuries of the Islamic era.

It organized and preserved whatever had come down to the population of Khorasan by either oral or written means, whether consciously or as often as not unconsciously, such as man's knowledge, his conception of this world and of the world to come, ethics and behavior, national sentiment, worldview, and—in a word—their social memory. What reached Ferdowsi were not simply Zurvanite and Mithraic ideas, or Zoroastrian and Mazdean didactic notions, and so on, but through the maker's arrangement—and sometimes lack of arrangement—it was all of these; that is, the accumulated social memory of an invisible past, and in another way of its religious and cultural beliefs, its customs and social norms.

For this reason I have tried to present the book as a historical work, but one to be read and studied on its own terms. It is not enough simply to dig into history and get to know it in order to understand and appreciate the Shahnameh. This book is more a poetic work than a historical one, and it's not the task of poetry to gather together knowledge of past generations; leaving aside a specific perspective and knowledge, information "whether conscious or unconscious" available to different generations will lead to different kinds of discovery and appreciation. For example, the social memory of a traditional society, in both its observed and unobserved aspects, passes from generation to generation, until it one day reaches particularly auspicious soil from which it causes a massive shady tree to grow, or it reaches a brackish marsh in which it abandons us to our own mirage. A tradition lives in searching to surpass itself, to leave itself behind; this is like the relationship between a river and its source—if it doesn't flow onward it becomes standing water. A dead tradition either mourns continuously over the corpse of what has gone, or it involuntarily and mechanically repeats the customs of the past.

A society's collective memory is, unconsciously, its history, a history that exists but is unaware of its own existence as history, and studying it is like researching and coming to know a man's unconscious soul, and as a result changing what was unconscious into something conscious by uncovering what was hidden. Digging into and coming to know a collective memory is also a process of awakening sleeping layers of the past, and bringing their richness into historical consciousness. If we imagine tradition as a mountain whose crags have risen up from the heart of the land and whose summit reaches to the heavens, Ferdowsi is in the heavens standing astride the mountain, on a rocky ridge. He shows the observer standing next to him the vast and varied view of the cultural regions before them; this resembles the moment when we stand on the top of Mount Damavand, like the sun shining over the world, and see beneath our feet to the south and north the dry plain of the Dasht-e Kavir and the green Caspian Sea. Ferdowsi is the highest mountain and Hafez—who developed to its utmost the art of lyric poetry—is the most beautiful garden in our world.

The history of the genesis and assembly of the Shahnameh, its previous sources and its subsequent fate, has until now, whether at a scientific or popular level, been studied mainly in terms of literary history, the investigation of manuscripts, and similar concerns. It is true that researches of a literary-historical nature, and the labors of respected scholars who have worked in this field, are the first condition for any knowledge of the national epic of Iran and its composition, and very useful scholarly research has been carried out along these lines. But above and beyond this, like every great work of art the Shahnameh is not a work that can be interpreted in only one way, and depending on the perspective and mindset of the observer it has different clear and also hidden aspects to it. The work of a poet like Ferdowsi is the creation of a new manifestation, a new perspective and aesthetic, the discovery of what is undiscovered; not, for example, the repetitive versification of a royal chronicle, forgotten myths, stories mixed up with legends, and bits of history. In one way his work is the "discovery" of inward, unconscious meanings within the history of mankind and the world, and in another it is the reflection of these meanings in language that is a mirror of untarnished beauty. And this role of the poet cannot be achieved solely with the help of "conscious" knowledge; if it could be, scholars would be poets. It is rather the poet's "unconscious" that leads this work to its auspicious end.

This is not to say that a poet depends on ignorance and a lack of awareness, it is rather the cognizance of unknown things, of things that cannot be known; of what works within us and forms us without our knowing it; of the importance and validity of the action of things that are unknown. For example, we see certain mythological motifs and cultural meanings in the Shahnameh which a thousand years ago were unknown to Ferdowsi, and which, influenced by archeological discoveries, by imaginative suppositions, by historical and etymological and mythological investigations and so on . . . have been brought to light and acknowledged. We can instance one or two examples of this: the relationship between the myth of Jamshid and the tradition of Now Ruz and its unknown sources, that is, the Zurvanite and Mazdean image of time in Ferdowsi's thought; similarly, the concept of an ethical viewpoint, and of acting in an ethical manner, or of an epic elevation of the material above and beyond the business of the visible world, whose origin and roots must probably be sought in Mazdean ontology and the existence of Ahriman and Ahura Mazda; these are things which the poet himself could not have known. Another case in point is the source of the concept of kingship, "political philosophy," and the notion of the exercise of justice, as it appears in the Shahnameh.

And so we are here dealing with two kinds of "ignorance," history's lack of awareness and the poet's lack of awareness; and there is another lack of awareness to add to these, which is the ignorance of the present writer. One of literary criticism's concerns is to account for these unknown things, to bring the unknown to light. *The Ant's Gift* is an endeavor, an attempt, to contribute to this project, insofar as the present writer's lack of qualifications for such a task will allow. During this search, in order to describe the underlying conceptions and concerns, at various points and in each case appropriately, Zurvanite and Mazdean mythology, the ancient and more recent recensions of the Avesta and Sasanian literature, or the Islamic beliefs of Ferdowsi's own time have been taken into consideration. But here the motive is not scientific research into the cultural knowledge of an interior mental state, or the given facts and reality of the outer world; rather it is an attempt to discover more about the worldview implicit in the Shahnameh, from its stories, narratives, and conversations—a search undertaken in the hope of a new apprehension of its truth.

But truth is linked to and involved with the realities of time and place. No truth exists inalterably, or outside of time and place (as has already been mentioned). Art too, like truth, exists in relation to a perceptible time and place, and the reason for this "relationship" is ahistorical; traces that remain from a given time outlast that time and in each subsequent historical era they acquire a new meaning (but they do not transcend time, firstly since they are originally products of time, and secondly, as we have said, since we have situated them "in relation to each historical era"). The aim of this endeavor is more that we see today—in this time and place in which we find ourselves—what can be gathered from the Shahnameh. *The Ant's Gift* is mainly an attempt to use the advantages of what is now known in order to find the "unknowns" of that time, and to look into the poet's unconscious, in the belief that this viewpoint will allow us to see the existence of the poem and the poet in a fresh light. The discussion is concerned with what we as modern-day readers can understand from the work of a poet from the past. In addition to the scientific researches of scholars of history and literature in order to understand the poem and its poet and his conscious knowledge, how can we salvage the testimony of his heart and his inner vision, "that which cannot be discovered"? How can his unconscious be our consciousness?

Until now the Shahnameh has been considered and studied mainly as a literary, historical, and national masterpiece, and also as a treasury of wisdom and prudent advice. Perhaps it is now time that, along with the success of these numerous and very valuable achievements, the Shahnameh should be considered in the way that Ferdowsi himself thought of "history," or for example in the way that Sohravardi considered the theory of sovereignty, or Hedayat considered Khayyam, and in his "Kafka's Message" our own times. Instructive examples of this kind (especially in the way Western scholars have reflected on their own literature) are not rare. But to think in this way requires bravery, not in the sense of fearlessness, of being negligent or ignorant of fear, but in the sense of conquering fear, of experiencing it and then emerging from its grip.

Leaving aside a small number of literate readers, for most former generations, the "readers" of the Shahnameh were an audience who listened to it, and the work was transmitted to them through intermediaries like oral storytellers or other performers, along with the knowledge and perspective appropriate to that particular time; they "read" through their ears. But these days if a reader wishes to study a text like this he can do so without any intermediary, and according to his own capacity and ideas he can use fresh methods, knowledge, and perspectives as a man arranges and rearranges pieces on a chessboard, and each time he will arrive at new meanings. New combinations of elements create new patterns of meaning, as a painter does when he applies various different colors to a painting's canvas. *The Ant's Gift* is one of these "patterns," a kind of reinterpretation of elements towards a rereading of the book, on the part of a well-meaning reader. What you see here is an interpretation and paraphrase of the Shahnameh according to two categories, what is consciously known, and what is not consciously known, as follows:

An explanation of the concept of "time," or for example the notion of the passage of history, the theory of sovereignty, fate and man's role, and similar matters, as Ferdowsi thought of them; an account of the poet's consciousness as it appears in the Shahnameh.

An inquiry into the hidden sources of these concepts and notions, which flowed like an unseen river in society's collective unconscious and in the poet's mind, about which the period's knowledge had no information, and of which the poet was thus unaware.

An inquiry into the return to the "first causes" and their unconscious transmission by the poet in the Shahnameh.

A sketch of the interpretation and transmission of the Shahnameh as presented in this inquiry, the poem's attention to "first causes," to the beginning of time, and its return to the end, "the negation of time," time as the destroyer. In Ferdowsi's thought, how can one escape from this trap? What is the nature of speech, the elixir against death, and balm for the pain of nothingness?

The idea of writing *The Ant's Gift*, and presenting it as an offering to the great poet of Tus, was conceived in my mind some years ago. My most recent complete rereading of the Shahnameh with a view to this end began—I am unsure why, as it was contrary to my usual way of going about things—with the seventh volume of the Moscow printing of the Shahnameh, with the reign of Eskandar, the Ashkanians, and then the story of Ardeshir. Looking back on that time now, I think the reason for this may have been the particular attention I paid, during the first years after the Islamic Revolution, to Ferdowsi's conceptions of sovereignty and politics. This rereading, what with writing down comments, filling up index cards, and making footnotes, took me over a year until I got to the end of volume six and the Kayanid dynasty, so that by Aban of 1366 (November 1987) I had finally read the whole work through. After this I was involved with other tasks for a while, though I was constantly thinking about the Shahnameh, until in the summer of 1380 (2001) I began writing this study. While I was working on it, in May 2002, at the suggestion of my good friend Ms. Sorur Kasmai, a private class was organized in order to study the Shahnameh, meeting once a fortnight, with each session lasting for two hours; eight friends took part at first, four of whom stayed until the end, which was in July 2004. The classes consisted of "written lessons," which were discussions of the chapters of this book recorded on tape. By relevant comparisons between different interpretations of the nature of truth and also of versions of reality in our culture and Western culture, the scope of our conversations widened to include references to Western literature.

Three chapters of *The Ant's Gift* have previously been published in *Iran Nameh* 20, No. 1 (Winter 2002); 20, No. 4 (Fall 2002); 21, No. 3 (Fall 2003); since these chapters now include additions and revisions inserted during two separate printings, they are now in a more complete form. After reading two chapters of the book, my good friend Jalil Dustkhah made a number of useful suggestions, most of which I have adopted. References to the edition of the Shahnameh edited by Djalal Khaleghi-Motlagh are indicated by V, for volume, followed by the page number (for example V1:12, meaning volume one, page twelve). For references to sections of the poem that have not yet been printed in this edition, I have used B, for book, followed by the page number, referring to the Moscow edition.

15 December 2004

The Ant's Gift

Time

I SHALL BEGIN with Now-Ruz, which Jamshid established and in so doing placed "time" on a new footing. In the Shahnameh Jamshid is the greatest of kings, and in mythology he is the first man.[1] Feraydun and Kay Khosrow are two kings who both cleanse the world of Ahriman's evil (embodied in Zahhak and Afrasyab) and bring about a rebirth, but Jamshid does neither of these things; rather he is the founding monarch, who with the help of "Clear Mind" (*rowshan ravan*), with the understanding and knowledge that is within him, confers order and a "civilized" stability on the savagery of man's life: for fifty years he draws iron forth from stone, and from this fashions weapons and armor such as cuirasses, shields, swords, and so forth; for another fifty years he develops the arts of spinning, weaving, the cutting of clothes, sewing, and laundering. Then for fifty years he establishes the occupations of priests, warriors, farmers, and craftsmen, and in this way social structures are formed. Then he sets demons to building walls, and raising towers and ramparts, houses and refuges; he discovers jewels and precious stones and fine scents; he reveals the secrets of medicine, boatbuilding, and voyaging by sea; he rises into the heavens on the backs of demons, and shines down from that height "like a sun glittering in the air." During his reign, no one was aware of pain or suffering, or of death. He was the lord of men and demons and of all the world. Then, "he saw no one but himself in the world" and he claimed godlike status, so that the divine *farr* fell away from him, and was transferred to Feraydun and Garshasp.[2] His greatness is indicated by the fact that he alone included in himself the achievements of the three great categories of myth and epic—the priesthood, warriors, and farmers and craftsmen.

In order to convey the greatness of the acts carried out by this king "whose face was as a houri's, a shining sun to behold" (Vendidad, Fargard 2) we must look in the Shahnameh and listen to Ferdowsi's words. Here I am simply making an inventory in order to describe this man who ruled over the earth and the heavens, men and supernatural beings, and who also by his decree brought "time" into being. The day on which, with the help of demons, he reached into the skies was the first day of spring, the dawn of earth's awakening, and the balancing of night and day. Jamshid celebrated this day of victory and we know that from a mythological point of view such a "celebration" is not simply a manifestation in itself, but also a symbol of the repetition of time, a returning to a former state, a renewal of the seasons within nature, and a regeneration of life. Jamshid named this day "the beginning of the new year, on the day of Hormozd, in the month of Farvardin." Time was now numbered and subject to measurement; days were considered units of time, having their own "identity and character," taking their place within the months. Years were marked by a beginning and an end, and escaped from the endless round of indistinct anonymity.

In this fashion, at the behest of Jamshid of the Clear Mind, the new perception of day—and of night which was created in conjunction with it—was no longer that of an empty shell of light or darkness. This is how day and night were named, how they came into being and were known, and so were necessarily named. Man's daily experience of life gave this eternal revolution content and meaning; worldly and infinite time were measured by us, who live our lives out in the world, and so time became "human" and finite; in other words, this entire concept, since it became involved with the passage of our brief life and with the nature of our destiny, took on the meaning of "fate" (or "fortune"). Although "time" and "fate" appear to be synonymous, "fate," rather than "time," implies the sadness and happiness, the successes and failures, of our life's unfolding.

> Fate is time, if you examine it / and no one has the means to judge it
>
> SHAHNAMEH B9:311

Hafez says: "Fate's broken promise gives me no time," and also, "Fate's faithlessness, the grief it brings, its deceit" are what troubles him; as others have done, he complains of the deeds, the tyranny, and the indiscriminateness of Fate's faithless cruelty. Seen in this way, Jamshid brought the indifferent, impalpable revolutions of worldly time down to earth, so that Fate became the warp and weft of our existence, the existential truth of we who live on the earth. We could evaluate our own life against that continual passing which has no beginning and no end, so that we would know not only the days of our arrival and departure, but in comprehending the past we could also become acquainted with the future, and with that which transcends all things, that is, eternity.

Jamshid of the Clear Mind, the sun-king and, as his name (Yima Khshaeta) indicates, the splendid and shining one, "set forth a new plan" for the beings of this world in this new time with its new ways. He is the first exemplar and paradigm of Man the Creator, one who recognizes no limits, and when he looks at his creative wisdom and skill he thinks that he himself is the World-Creator. He loses his God-given glory and becomes a homeless wanderer for many years. Finally this sun-king, like the sun setting in the ocean, hides away in the depths of the China Sea, but—like the sun rising out of the sea—he is dragged out of the water and cut in two with a saw.

In the Avesta, Jamshid's downfall comes about because of "the lie," his rising in revolt against the ways of the world and its Creator. But in the Shahnameh, Jamshid is defeated because of his pride, and it is this that brings about his end. In our mythology "Az" (Greed) is an insatiable demon that devours and destroys everything, including, in the end, itself. In the world of the Shahnameh, whose roots derive in part from a much older system of thought, the desire for more and the ambition to rise above others that is felt by those in the grip of Az, destroy their wisdom, to the point that no act or possession can ever satisfy them. Jamshid is the first of those in the grip of Az; he says to the priests, the sages, and the wise men,

> I have made the world splendid with my virtue,
> The earth is as I would wish it to be
> Your food, sleep, and rest derive from me
> So too clothes, and your well-being, are from me
> Greatness, the crown, and kingship are mine,
> Who says there is any other king than me?
>
> V1:45

> Jam rose up in the path of Ahriman and demons, and said, "I created water, I created the moon, I created the land, I created plants, I created the sun, I created the stars and I created the heavens, I created the beasts, I created mankind, I created all things that have been created." He spoke the lie, affirming this (belief) that he had created (the material world).[3]

But how can this belief be overcome? In creating thought and the concept of creation, Jamshid's "Clear Mind" is tantamount to the human equivalent of God. And if creation is not perceived and recognized, what is the world other than a body without a soul? If we take the insistent repetition of "I" into account we can think that here is the first man, or greatest king, to reflect on his own nature and being—and finally on thought itself—as the creator of things, or who considered thinking as the origin of what it is to be human. Without such awareness the two human concepts of "being and nothingness" cannot be distinguished from one another and neither can be recognized. In the same way, in the Avesta (as we shall see) the creation of "life" cannot happen without the help of human qualities. And Jamshid is the greatest recipient of divine glory, the king who is the "maker" of a world that, if it were not fashioned according to our wishes, would not be a place of gratification and comfort so much as a confused chaos of unbridled nature.

In the Vendidad (Fargard 11) Zoroaster asks Ahura Mazda, "Who was the first human with whom you conversed? Which person was it to whom you first revealed the faith of Ahura and Zoroaster?" And Ahura Mazda replies,

> Jam, whose face was as the sun, possessor of fine flocks, was the first of men before you . . . with whom I conversed, and at that time I revealed the faith of Ahura and Zoroaster to him . . . then I who am Ahura Mazda said to him, "May you be the knower and preserver of my faith (in the world)," and then Jam whose face was as the sun replied, "I was not born and raised that I should be the knower and preserver of your faith (in the world)."

Since Jamshid did not agree to be an observer and promulgator of religion—because this was not within his nature or knowledge—Ahura Mazda said, "Then make my world abundant, make my world grow great, be the protector (of the world's inhabitants), their leader and watchman."[4] Jamshid agreed to this, and Ahura Mazda gave him the gold-inlaid symbols of sovereignty, and Jamshid became the ruler of the world,[5] and Ahura Mazda taught him how to augment the earth's crops and increase its herds and make the world flourish.

In this way, in faith and tradition, for a long time before the appearance of the Shahnameh, Jamshid was the first man who conversed with God, and through the wisdom of his innovative leadership the world, as the Shahnameh explains, became fruitful. And this is the origin of awareness, since on the one hand awareness takes shape through language, and on the other in this shared language each person becomes aware of the existence of others—and as a result of this he becomes aware of his own existence, because as long as there is no mental concept of "the other" or "not oneself" we can also know nothing of ourselves, even at those moments in which we look at our image in a mirror.

In this exchange Ahura Mazda offers Jamshid divine and celestial awareness (religion), so that he may disseminate it throughout the world, but Jamshid does not accept the responsibility. And the acceptance or rejection of something—not because impelled to do so by instinct, but due to his will and determination—is that within him which makes him aware of himself. And it's only in man that this results not only in a search for the knowledge of God but in investigating further into this state of "not knowing," as far as that perilous place of absence and nothingness, and so hurrying forward to the invisible world of "blasphemy," the place where God is not, and, unavoidably, one is God oneself. In this unknown nowhere, death is the lord of life, and every Jamshid in thinking that he himself is God comes face to face with his own fate: that he is a man, and mortal.

In another sense, when Jamshid refuses God's suggestion he disobeys time's Creator, and the punishment for this stubbornness is, inevitably, that he is forced towards "No-Time"; that is, to the realm of death, and it is because he is mortal that he is aware of life. In Iranian mythology two other examples of the first man can be found: Kayumars (Gayomard) and "Mashi and Mashyaneh." The name Kayumars (Kay = Giah = "living," mars = martan = mira = "mortal") as a whole means "a living being that is mortal." As for the pair Mashi and Mashyaneh, "each of them at first thought that he was (the first) human."[6] Man is the being that is aware of death; the knowledge of death is a part of his essence. In a situation where death did not exist, what concept could there be of not-dying, and how could an immortal being know what it is to be alive? But if there is God, and Jamshid is "not-God" and in him death exists, as God's interlocutor he is another source of the awareness of life. Given this state of affairs, perhaps this is why Ahura Mazda wanted him to devote himself to the flourishing of living beings and his land. And so since Jamshid is the first interlocutor with God and the first who is disobedient to Him, his too is the first awareness and existence that acts according to its own desires, and because of this, whether it be spoken or unspoken, he is also the first man; and "to be a man" is the perception of time that flows in us and bears us away; it is the presence of death in life.[7]

Man is the creator of the world of which he is aware and whose appearances he discovers, sees, and recognizes (not of the world as such, in itself, which lies beyond our knowledge). Without awareness, this world of "appearances" cannot be perceived. Awareness is a necessity of its existence. And this awareness of time recreates the knowledge of night and day, as well as the connection between the turning of the seasons and the passage of our lives with the earth—or better to say with our "fate"—and brings into existence the world's activities. It is the presence of death that precipitously drives man to live. Seen in this way, Jamshid is not only the originator of Now-Ruz and the orderliness of time, but in his role as the first man to be self-aware he is the origin and founder of the world of mankind; in him death is the source of being, and the first glimmer of dawn.

In the world of religious thought, apart from man God is the only possessor of awareness. Man who has been created in the "image" of God, and who receives his soul from His breath, is in the world without awareness, as the agent of his creator. And so this being who is aware in an unknown world sees "this potter who fashioned the world" as a foolish man does, or like Khayyam he asks God the why and wherefore of His claim to be the lord of the business of creation, or like Mowlana drives himself with selfless haste to fly upwards in order to be one with that "Soul of souls." In the midst of all this there are those who like Ferdowsi turn "to left and right," in every direction, but can find "neither head nor tail in (the affairs of) the world." In all these states—and in religion and mysticism and philosophy—man strives to discover the nature of the relationship between God and his own divine essence, and in this way to find his place in the two worlds.

Long before all this Jamshid too searched for his divine essence, and thought it was God. In Iranian mythology the divine essences were the highest celestial power of the pure and noble; they exist in paradise with Ahura Mazda before the birth of every person, and after his death they return to their place there; they take no part in a man's evil deeds, and in the worldwide battle against evil they are, by their own choice and volition, the allies and associates of Ahura Mazda. Of their many and various attributes, pertaining to both worlds, I refer here only to the eternal nature of the essences, and how they are the originator of "time." Ahura Mazda says to Zoroaster that it is from the "glory and splendor" of the powerful essences of the just and good that "I sustain the heavens and preserve the wide earth's magnificence":

> It is from their glory and splendor that the waters bubble forth
> from their sources forever . . .
> It is from their glory and splendor that the sun follows its
> course
> It is from their glory and splendor that the moon follows its
> course
> It is from their glory and splendor that the stars follow their
> courses[8]

If we understand that the succession of night and day and the moon and the sun has inevitably comes from the turning of the moon and sun and the passage of the stars and the movements of the heavens, then the "coming into existence" of time from the glory and splendor of the essences of good souls from mankind—as in the case of Jamshid who made the earth flourish and the beasts multiply—happens with the aid of Ahura Mazda. And of course the creator of time is none other than Ahura Mazda. But this "time" is motionless and remains within itself, and it is the cooperation of the victorious essences with Ahura Mazda that bestows life and movement on this and the rest of creation. And so without mankind (the essences of the good souls) the heavens will not turn, and nor will time, just as we have seen that it is Jamshid's association with Ahura Mazda that makes the earth flourish and be fruitful. But the sense of time and its conception depend on awareness, mankind's awareness as manifested in his culture. From the blessings of culture (i.e., knowledge and wisdom) mankind gains control of the world into which he has fallen, he gives his existence to this environment, he delivers the "microcosm" from its wandering in the "macrocosm" and in the same way that he gives meaning to existence he remakes himself. All this is his "awareness," and if Jamshid in the Shahnameh "discovers" time this is because he is a king who knows culture and in consequence possesses awareness. If awareness, as it is in humankind, did not exist, time too would not exist.[9]

In short, Jamshid is one of the most important of mythological figures, in that this man—in his acts of creation—is so linked and involved with God that it's as if the difference between the two were no more than a hair's breadth. And so it is no surprise that this king of the earth and time, and the most powerful of men, should be deceived by his own achievements and that he should imagine he is God; or that a demon should appear within "high-flying" self-indulgent Kavus in his search for the secret of time, and deceive him:

The face of the earth is as you would wish,
    You are the shepherd and the nobles are as your flock
One task remains, so that in the world
    The memory of you will never be hidden
The sun hides a secret from you,
    How does it travel over all vicissitudes?
Of what nature is the moon, what are night and day?
    Who is the ruler of the revolving heavens?

V2:95

Even though man is linked with something higher, and with an unknown that is yet further off, and flies toward a self beyond himself, he is not God, and the difference between these two has been eternal from the moment of creation; God is deathless and beyond time, and man is mortal and within time, and we know that our lot is to last for the space of no more than a few days. Jamshid's "space" turned out to be that he boasted of godhead, and believed that he had escaped from the snare of time; God and man set him at liberty, and for a hundred years he wandered in secret over land and sea, fleeing from his own "time," until the day he was captured and suffered the most terrible of deaths; his body cut in two with a saw.

Jamshid's reign was brought to its disastrous end by Zahhak, whose thousand years of injustice were ended by the great Feraydun. He assumed the throne on "the auspicious first day of the month of Mehr," in a time "without sorrow caused by evil," at the beginning of a new season, when the world was renewed by justice. The Shahnameh says that the month of Mehr commemorates him, and that the Festival of Mehregan was instigated by him.

Just as Jamshid celebrated the spring equinox with the festival of Now-Ruz, so Feraydun established the festival of Mehregan to celebrate the autumn equinox; each of them did this at a moment when day and night are equal—as two pans of equal weight on the scales of time—one in the glimmer of nature's dawn, the other as she moves towards sunset and sleep. In this way, Feraydun is the second great king of the Shahnameh whose instigating hand brought order to the passage of time. This is so not only because, contrary to Zahhak, in the five hundred years of his reign "not on a single day did he commit evil," so that the passage of time took on a new quality, but more because he made the beginning-time of Jamshid's reign "historical," and set it on a new path.

Like Jamshid, Feraydun is king of the world, and we know that he divided his realm among his sons Iraj, Salm, and Tur, as a result of which the three countries of Iran, Rum (the west), and Turan developed three separate histories. And so history now requires geography. For men to become the protagonists of history they must first possess their own place, within which alliances can live together and with one another, so that this shared life is their history. Even the wanderers of the desert, for as long as they have no land within which they can "wander," cannot take on the appearance of a tribe with its own history and identity.

At Feraydun's instigation—for good or bad—Iranians became separated from the inhabitants of Rum and Turan, and our epic history began. For we Iranians, from then on, time passing took on a new dimension. The concept of "Iran," as referring to a place where for a long time people had spent their lives cheek by jowl with one another, and so shared cultural likes and dislikes, and whose destinies were interwoven together, came into existence. With the appearance of history, an area is not simply a collection of various particular geographical features—its mountains and knolls, its plains and foothills, its deserts and wildernesses or rivers and forests; the land is not simply earth, it is the destiny and dwelling place of a people who are called Iranians, or the people of Rum, or of Turan. Peoples who are distinct from others have their own identity, the means by which they are known.

If it is true that man is a social animal, an individual comes to know himself through his relationship with the other. The other is my mirror, and it is because of his existence that I become aware of myself, and it is the blessing of this connection that gives my existence meaning. "The social animal" inevitably lives in one place (society), and it is there that his time is spent. For us that "place" is Iran, and that "time" is the history of Iran.

After centuries have gone by it is natural that there should arise a kind of bond made up of language, beliefs, and customs, a kind of harmony of activity, behavior, and views of the nature of both this life and the life to come. When countries are established it is only the geography that does not change; by setting out on the road of history, time, and existence, each individual finds himself involved with the time of others and in this way the conditions of society and cooperation come into being. It was Feraydun who, by establishing countries, history, and time—and, in a sense, destiny—united the people of each tribe and nation. Leaving aside theoretical and debatable differences concerning the motherland, nation and nationality, and their antecedent histories in the West and in Iran and elsewhere, for us, and for our enemies, the concept of a motherland or birthplace is equivalent to the place where our people are linked to the surrounding world, bounded on the one side by the stone inscription at Naqsh-e Rostam in which Shapur the son of

Ardeshir the son of Babak names himself the king of Iran and Aniran, and on the other side by defiance of Afrasyab's armies face to face with Rostam:

For the sake of our country and our sons,
  Our wives and children and relatives,
All of us shall sacrifice our bodies in death—
  Better this than that we give the world to our enemies

V3:261

Similarly, it is obvious that Rostam and Esfandyar were compatriots when Esfandyar answers Rostam's suggestion that they fight in single combat (rather than have their armies fight en masse) by saying:

May it never be my way
  Since such an act would be unworthy of my faith
That I give Iranians over to slaughter
  While I assume the world's crown.

V5:379

Whatever tribe or clan or ethnicity Iranians belong to, whether we call ourselves *dehqan* or *tajik* or *'ajam*, we have lived with the ugliness and beauty of our destiny, wherever it may take us, from ancient times until now, with a shared identity, social structure, and order.[10]

Passing on from this short parenthetical remark, let me return to "time." "The great Feraydun was not an angel," and Ferdowsi says that his goodness lay in his "justice and generosity." The generosity of this king toward his sons, and the inevitable establishment of different countries, which marks the beginning of a new era and another kind of "social history," is a part of our mythological narrative. He bestowed the world on his sons, in order that his realm not be dispersed, and so that the populated world should remain in his family's possession:

Since the world was given to me in this populous state
  I did not seek to disperse its peoples

But I said thus, that I would give
The government to three clear-sighted men
V1:113

But with this just "gift" he sowed the seed of fratricide (and of Iran and Turan) among them. The battles of the descendants of Iraj and Tur, Iranians and Turanians, two tribes from one family, take up more or less the whole heroic period of the Shahnameh. Our epic, heroic history began with slaughter engendered by envy and greed, and ended with the death of Rostam, tricked by his villainous brother, in the depths of a pit. By the conjurer Fate's sleight of hand a history is brought into being that is completely contrary to the wishes of history's maker, one that is overflowing with injustice, dissension, and greed. In our history it is as if Ahriman continually waits in ambush for Ahura Mazda, and darkness cannot be separated from light, except for short periods, and then only with heart-wrenching effort and at the cost of the loss of sons like Iraj, Sohrab, Seyavash, and Forud, or the sons of Gudarz, or Esfandyar, who in a dream of the true faith and the hope of sovereignty lost his life in an unjust battle.

Now that his goodness has brought forth evil, Feraydun's only wish is the destruction of the criminal fratricides who have done this and so to tear out injustice by its roots and avenge its oppressed victim. When he has accomplished this, Feraydun's work is over and his "history" has reached its end, and a new reign will create a later "meta-historical" time. The successor of these two former time-fashioning kings was Kay Khosrow, who came to earth with a mandate from heaven and "Made his throne splendid as Jamshid and Feraydun had done." Kavus, the mad "high-flying" king who had wanted to know "What kind of a thing the moon is, and what night and day are," gave his heart into a demon's hands in order to plumb the secret of time, stretching out his hand towards the heavens, and fell out of the air with his chariot and throne and crown down to the earth. But

In its astonishment the world did not destroy him
But kept him alive in secret

Wanting Seyavash to be born from him, and so
He had to strut and stride in the world a little longer.
V2:96–97

"A little longer" so that, according to the Denkart, from Seyavash's loins Kay Khosrow would be born, and bring to an end both Afrasyab's life and the injustice he had perpetrated. For the sake of Kay Khosrow's divine essence, "Neryosang" asks God not to take Kavus's soul when he falls to earth. For the blessings that these future beings, who have not yet descended from heaven, will bring, Kavus remains alive.[11]

And so Kay Khosrow—in epic as well as in religion—is the possessor of a heavenly mandate to which Kavus swears fealty. Zal and Rostam bear witness to this, and the written oath is entrusted to Rostam. Later Rostam says, in reply to Afrasyab's proposal of peace between them, that the command of God "Has diverted your downfall and defeat from my hands / For Fate keeps a secret with me" (V4:249). The secret Fate keeps will be revealed by Kay Khosrow.

The story of his wonderful deeds must be read in the Shahnameh, which shows how during his reign "the world was filled with virtue and security." He traveled throughout the whole country, administering justice as he went, until he reached Azerbaijan and its fire temple Azar Goshasp, which he himself had founded, and there he prayed for victory over Afrasyab, and the uprooting of evil. Then he asked his nobles and his soldiers to support him in his campaign, since in this celestial battle

Whatever blood is spilled in revenge
He (Afrasyab) is guilty of it, and will be punished
If someone from this army is killed
His dwelling place will be the high heavens
V3:10

Those who kill are innocent, and those who are killed are martyrs who dwell in heaven.

It is as though the long battles of Kay Khosrow and the Iranians against Afrasyab and the Turanians are an earthly replica of the worldwide war of Ahura Mazda against Ahriman, since even before "His good Fortune came from above, and was ever effective (V4:309)"; from the beginning we know that he possesses "ability, lineage, nobility" and wisdom, such that no one "had ever seen his like in the world" (V4:309).

The blessing his deeds confer, and his active good fortune, mean that Kay Khosrow has been chosen for a heavenly mission, and because he is the bearer of a heavenly mandate his "time," like his fate, is celestial and predestined. A time has to come that will end the era and so return to a former place (and time); this is neither the time of being and the individual, nor of history, even though it becomes manifest in an individual being and within a historical existence; this is heavenly time or, in other words, sacred time, which cannot flow within a person or the world unless that person and world immerse themselves in the current of eternity.

Nevertheless time is a topic from the other world, one that has either always existed and will do so (Zurvanism) or has been created by Ahura Mazda and flows within us in all of our conditions, our being and not being, and which has its source elsewhere. But for each person in this world the circumstances and nature of "time" are related to his role in the world. Jamshid and Feraydun both came in order to act; they did what they came for, and went; their time came to an end. But Kay Khosrow's "time" is of a different order and nature. As with the appearance of Zoroaster in the midst of finite time he appeared in order to put an end to this process. The day that he comes to the earth is "a day of new customs and a new festival." And on that day that he left the earth he was still alive, and hastening to see God:

A wise man will smile at such a deed,
    That a man should go before God while alive

V4:368

At the height of his power, after enriching both faith and the world and tearing up injustice by its roots, Kay Khosrow does not forget Jamshid's arrogance and Kavus's foolishness, and he is afraid lest he suffer a fate like theirs, that he be ensnared by egotism, and the insanity engendered by power. While in the midst of his heart's anguish, a divine messenger, Sorush, appears to this "attentive soul" in a dream and advises him to leave "the dark earth." Unlike his predecessors he is immortal; his time does not come to an end until the "end of time," when there is no more time, and as death is the predestined child of time, when time does not exist death too does not exist, and Kay Khosrow lives eternally. He does not die but, fearful of sovereignty and heartsick at the thought of world dominion, he goes "while still living before God"; he returns from the earth to the heavens, whence he came, and there he remains until the last days as the helpmate of Zoroaster's child, the deliverer.

A detailed account of the ins and outs of this "journey" can be found in the Shahnameh, the source that provides the most comprehensive version of the narrative. Here I shall only mention one such detail that is connected to the subject of time, and this is the raising of an unknown person to sovereignty, Kay Khosrow's placing this person in his own position, and the "subjection of all the realm of Iran" to Lohrasp, "an ignoble wretch" who, as Zal says, once came—from where?—to Iran with a single horse! How could the "well-born nobles" obey such a worthless person? "How could he be enthroned as their king?" The nobles and champions agree with Zal and, in spite of their unparalleled loyalty to Kay Khosrow, defy him:

A cry went up from the Iranians,
  "From now on we shall serve no one,
None of us will be present at banquets or battles
  If fate is to exalt Lohrasp in this way."

V4:359

But finally they calm down and comply, since Lohrasp is a descendant of Hushang, and is wise and possessed of divine glory.

This accounts for his lineage and nobility of family. But, more important than this, it is he who

> Will eradicate all trace of sorcerers from the earth
> And bring forth the way of God
> Time will grow young again with his counsel
> And a pure son will be born to him
>
> V4:360

His "pure son" is Goshtasp, within whose reign the prophet Zoroaster appears; Goshtasp embraces the new dispensation and is Zoroaster's ally and supporter as he spreads "the good faith." This is why in the traditions of Mazdaism he is a sacred king, although in epic he is the opposite of this, a man who for the sake of sovereignty was ungrateful to his father, and who betrayed his son and sent him to his death.[12]

By raising up an unknown but devout man, Kay Khosrow, through the sovereignty of this man's son, has smoothed the way for a prophet to come, so that his sons, after three thousand years have passed, will take time to "the end of time," to that place where Kay Khosrow himself dwells.[13]

What is recorded in the Shahnameh and takes place in the world is a reflection of what is recorded in the Avesta and takes place in the heavens. After Ahriman attacked heaven and the light, in order to achieve victory in this universal war Ahura Mazda, who knew all things and from the beginning foresaw the end, created the world; men's divine essences rushed to his aid, and in this way, as we know, the world took on life. From the movement of the sun and moon and stars time appeared. From eternal (limitless) time Ahura Mazda created a period of finite time (as a divine interlude) of nine thousand years, so that through the progression of events in irreversible sequence time would proceed to its conclusion, to resurrection and the last days. In this way the defeat of Ahriman at a fixed moment was predestined from of old. If this time had not existed, Ahriman's life would not have come to an end and deliverance would not have occurred. Like mankind and the world, time is the armor and ally of God in the battle with demons, and in Ahriman's unavoidable destiny.[14]

In epic and religion, time goes forward in a similar way to the unfolding of fate. In religion, after the final victory and resurrection, finite time is joined with infinite time, and motion with repose, and we rediscover divine peace and the first heaven. Similarly, in epic, finite time takes shape in Jamshid and Feraydun, or to put it another way, in these two the course of fate in "an epoch of mingling" can be seen, and in Kay Khosrow the victory of infinite time.

Infinite time, as its name indicates, is not circumscribed, and so even in the world of imagination it takes on no form; it has always existed and will always exist. But finite time is circular, like a wheel, or like the rising, passing, setting, and rising again of the sun. In this time, after four epochs of three units, each of which is three thousand years, the end reaches the beginning again and the process concludes. In this rotation, time predestines man's fate, but the fate of time (finite time) cannot arrive at Ahura Mazda's auspicious and victorious end without the help of humanity's divine essences. And so in this closed-off arc of world time, it's no surprise if thought too has the "form" of a circle, with the beginning reaching the end and then returning to the beginning: "What can it do, since like a compass it cannot swerve from this rotation / but meets with whatever lies within the circle of days"?

The worldview of Iranian mythology is "historical"; the world has a beginning, a middle, and an end; creation, the appearance of Zoroaster, resurrection and the last days. This way of considering time in the Avesta has stayed intact in the Shahnameh, albeit in different forms. Jamshid's role in the "discovery" of time depends on the reality of being, in that an individual through confidence in his own being recognizes time, and this recognition of being inevitably appears together with the recognition of non-being—death. And so Jamshid, within whose reign there was no trace of either pain or old age or death, "recognizes" death, and because of this, despite his long successful life, becomes a wanderer who hides himself away for a hundred years, even in the furthest and strangest places like the depths of the Sea of China. Perhaps it is this very awareness, this continuous presence of death, which pushes Jamshid more and more towards life—the antidote to death is to live as thoroughly as possible. And for a world-ruler like Jamshid, life exists in the "ordering of the world," in the establishment of civilization and culture. Jamshid changes a time of self-absorption and negligence into a destiny without pain or old age or death: "Destiny was happy with him, and he too was happy" (V1:42). And happiness is a human state; it's not a stranger to us. "Ahura Mazda created happiness for mankind," and both for this reason and because of its social results Jamshid's "individual" role is general and permanent and goes beyond the closed circle of his own individuality, even though Jamshid is king of the world. But Jamshid's time has no "history"; with his defeat everything disintegrates and before he has departed Zahhak is seated on the throne.

In contrast to Jamshid, Feraydun's time has two historical aspects, in that he brings to an end both the thousand years of Zahhak and also the period of his own sons' injustice, and after this the history of our people continues until Afrasyab's attack on Iran. Jamshid strives to bring order to his own time, whereas Feraydun brings order to his historical past, which is the history of Iran. In him the past and its history are identical. But Kay Khosrow has two kinds of destiny, a historical one and one that is beyond history; while he lives he leads time toward its deliverance, and before he departs he smooths the way for the coming of Goshtasp and Zoroaster, the propagator of faith. The appearance of this prophet is itself another stage on the journey towards this final goal. Kay Khosrow's time, with its impetus toward the future life, hurries toward the resurrection and his return to renew the world. With the prophet's support and by smoothing of the way of faith, Goshtasp wishes to redirect the course of earthly (finite) time. But there is Esfandyar! In the Shahnameh he, unlike Kay Khosrow, is eager to rule and impatient for power; with military might and heroic strength he strives to spread the true faith—at the price of another's freedom and reputation—so that heavenly time will appear on earth as soon as possible. We know the disastrous result; the simorgh has told Rostam that whoever spills Esfandyar's blood will not survive and in both worlds he will be helpless, wretched, and despicable. The obstinate quarrelsomeness of Esfandyar, who as a prince wears a crown and as a warrior a helmet, destroys both of them.[15] After the death of these combatants comes the unexceptional reign of Bahman, and then a little later the distress and destruction of Eskandar's invasion. At this point the heroic era of the Shahnameh has come to an end, and along with this the nature of "mythical-epic" time reaches its end and gives way to the forms and narratives of history.

Mythology and religion say that in the heavens there is peace and tranquility. In a place without the revolutions of the moon and sun and stars, there is no movement and there is no time. Where there is neither time nor movement all times are one time—eternal time, that includes both beginning and end and all localities, that is without movement and exempted from the passage of the seasons, a unique place that can be seen in Kay Khosrow's world-revealing cup.

But within this idea, it seems that time is "older" than God, because "Hormozd himself came into being through the movement of creation,"[16] and before that did not exist. "Hormozd was not a God before the creation, after creation he became a God, a seeker of benefits, wise, an opponent of evil, manifest, one who bestows order and prosperity on all things, and is the guardian of all things."[17] In the same way that creation occurs after the help and support of the essences of the good, it comes into being with movement, and with the revolutions of the moon and sun and stars time appears, and existence becomes susceptible to time. Does Ahura Mazda therefore become a "God" after the creation and the fall into the cycle of time; and does his power, like his knowledge, only become complete after the final defeat of Ahriman? From a glance at what has been said it seems that in every situation Ahura Mazda is a being that is "coming into existence," one that only after three cycles of a thousand years, and the end of the Saoshyant's mission of salvation, becomes permanent as "an extant being" forever, possessed of complete power and knowledge.

In epic too we see this ultimate sovereignty of time, in both the heavens and the earth it's there before the coming of those who have not yet arrived, and after the departure of those who have left. The warp and weft of time are such that they are woven together and torn apart from one another; in every epoch a new design for this weaving appears, which is the destiny of this time's children, and their "fate." The humans who create time (Jamshid, Feraydun, Kay Khosrow) are themselves creations of time; the one who creates is created. The destiny and fortune of Jamshid, Feraydun, and Kay Khosrow, like that of Zal, Rostam, Sohrab, and the others, have taken shape before birth and survive beyond death. In one of the battles the Iranians, under the command of Tus, are defeated and ambushed on Mount Hamavan, where many of Gudarz's sons are killed. At night Seyavash appears in a dream to Tus who is "heartsick, filled with sorrow and anguish," and smiles and says,

Leave these Iranians here
 And you will be victorious in battle
Don't grieve for Gudarz's kinsmen
 For there is a new rose garden here
Beneath these flowers we shall drink our wine
 I don't know how long we shall drink such wine.

V3:149

Concern over the passing of time does not disappear, even in the heavens and after death. Seyavash and Gudarz's kinsmen are in the rose gardens of heaven, but they don't know "for how long" time is given to them, and when their days shall come to an end. In the Shahnameh time is always present, both in the world and in futurity, or perhaps it is better to say that each event appears within time according to its own "fate," and after a while disappears. Time is essential to the world's nature, and the creatures of the world are subject to time.

Such is the world in its form and nature
From his mother no man is born other than for death.
V1:252

Because time is apparent in the courses of the heavenly bodies, those who understand the nature of these courses, the astrologers, can perhaps, through their knowledge of time's nature, be aware of others' fate and see the as yet unrealized future. Zahhak and Afrasyab both foresee the wretched end of their days, as Goshtasp foresees Esfandyar's death. The hidden secrets of the auspicious and inauspicious aspects of Iraj's, Sohrab's, and Seyavash's horoscopes must be sought in the revolutions of the heavens, and Manuchehr orders "astrologers and wise men" to "inquire into the workings of heaven" in order to see the fate of Zal's son. After a three-day interval they tell the king, "We have considered the turning of the heavens," and a hero will be born from the daughter of Mehrab and the son of Sam who will be unique in his feasting and fighting, whose "sword will make the very air weep" (V1:246–47). And in contrast to this, when Zal's other son, Shaghad the fratricide, is born, all the astrologers tell Zal that this son will annihilate his clan (V5:442). It is as if this most ancient of heroes, a white-haired man who is old before he enters the world and who lives through almost the whole of the Kayanid era, from Manuchehr to Bahman, which is like the infinite time of mythology (Zurvan), contains within himself the good and bad seed of Rostam and Shaghad respectively.

Besides the turning of the heavens, men also see their end in dreams. The dreams in the Shahnameh show that the secrets of destiny are not only in the height of the heavens, but also in the depths of our being, in both the distant stars and the secret locations of the soul.

Since our coming and our going appear in time, without which no one either comes into the world or leaves it, while we are alive fate counts each of our breaths until it consigns us to death. No one dies "out of time," which is why in the Shahnameh "time" often means "death," as is said of Piran, for example:

He armed himself and hurried from Turan
For Gudarz's javelin would be his time

V4:157

And this "time" cannot be changed. Human

Said to Piran, "There is no avoiding heaven
And what time has in store."

V3:216

Similarly, one cannot flee from it. During the battle with Esfandyar, the simorgh tells Rostam to ask pardon from Esfandyar and to weep, so that he might give up their quarrel, but if his "time" has come to an end, "Certainly he will take no notice of the request for pardon," and will give his body to death. And concerning the manner of his killing of Esfandyar, Rostam says,

I have made his time within my bow
When his days are at an end I shall shoot

V5:417

The journey of our life is involved with time not only from its beginning to its end, but also before it begins and after it ends; it is time that molds our lives' substance, kneads the dough of our destiny, and holds and forms it like a pearl within its shell. In the midst of such compulsion, where can the incredible notion of freedom of action or free will be found? The life and death victories of epic heroes, in their unrelenting struggle against enemies and the faithless world whose nature encompasses our death, take their origin more from free will than from martial strength or warlike prowess.

We realize that this contradiction between time's compulsion and human free will arises from the order of Aristotelian logic; it is not that mythological scheme of logic with which we are familiar, and which has a different "logic" of its own. For example, in *The Iliad* and *The Odyssey*, the fates of Agamemnon, Achilles, Ulysses, and the other warriors depend on rivalries and arguments among the Gods and Goddesses, on their jealousies, their arbitrary support and enmity, and their capricious whims. Belief in the Gods and in a world beyond the scope of our thoughts, senses, and perceptions, and knowledge of that world—if it can be known—requires an intuitive insight, not that prosaic knowledge with which our own minds are involved. Believers, mystics, and adherents of insight and inward knowledge achievable by other means, have turned their attention toward the heart's understanding, inner discovery, and the mirror of the soul and its purity, all of which is outside of our present concern, besides which what has been said mainly concerns notions held by a contemporary reader. From the poet's point of view, man cannot escape the will of God; our understanding and judgment of the divine can go no further than an evaluation of what is there, and all man can do is accept the reality of God and believe in Him.

Sometimes in mythology, as we have seen at the beginning of creation, the divine essences rush to the aid of Ahura Mazda and choose good in opposition to evil. And for just such a prophetic mission each of them, in his own time, comes into the world, fulfills his heavenly mission, and returns to the heavens; in them time's compulsion (destiny) and how one lives (a man's life narrative) are the same. But in the Avesta we don't find any sign of malevolent and evil beings in opposition to the divine essences; we only know that trickery seeks out those who choose the demonic and makes them follow the worst of beings (Gathas, Yasna 30). The malevolent also, in their earthly existence, live out their worldly lives' narratives according to this ancient Fate.

In both these situations, good or bad, life narrative and Fate work together as one and there is no contradiction, except for the unanswerable question as to why and how people who have not yet come into the world can be deceived by Ahriman and turned towards the demonic. Is it in the nature of creation that men, like those "two heavenly beings born together in thought, speech and deed, one good and the other evil" (Gathas, Yasna Hat 30), should from the beginning have two forces appear in their makeup, one good and one evil? In such a situation what is morality's true judgment concerning "those who are evil"? According to such a point of view is the existence of "evil" in their creation still an unacceptable argument? Or is the explanation of such a problem fundamentally irrelevant, since ethical concepts and meanings—leaving aside religious considerations—are more or less a new affair? In the remote past ethics were solidly founded and built up on the ground of faith, and took their meaning from a religious and mythical worldview. Zahhak, or Afrasyab and Garsivaz, are murderous unjust sinners worthy of punishment in both worlds, because they have been deceived by the devil or are demonic, not the other way around. It is because they followed "the lie" and the demonic that they are criminals, not that they became demonic because they were criminals. In other words, their fate was cursed, and they became malignant and lived out their lives and came to a wretched end, because of this initial choice. In them their life narrative is a prisoner of their fate and no logical connection can be found between their sin and their punishment. According to the concept of free will, a sinner was able not to sin, and since he has violated this ability, this self-control that forbids an action, and discounted it, he deserves to be punished. But here this is not the case; in this conception that has survived from the remote past there is no boundary between choice and compulsion, and one cannot discover the source or cause of that first decision. But from another point of view, we can ask what would have happened to the martyrdom of Seyavash and the spiritual advent of Kay Khosrow to renew the world, if in the absence of this Fate there had been no Afrasyab? Without the existence of the Jews how could Christ have been crucified and have taken upon himself the sins of mankind, and how could God have known man's sufferings? And how could he have become our fellow-sufferer? Is evil the twin of good, and the existence of one impossible without the other?

But ethical time accepts that in the thoughts and actions of existence there exists within man the possibility—with a modicum of will-power—of knowing good and evil, so that he can weigh the claims of "right and wrong" and choose one of them, and it rejects the notion that those who are good and those who are evil simply go along their own way. Furthermore, since absolute good and evil exist in the realm of the simorgh and alchemy, the goodness of good and the evil of evil can only be found in spiritual individuals (Seyavash and Kay Khosrow) or satanic figures (Zahhak and Afrasyab), in angels or demons.

The mind of a man who lives out his life in the world of myth is connected to and mixed in with nature and its celestial and transcendental manifestations, manifestations that raise him up beyond the realm of nature; he is connected to earthly beings and the celestial Amesha Spentas—the world of earth and the world of the heavens—for which there are expressive symbols: (1) the world, (2) cow (and the useful animals), (3) fire, (4) metal, (5) earth, (6) water, (7) plants.

Each of these possesses a celestial representation, a spiritual reflection, of his own ideals, as follows:

(1) wisdom, goodness, (2) good thought, (3) justice (the order and welfare of the world), (4) ideal kingship (might), (5) patience, (6) health, (7) eternal life.

And in another aspect they are representations of the divine, and the Amesha Spentas: (1) Ahura Mazda, (2) Vahman, (3) Asha, (4) Shahrivar, (5) Armiti, (6) Haurvatat, (7) Amurdad.[18]

In this way it can be said that the earth and the heavens, the world and the divine, the body and the soul exist together on three levels and that "the eternal witness casts aside the veil from its shining face in three mirrors."

Those who have this view of the world, consciously or unconsciously, see and know themselves according to this perspective. A person who is immersed in the realm of myth—the man of myth—has not yet reached that stage in which he can consider and know his own thoughts and actions outside of this viewpoint. But since a man's actions, whether his fate be good or bad—and this is especially true of great personages, kings, and champions—have an effect on others (whether or not man has a notion of personal ethical responsibility), the injustice of Zahhak and Afrasyab, and the justice of Feraydun and Kay Khosrow do not remain unrequited. A man cannot be considered responsible for the murders committed by justice and time, fate, or the turning of the heavens.

Good does not come, o champion, from wisdom
For each famous man who is obedient
You give him to death in his bewilderment
And blame the turning of the heavens.

V4:142[19]

He cannot be blamed since, as we know, a man's good and bad acts not only affect others but are also a result of the battle between Ahura Mazda and Ahriman, and the turning of the world; and so he curses the "turning heavens" as criminal. When Seyavash is killed, Farangis acts, we can say, as the mouthpiece of Fate when she warns her father that "spilling blood is not a game":

Shining day wears black, vengeful for Seyavash,
And makes Afrasyab's day accursed
It is your own body you are oppressing
May you remember my words!
You are not out hunting for onager
Or violently bringing down deer
You are snatching a prince from his throne
And the throne and crown will curse you

V2:255

By killing an innocent person, Afrasyab harms his own body first of all, and so this poet who cannot endure injustice has Fate, and the crown and throne, curse him. The poet has selected and recited our mythological and heroic tales in a way that—although, fortunately, they do not explicitly inculcate ethical lessons—shows him to be a great and wise master of ethics, and this is why he is called "Hakim (Sage) Abol Qasem Ferdowsi." His wisdom is, in the highest meaning of the word, ethical, not philosophical, a discipline with which we know he has nothing to do. The whole of his book from beginning to end is in praise of the ethical essence of this wisdom, and willy-nilly he has woven its warp and weft into the book's stories, and portrayed himself within them. From another point of view, we know that the Shahnameh, unlike *The Iliad* and *The Odyssey,* is not a youthful, unadorned epic that insistently celebrates the naked will and instinctive strength of its heroes. The epic tales of Iran, intermixed with myths and Avestan beliefs, passed through the Parthian and Sasanid eras and four centuries of Islam and, after being brought together along this long road as an immense history modified by culture, thought, and ethics, they reached the hands of the wonder-worker Ferdowsi. The book is the masterpiece of such a poet, and it issues from such a background. And so it is no surprise if we find there the ethical values of later eras in its opening tales and its ancient personages.[20]

In "mythological-heroic" epics such as *The Iliad* and *The Odyssey,* the *Mahabharata* and *Ramayana,* and Wolfram von Eschenbach's *Parsifal,* since the narrative of men's deeds is mixed in with demons and gods, the will of the powers of heaven and hell plays a leading and evolving part in a narrative, and—although not always—leads it to the end that it desires; Fate triumphs over the narrative. Eblis involves Zahhak in the life we all know, and twice Sorush prevents Feraydun from killing him, so that he can be fastened beneath Mount Damavand where he will stay until the Last Judgment; Zahhak's beginning and end are in the hands of hell and heaven.

When we pass from mythology to epic figures like Afrasyab or Kay Khosrow, the presentation has two aspects; man and demon, or man and angel, in each case with their characteristics mixed together. An unavoidable mixture of the limited and unlimited, reality and fantasy, can be found in them, as they exist in a world both natural and supernatural.[21]

But in heroic epic, men like Gudarz, Giv, Bizhan, Sohrab, Zal, Rostam, Esfandyar, and other heroes, or women like Farangis, Sindokht, Rudabeh, Tahmineh, Manizheh, Sudabeh, Gord-Afarid, and Gordieh, and also those disappointed heroes famous for their wisdom like the Turanian Piran Viseh—none of these figures accepts their fate; they struggle to construct their lives as they would wish and by their own efforts. Heroic epic is concerned with a new kind of fate derived from social developments, in which man, although he is not yet detached from the realm of myth, nevertheless insofar as he is involved with it, at least—as an individual who is strong in himself—tries to extricate himself from it. (By saying "individual," I do not mean the more recent concept of individuality based on rights and political participation.) In the era of epic, the hero uses his strength of will and the capabilities of his body and soul to try to subdue the stubborn world, as though it were a fractious horse tugging against its reins.

Epic poetry is a reflection of the culture of its time, and it constructs man and his history, in which the tribe or people or representative sections of society are shown as they take shape and come into being; man takes his place in history, and time's immensity is measured by the individual in history, and in such an era kings are the "makers of history." In former times, the effects of cultural and economic forces, and the secret workings of society, were unknown. From another point of view, in a pastoral economy and in the lives of those who wander the deserts, in which the back and forth struggle for land and grazing were daily occurrences, the role of force and raw savagery, of war and slaughter, and tribes' rising and declining fortunes, could be seen much more clearly. It is from this circumstance that the realm of epic poetry, the passing of kings and princes, of great ladies, heroes, viziers, priests and astrologers and so forth, appears; such figures who manage the world's affairs are like beings above and beyond society who bring in their wake all those who are nameless and anonymous.

In this period man is not a stranger in the world, he has not fallen far from the Creator or his creation; his feet are firmly on the ground, and he has a refuge in the world above; his God is "alive." But he is conscious of his separation from the world beyond, particularly through his constant wariness of death, and to affirm his own being he stands vis-à-vis the world so that at the moment of death he constructs his own fate. This is because, in the turning of the world where he has fallen, he has no desire to be "a plaything of the heavens," and at the cost of his soul he strives, according to

Ferdowsi, to go above and beyond the heavens and their stars. This is the business of those magnanimous souls who are not afraid of momentous and terrifying trials; examples of this are Rostam's and Esfandyar's Seven Trials, the killing of demons, sorcerers, wolves, lions, and dragons, surviving deserts and snows and intense cold, thirst and intense heat. Like Esfandyar, when Rostam meets up with a sorceress he complains bitterly of his hardships:

> Rostam is wretched and a wanderer
> Who has seen few happy days
> Everywhere is his battlefield
> His orchard is deserts and mountains
> He fights against lions and male dragons
> He cannot escape from demons and deserts.
>
> V2:30

And this pain and hardship that he himself has chosen crosses all barriers. In his battle with Esfandyar, the simorgh tells Rostam that whoever spills Esfandyar's blood will suffer torment in both worlds, before death and after death. "If you agree to what has been said / You are now valiant against your enemy" (V5:402); the condition of his honor, of living as he would wish, is his acceptance of such torment. And Rostam says, "Being killed is easier for me than the shame / If I should survive this battle" (V5:401).

This death is preferable to shame; unlike Seyavash's "martyrdom" his motive is not a worldly or a heavenly role, or the reward of the world to come. Death is accepted simply to save his "name"; it is like the self-willed death of Bahram, who after his victory returns alone to the battlefield, to the willful struggle which is where his "name" lies, so that his "name" will not fall into the hands of his enemies even though he himself might, which he does.[22]

Sometimes the epic hero, at great cost, urges his will on to action, so that he is not merely the captive of Fate but struggles and strives against it, and—in opposition to destiny which holds his death in its hands—tries to turn Fate to his own life narrative's purposes, and to reconcile his will to heaven's demands. In him, the sources of his will's potency lie hidden in the strength of his soul and spirit rather than in the body's capabilities. However much the epic hero struggles against the world around him, he is at peace with himself. In his era, arbitrary power is still not absolute and all-inclusive, and structures, constructions, laws, and complex requirements are not so omnipresent, and not so strict and strong, that a man's will is the captive and prisoner of their intricate web, as they were to be in later periods. And so a hero's victory lies in the wager of his struggle in battle, when he is face to face with death and wrestles with his own fate, and chooses either "name" or "shame," and in this way gives meaning to his life narrative and even to his destiny. When Gudarz is old he says to his young son Giv,

In treasure there is suffering, and in suffering there is "name"
And so your "name" is better than treasure
If you will not remain here eternally
That "name" is finer than this fleeting world.

v2:414

With "effort"—in the meaning this has in the Shahnameh—a hero can push back against Fate, and by putting his body and soul in danger he can be the master of his own life narrative. But no matter how extraordinary this effort is, without "fortune" (supposedly another aspect of Fate) effort is not able to guarantee victory and a safe outcome. We can take as examples Piran and Afrasyab, one good and one bad, but both thwarted in their desires; or Sohrab and Forud, both young and both dying young. When Anushirvan asks the wise sage Bozorgmehr "Does greatness lie with effort or with fortune?" he answers that fortune and ability (heroism and determination) are like body and soul, partners and aids to one another:

This body is but the covering of a man
If fortune is awake and striving
Greatness will not come from striving
Unless good fortune is its guide.

v8:199

For victory in life and death the guidance of "good fortune" is essential, and its existence or nonexistence lies beyond our wishes and efforts, coming as it does from another and more distant world. Through ill fortune, Piran and Afrasyab come from Turan, Sohrab is deceived by his own ambition and others' lies, and Forud is sacrificed to Tus's carelessness and imprudence. In epic, as in mythology, the world's innumerable inner and outer forces are beyond our knowledge and ability and have their effect on the making of a man's life narrative, shaping it according to their own demands. In the combat between Piran and Gudarz, the Turanian recognizes the turning of Fate and sees that death is inevitable:

> Piran saw the nature of this moment
> He knew that this turn of events was from God
> But out of valor he strove
> Fighting against the turning of Fate.
>
> v4:128

Even today when we no longer believe in gods and the influence of heavens and stars, we are still caught in our own time and place, whatever area of the world we come from, whatever family or society or environment, with whatever conditions of body and soul and so forth. Our fortune—or Fate—has been formulated before us and without our will. And good or bad "fortune"—like Fate—comes from infinite time that has neither beginning nor end; having itself come from the headlong turning of the heavens and stars, the endless inconstant rush of day succeeding night.

> And furthermore the world is a fable and wind
> Such as a dreamer sees in his mind
> And when he wakes his eyes do not see it
> Whether it was good he saw, or pain and anguish.
>
> v8:199

The fleeting world is like wind and a fable, like a dream that stays in the mind, and in both states being, existence, is unstable; it's as if time has so interwoven itself upon itself that at each moment the world in which we are attaches itself to the past and by the time you open your eyes you see no sign of either good or bad, what has gone and what remains, what is visible and invisible; like time, being and non-being are within us who are ourselves becoming the being of non-being.

Time is the "container" of Fate, but just as Fate or Fortune appear in time—that is, in the life of man—and come into being in time, in the same way these two concepts, without any why or wherefore, are considered as one with the essence of time, and like time are unchangeable. From another perspective, since each moment of time begins and ends in itself, whatever falls into time also has no other fate than this. Death is a crossroads, and all, human or inhuman, no matter which road they travel along, arrive as one at this deadlock of time. Zahhak and Feraydun, Garsivaz and Seyavash, the White Demon and Rostam "are all born from their mothers for death." Even the end of this history of valor and honor, the death of Yazdegerd, is wretchedness and oblivion. The Shahnameh is an epic of failure; this is the reason that some scholars, especially non-Iranians, consider the Shahnameh to be congruent with an "Eastern mentality," a product of "predestination" and "Fate." And it's true, the Shahnameh is an epic of defeat. But as Rostam has said, "To save his name, a hero not only does not flee from death—which is the weapon with which time hunts down our souls—but in order to assert his free will he turns towards it, even when he knows and sees that the end has come." At the moment of death, the hunter has become the trapped prey, and asserts his will at the cost of his life. The Shahnameh is an epic of freedom within what is predestined. Free men and women exercise their free will and rely on its formidable might, and their valor is in accepting this, not in bodily strength.

In the Shahnameh, from the beginning to the end, sovereignty is a mark of what is stable and lasting, and as we know a hero can only bow his head before his king; even a hero like the great Rostam must do this, despite his own wishes, before a weak king like Kavus. Be that as it may, the hero's will is not limited in any other social fashion, and this is because in terms of his clan or country—as for example Sam the son of Nariman, Rostam the son of Dastan, Tus of the Nozar clan, Gudarz of the Keshvad clan—he is its social leader, its free prince. And so a hero's life narrative is limited only by the conditions of his existence (fate or fortune, time or death) and his own physical being (his "name"); he is bound by the heavens and by his own being, not by social conditions. Therefore, we can say that the predestination and compulsion presented in the Shahnameh are predicated on a simplicity that does not delve into the inner layers of its narratives. The characters created by Ferdowsi are trapped within their freedom, and they are noble more than they are free.

Within the structure of epic narrative, time remains an extraneous entity; it is not something within man's makeup, in the way that as it passes it forms, nourishes, and builds us up, and destroys us. As soon as Sam, Zal, and Rostam appear they are already heroes, just as Gudarz, Giv, Bizhan, and so many others are; during the childhood of Sohrab and Seyavash we see them at the age of fourteen, when in their strength, heroism, and fighting ability they are already fully realized, as a full moon is fully realized, and like "mortal mothers and fathers" they are completed and fulfilled.[23] When Rostam is still a child he tames an elephant with his hands and fists. Farangis and Sudabeh, or Kavus and Afrasyab, remain as they were from the beginning to the end of their lives; the mental characteristics of epic characters do not change or develop with the passage of time; time does not exist in them, it remains outside of them, and they are untouched by the turning of the heavens, from whence their lives are brought to an end, and the poet reminds us with his repetitious language that time has passed: "and so the heavens revolved a number of times . . . and so the skies turned . . . when a few days had passed by for the king . . . and so many years passed for him"; it is as if our concern is with disconnected moments of time, not with the developments and passage and changes of the world's state and man's.

Despite this image of time in epic poetry, the Shahnameh has been chiefly known as a "historical" text that deals with the particulars of forebears, the description of events of great consequence, the comings and goings of kings, wars and victories and defeats and such matters. From this point of view the Shahnameh's take on epic time is "outward"—outward in the sense that it is concerned with God and demons and the world in which we live.

But although time in the Shahnameh has the appearance of being outward, its origin is inward, so that it is apparently a self-contradictory entity. From our perspective we are so within time that no conception of existence is possible without it. But from another perspective, for this very reason, this external matter has sent down roots into our mind's subconscious and every thought, whether known or not, is formed within its confines. It brings what is "outside" of us to us, and as it has brought it so it takes it away; within it our death is a destructive enemy and an unwanted fate.

In narrative literature (including epic), where the narrator is a knowledgeable and impartial observer and makes a story out of what he sees and knows—for example, in a *qasideh* (panegyric), Naser Khosrow's *Safarnameh, Kalileh and Demneh,* or the *Golestan* and *Bustan*—time is an outward matter, and the poet or narrator reminds us of its existence: "In the beginning of my youth, as it happened and you know . . . I remember that in the days of my youth I would wander the streets and . . . one night I remember that my beloved came out of the door . . ."; or "I remember one night when my eyes didn't close . . . I heard that an old man stayed awake all one night . . . at dawn he raised his hands towards God . . . ," but this same narrator in a ghazal has a completely different perception and understanding of time.[24]

In lyric poetry the poet is not a "knowledgeable and impartial" narrator; "aware or unaware" of himself he seeks and is involved in the truth of existence. Love, like death, the destined child of time, is the most obvious manifestation of this unavoidable truth. The lyric poet experiences time, like love, in the depths of his nature, and his sensibility arises from these two. Time that played such a part in the narratives and tales of Sa'di finds another meaning completely in his ghazals; it doesn't pass according to the horizon and the rising of the moon, but in the region of the soul; it becomes inward, and its duration, its passing, whether slow or swift, depends on the poet's state and his relationship with the beloved:

> How long the night of lovers is without the beloved
> Come to me so that night will start again from the dawn

or

> A year together with him was a day you would say
> And now waiting for him a day is as long as a year

How long night is during separation, and when with the beloved how short—it has no sooner come than it has gone. The union of lovers changes time, so that its hurried passage seems to bestow the quality of eternity; for example,

> Between you and me time has passed in eternity
> A thousand years are as its first year

or

> For all my life I will not remove my head from this drunken state
> For I did not exist when you entered my heart

And from another perspective:

> The scent of love will come from the dust of Sa'di of Shiraz
> A thousand years after his death if you but inhale it

In one state love is eternal and precedes life, and in another it is unending and remains after death and denies the passage of time; it is a flight that, through the blessings of a lover's soul, outsoars the two directions of time and the four directions of space.

> By the soul of the friend who has no faith in Sa'di
> In the world there are other places than the street of the friend.

Compared with the "street of the friend" all other places are worthless and transformed into an anonymous nowhere. But in separation from the friend both time and place are destroyed, and living is "a death that is called life" that passes in a void without place or time:

You know that as we live through our days
    The day that passes without you is the Day of Judgment.

And the night that passes without you is a perplexing delay, "you are unlike other nights, a night of such duration"! And so it is no surprise if the poet is continually afraid that this hurrying forward will lead him to the night of separation and ultimately to the place of eternal oblivion.

I do not know if this is the night of power or the morning star
    Whether you are before me, or a vision of my sight
O sky, keep the door of the morning closed for a moment
    To the sun, for the night is sweet with my full moon
Alas for the scent of the garden, for sleeping in the orchard,
    Would that I felt no anxiety provoked by the nightingale of
        dawn
I see you with these two eyes tonight
    Alas that tomorrow I should see another . . .

The lover's time is not in the horizon that he questions in his bewildered state, so much as deeply within himself:

You left and took my heart and gave me over to grief
    Day and night I think of you and I don't know where you are.[25]

In the novel that, as Gyorgy Lukacs says in *The Theory of the Novel*, is the bourgeois epic, narrative and character arise and develop from the context of social origins and are linked to and continuous with the past. In Sa'di's ghazals the lover becomes aware of time's conditions, its hurrying and delay, through the blessing of the beloved's existence. Here no other way can be found than that of the lover, the friend, and it is only in this way that nature, society, intelligence, and other elements that impinge on us are known. Man as a social being is made and known with and in time. The modern novel, in its conception and understanding of time, even goes beyond this. "Personal" time is the basis of Thomas Mann's novel, *The Magic Mountain*. In Marcel Proust's *Remembrance of Things Past* there is a desperate struggle to recreate and render alive again time that does not exist except in an active memory. In *Ulysses* time is subject to the evolving processes of the mind; it is a person's individuality that draws time after itself. And in Kafka time is either hidden (*The Trial*), or at each moment is the prisoner of either social or personal circumstances (*The Castle*).

Creation

IN PERSIAN MYTHOLOGY man comes to the world in order to be God's ally in the battle against evil. This is why he is created, and Ahura Mazda has created this world—which is the battlefield of good and evil—in order to achieve victory over Ahriman. I will not go over again material that has been covered earlier; here the discussion concerns the nature of creation, not why it happened. How did this vast field of battle, this workshop of destiny, come into being?

Before the creation Ahura Mazda was "all-knowing," but remained unmoving within himself. Wisdom (the ability to think and know) is the soul of the God who knows (Ahura Mazda) and is in his essence. Knowledge without wisdom, knowledge in itself, and a God without knowledge, are not God. Ahura Mazda is knowledgeable in his wisdom. According to the Bondahesh, "Hormozd was aware (knowledgeable) of Ahriman's existence" (Bahar, Bondahesh, 34). Knowing certainly comes into existence through thinking. Something must be thought of before it is known; a lack of thought cannot lead to knowledge. In his awareness (or knowledge) of himself he thought and knew of the existence of Ahriman and what his end would be, and created finite time so that he would be brought to an end, and that one day—the day of Ahriman's death—this would come about. "He had no choice but to create time in order to prevent Ahriman's activity." Before creation "both celestial beings (Ahura Mazda and Ahriman) were limited within themselves, and whatever knowledge Hormozd had was limited" (Bahar, Bondahesh,

34–35). Hormozd is limited to, and confined within, his own boundaries. Perhaps this is one reason why the Bondahesh says, "Before the creation Hormozd was not a God, after the creation he became a God, ambitious, wise, opposed to evil, manifest, the giver of order to all things, the one who makes all things prosper and cares for them" (Bahar, Bondahesh, 34–35).

Here we can say once and for all that according to the Bondahesh Hormozd is possessed of "human" qualities, and is one with and sympathetic to man as he wanders between heaven and earth, and life and death: he is the provider of benefits and wisdom, and he bestows blessings in the battle with evil, and in the ordering of the world and its inhabitants. He is a God who is himself ensnared by Ahriman, in the tumultuous clash of good and evil, and is an ally who anxiously cares for his creation.

Both Ahura Mazda and Ahriman existed in infinite (limitless) time. After Ahura Mazda became aware of Ahriman, he created the heavens and the earth (the world) in order to fight against him. "At the moment that Ahriman became bellicose, Hormozd simultaneously created a God with the body of a fifteen-year-old youth, who was shining and had white eyes, and was tall and powerful, and his power was derived from his skill, not from thievery or cruelty . . . Hormozd's role was to actualize the creation, and it was through his knowledge that he was able to create" (Bahar, Bondahesh, 47). He is a wise—aware, knowing—God. Here and in the Shahnameh the conception is very close, and at times identical.[1] Sometimes wisdom can be considered as the instigator of thinking: it is from wisdom that thinking becomes aware and knowledge becomes manifest, just as the sun's rays awaken the gray, silent, formless, and colorless dawn. Before Ahriman's attack, Ahura Mazda's wisdom and knowledge were finite and contained within himself, and the creation of celestial beings (Amesha Spentas) was carried out "without thought, movement, or comprehension" (Bahar, Bondahesh, 34). After Ahriman's attack, Ahura Mazda became aware of and thought about himself. Creation was wisdom's awareness of itself;

that is, it was a "self consciousness" and an awakening of thought that became aware of itself, self-conscious, a setting of knowledge in motion (becoming active, a passing from potentiality to activity), a putting to work of awareness, and by thinking of it making it capable. Before this, knowing remained inactive and asleep (perhaps this is why it is said that knowledge is power; but even if this were not the case, the way to capability and power, and as a result to unachieved failures of capability, would have appeared).

The world, the heavens, the earth stretching far and near, are a manifestation of God's thinking awareness. In this way space (the world) is created with time, and each is a twin of the other. And so the earth with its spring and autumn succeeding one another, and the heavens with the moon and sun and stars, turn like a wheel upon themselves, each day and each night, each month and each year, and so fabricate time and destroy it. "Space" without time has no movement, and movement needs time. And time without movement has no visible manifestation; only with movement does it become susceptible to perception. These two are necessary to one another, they are two faces of the one "being"; in their creation Hormozd wove the warp and weft of world history, and in this way he also set out the narrative of his own reality, and the destiny of Ahriman.

Ahura Mazda (in his capacity as the lord of knowledge) is "all-knowing." Wise awareness, or the wisdom of awareness, constitutes the nature, the seeding ground, of Ahura Mazda; the seeding ground of the fullness of time and place where thought's seed flourishes and flowers. We can say that before Creation Ahura Mazda was unconscious of Himself, silent and sleeping, and became self-aware with the attack of Ahriman. This is because a precondition of self-knowledge is the existence or at least the conception of another being, and here Ahriman is that "other" for Hormozd, and the stimulus for his role (as creator). In coming to itself, to thought, this latent awareness finds life and lives; that is, it descends into the circle of time. Ahura Mazda is a "becoming" God, not an "existing" one; his strength lies in the state of becoming, and does not end except with the end of world history in the last times, and with the annihilation of Ahriman. Ahura Mazda exists in time and is thus the God of "history."

We shall merely refer to the fact, and pass on, that infinite time has neither beginning nor end, that it is perpetual and constant. By creating finite time Ahura Mazda impels it, puts it into action, lays the foundation for world history, and in so doing makes himself "historical," and with the development of unfolding time what was "all-knowing" also becomes "all-capable." And this only comes about with the passing of time, in world history.

In short, the thinking God is the God that is thought, and the thinking world is the world that is thought, the awakening of thought that precipitately appears and thinks itself. This thinking oneself is the "becoming" that accepts being and the appearance of the world. In its visible form the world becomes understandable, and in its timely aspect—since it is historical—it is the container of time; place takes its form in time, and becomes apparent. As Bozorgmehr says in response to the question of a wise sage, "He answered thus, 'In wisdom / There is nothing valuable but thought'" (B8:123).

It might be asked how this spectacle of fortune and activity, of epic fighting and feasting, came to be thought so that it took on existence and visibility. "The first creation that (Ahura Mazda) fashioned was good-conduct; when that celestial being thought of creation he bestowed goodness upon his own being, since Godhead was his through creation" (Bahar, Bondahesh, 35). And so Godhead comes from creation, and creation from thought. It is "thought" that gives birth to the reality of Ahura Mazda, and to the source and origin of the world in which we have our being. To put it another way, the world is thought become external, the visible form of God. He thought Creation, and made his own reality "good." And we know that his good reality takes the visible form of light. And so, "Hormozd made the substance of good-speech from light, and from good-speech the intensification of divine justice became apparent, which is the Creation; since he created infinite reality from infinite light, and made in infinite reality all things that are created. Infinite reality is outside of the passing of time" (Bahar, Bondahesh, 37).

In the same way, within this thought (as with infinite time) the conception of infinite space that is "outside of the passing of time" can be understood, since Hormozd's self is both in and from this, and he caused the world and its inhabitants to arise from this. "Out of his own self, from the substance of light, Hormozd brought forth the being of his creations" (Bahar, Bondahesh, 36).[2]

Ahriman also fashioned himself from the substance of darkness. Man and the creatures that are good came finally from the being of God, but by degrees. First they came from the light of "good-speech," and then from the righteousness of infinite light, and its infinite being. All creatures came into existence from infinite being; this is the journey from the heavens to the earth, from the soul to the body, from pure thought to the obdurateness of stone.[3]

The Avesta considers the following to be the first creations of Ahura Mazda: Bahman, Ordibehesht, Shahrivar, Sapandarmoz, Khordad, and Amordad (Dustkhah, Avesta, Yasna 16). He first created the heavens: "and his first material creation was the heavens, and then material forms . . . among the material creations that he created in the heavens were the six (Amesha Spentas), and the seventh was Hormozd himself, since Hormozd is both of these, first heavenly and then materially" (Bahar, Bondahesh, 37). We have already encountered the Amesha Spentas, both in their spiritual manifestations and earthly forms.[4] I shall not go over again what I've already indicated. We know that this world is the bodily manifestation and physical appearance of the heavens, and Hormozd himself is both worlds.

In other places, the appearance of the world from the heavens (the antecedence of the spiritual world to the physical world) came about in this way; first, from the "thought, speech, action, awareness, and choice" of the heavens, the sky appeared in order that the world should be the dwelling place of demons and of Ahriman, then water, earth, plants, and flocks appeared, each with their own function, and virtuous man was created in order to destroy Ahriman (Bahar, Bondahesh, 39–40).

The ceremony of creation, which is a journey from what is abstract to what is conditional, and from the heavens to the world, is recounted thus in the account of the nature of creation's stages: first, the seven kinds of Amesha Spentas; next, gods such as Mehr, Sorush, and Neryosang; and then the sky and the earth, water and plants, man and horses. Then it is the turn of specific men: the first person who paid attention to the words and teachings of Ahura Mazda (Kayumars), and the first person who cultivated good thoughts, speech and deeds (Zoroaster) (Farvardin Yasht, sections 23 and 24). In the same way, "*fareh*" in man, which is like the "*faruhar*"—essence—of the heavenly sphere, was created before the world, which is its embodiment, so that it could aid God in his completion of the two worlds.[5] We know that these essences come to the aid of Ahura Mazda in his battle for the world, and we know that if their aid had not been there the creation would have remained incomplete. Here the celestial essence of man was allied to God, and of its own free will, in order to aid God, it takes on bodily form, comes down to the earth, and after the body's death is reunited with Him. In another version, this same passage from the heavenly sphere occurs when thought is united with the body: "Hormozd said to Mashi and Mashyaneh, 'You are men, the father and mother of the world's inhabitants, I have created you with sound judgment, see that you bring this sound judgment to bear on your activities. Think good thoughts, say good words, perform good deeds, do not have any business with demons.'"

When each thought of the other, the first thought of each of them was "He /she is a person, a human being." As soon as they existed, their first act was to think (Bahar, Bondahesh, 81). In the same way that the creation of the world was the coming into being of God's thought, so being human arose from that first moment of thought; by thinking God becomes the creator and so on and so forth, and by thinking man creates humankind, the knowledge of good and evil, and an awareness of good thoughts, good-speech, and good deeds. This is why, before anything else, Ahriman "attacked their thinking, and defiled it" (Bahar, Bondahesh, 81). On the other side, in creating man the Creator first endowed them with wisdom drawn from his own nature.[6] In his relationship with God, the wise man in his splendor benefited from his awareness of his thought. The source of truth, the essence of man's being, is in wisdom, and his first act is to put wisdom to work (that is, to think). To be a man, as to be God, depends on wisdom and thought, and he who thinks is one who is knowledgeable and who creates. In response to a wise man, Bozorgmehr "Answered that in wisdom / There is nothing worthwhile but thought" (V8:123). At the same time, it must be borne in mind that each act of thought does not necessarily result in knowledge. The outcome of Ahriman's thinking is "evil knowledge," sorcery, and witchcraft.

The omniscience of Ahura Mazda, through the blessings of which he saw the end-times, and created finite time, is miraculously contained within prayer, or celestial speech (*Yata ahu vairiyo*), "from which the beginning and end of creation became apparent; and this may be called religion, since religion was created simultaneously with the creation" (Bahar, Bondahesh, 37). And so speech (prayer), which is the mirror that displays the beginning and all that is subsequently enacted, is the representation and embodiment of religion (knowledge and wisdom), and for this reason, "was created simultaneously with the creation" (Bahar, Bondahesh, 37). Thought can be thought through speech (the divine word); or in other words, thought is born, nourished, and becomes apparent in speech (this is a lengthy subject which we shall return to later).

And so this world is the battle of thought between Ahura Mazda and Ahriman, and the predestined way that this is played out at a certain time. As regards the fleeting world and time, "creation is stronger than both of them; Hormozd's creation, and that of Ahriman . . . time is the discoverer of their deeds . . . time knows more than the knowledgeable . . . it is through time that our families are destroyed . . . no mortal man can escape it; not if he flies upward, not if he digs himself into a pit, not if he dives beneath streams of cold water."[7]

And as we have indicated, this time "cannot become apparent without the movement of space . . . these two are necessary to one another and are two aspects of one reality; time is the soul that bestows being on space and the force that sets its turning in motion; and space, with the earth and the sky, the heavens and the stars, is the turning wheel of time. The two turn as one, each firm in the other, but transient, bound together in their passing, whose endless elapse and return brings us into being, whether we will or no, and bears us away, and which is faithful to no one and to no thing."

We also find such a picture of the world "in the grip of time" in the Shahnameh of Ferdowsi, a Muslim of the fourth century Hejri. Four centuries is too brief an interval for ancient beliefs that are deep-rooted in the soul of a tribe or people, whether they are concealed or openly present there, to be erased from consciousness. Even today, a thousand years after Ferdowsi's time, fragments of ancient thoughts and beliefs still linger in our hearts, and to write about this, if such an opportunity presents itself, would be a contribution to the cultural history of Iran, but this is not our present concern. Leaving this aside, despite all their manifold differences Mazdaism and Islam both believed in a God higher than the reality of this world, in creation, in a prophet and a divine book, in man's divine essence, in the transience of this world, and in a judgment day. And this has inevitably facilitated the entrance of Zoroastrian material into Islam. This is especially so since Ferdowsi was a Khorasani Muslim; that is, a believer in either the twelve or seven imams of Shi'ism. Khorasan was one of the Esmailis' foremost areas of concentration, and someone like Ferdowsi was not unaware of elements derived under another name from pre-Islamic Iran. Consciously or unconsciously, the blood of the past flowed in the veins of the poet's soul. In the same way that the new religion's places of worship were built on the ruins of ancient temples, the thoughts, customs, and traditions of the former faith had a formative influence on the organization and elaboration of the new faith's worldview.

As well as all this, perhaps the most effective means by which the ancient culture's conceptions were transmitted were the translation of Pahlavi literature into Arabic and Persian, the widespread prevalence of oral tales and folklore, and the awareness of the former history of Iran that was still alive in people's memories. A glance at the thousand lines of the Shahnameh written by Daqiqi shows how strongly established the old traditions were. Both poets were dealing with the same culture. If we leave aside their relative poetic abilities, we find the same conceptions of mankind, heroism, bravery, and honor, the same values and tropes, in the work of both.

At that time, even if Mazdaism and the sects that derived from ancient beliefs (Manicheism, Buddhism, Mazdakism, and perhaps atheism) openly or secretly lurked here and there in corners of Iran, the religion of everyone was, with a few exceptions, Islam and its book, the Qur'an. In the Shahnameh the conception of God and the creation goes back to two sources that have different origins, and sometimes reflects the perplexity of someone caught between two conflicting systems of belief. This is apparent in the past of the *dehqans* of Khorasan in the fourth century Hejri, which on the one hand went back to the beliefs of ancient Iran and its mythology and religion, and on the other derived from the Qur'an. For this reason, in order to understand some aspects of the world's affairs, to resolve their bafflement at the way the heavens turn, at the wisdom of the Creator and the disasters wrought by fate, and even more so at those questions that have no answer, it was not enough for them to turn only to myths and ancient beliefs.

Here we should also mention another significant point; whatever was derived from the heritage of ancient Iran and Islam and reached "the new historical era" was sown and nourished in one world of thought and feeling, and came to rest in another; it is as if two streams that rise in two widely separated mountains should after many long years become united as a river that irrigates a new landscape, so that the "water" both is and is not that former "water." It is the former water because it has come from that stream, and it isn't because it now flows through another agricultural area that is subject to different weather conditions, and therefore reaches a different state from that which it was originally. And now after this reminder we can consider the concept of the creation of the world that is present in the Shahnameh, which opens with precisely this subject.

In the Shahnameh's preface, which describes the world's creation, we see that God, effortlessly and without trouble or hesitation, creates the world from nothing. In demonstrating His might He creates the four primal elements—earth, air, fire, and water—out of which arose the fleeting world (V1:6). Out of these elements "came the swiftly turning heavens," which with their eternal revolution produced amorphous time that took on form, so that day and night became apparent. Then plains, mountains and seas, plants and trees, the stars and light, moving and living creatures appeared—but all these lacked speech and wisdom. Then came the turn of man to be created, the resolver of problems, the lord of the animals and king of the earth, the possessor of speech and wisdom; in contrast to other living creatures, "he knows good and evil and the results of his actions," and answers for his acts to the Creator.

At the opening of this extraordinary work, the God of the Shahnameh is the creator of "The soul and wisdom, the giver of provision and guidance." He has given a soul and a time, and a place for them to exist, to all sentient creatures. But wisdom, the naming of creatures, guidance—these are the properties of man. It is naming that, in speech, bestows being. Without speech there is no name for anything; in order to know each being, it must inevitably be named. God is "the master who creates speech" so that the things that He has created can be known and recognized. To name, an act that comes into being through the blessing of speech, is to recognize, since it is through speech and naming that things can be recognized. And to recognize is to recreate, since when creation passes from potentiality to action the thing created is recognized; that is, it reaches the stage of actuality. Wisdom too depends on the existence of speech, on the existence of mankind, since it has no embodiment other than in speech. It is thus that it takes form, that it is born and nourished, that it passes from one to another, from Ferdowsi to us. These two are body and soul of one another. The way to wisdom cannot be found without speech, and speech without wisdom is an empty husk.

But that word "guidance"! Guidance as to what is good and bad is one of wisdom's gifts: "Wisdom is a guide, wisdom delights the heart / Wisdom takes us by the hand in both worlds." Wisdom enables us to distinguish between good and evil, so that we can find our own way. For this reason, only man, and no other creature, lives in terms of good and evil, and is the lord of the world's animals that have neither wisdom nor speech. The poet says that if you seek "wisely . . . the meaning of mankind" and wish to know what it is to be human, you will see that

> You have been fashioned from two worlds
> Brought up between many states
> First for you is thought, then judgment,
> Do not take your being as a joke
>
> V1:7

The "first thing" for man is his thoughts, and the "last thing" is the Day of Judgment. It seems the ancient insight of Hormozd to "the father and mother" of mankind is repeated here; that mankind is, before all else, "thinking," that it is through thinking that he knows he is human, and his first deed is to think (Bahar, Bondahesh, 81). Man is fashioned from two worlds, and through the blessing of wisdom he is the lord of creation, and on the Day of Judgment he must answer for his good and evil deeds before the Creator.

It is clear that one who is endowed with wisdom must be free to choose between good and evil. Bring free is an unavoidable condition of being responsible. But it seems that this entity "fashioned from two worlds," and the possessor of the highest thought, is not free; he is subject to another, one who is mightiest of all the mighty, because after the two lines quoted above the poet immediately makes clear his uncertainty and bewilderment:

I heard from a wise man other than this—
    What do we know of the Creator's secrets . . . ?
Look at this swiftly moving heaven
    From which come both pain and the cure for pain
The passing of time does not wear it out
    Neither pain nor suffering harms it
Nor will it cease from turning
    Nor does it suffer destruction as we do
Know that from it comes increase, and also time's passing
    Evil and good are in its keeping

V1:8

The wise man's words are that same secret which the poet's thoughts repeatedly express in this great book: not only is the turning of the heavens not worn away by the passing of time, but it is the originator of time and fate, and both brings us into being and wears us away.

As the world is created the characteristics of time become apparent, and as man is created we immediately look to this "swiftly moving dome" from which our troubles proceed and by which they are cured. Time is the central concern and context of the world of our poet's thought. Some indication of this hidden perspective can be discerned in the prologue to the Shahnameh. The book begins "in the name of the lord of the soul and wisdom." After this mention of God comes a passage in praise of wisdom which is the greatest of God's gifts to man, his heart's guide and the light that leads him through this world and the next. After this comes the creation of the world and of mankind. In creating the world, the Creator makes "something" appear from "no thing," from nothingness. But what is this "something"? It is the stuff of the four basic elements: fire, air, water, and earth![8] These were mixed together, the process was set in motion, and the dome of the heavens became apparent; the twelve divisions of the zodiac and the seven heavens began to move; the "wheel" of the heavens started to turn and the time of this fleeting abode (the transitory world) was initiated. After these four elements take on form and structure and the evanescent world comes into being, we reach the account of the creation of mankind. Here too, as we have seen, before man's place in creation can be known there is mention of the "swiftly moving dome" that fashions time and our fate. After the two accounts that concern the creation of the world and man comes the account of "the creation of the sun and moon" with its description of their movements and the passage of day and night; then once again we turn to a discussion of time, and here we deal with visible, corporeal, palpable, worldly, and quotidian manifestations of time. The poet cannot conceive of a world without time, without the processes of coming and going and disintegration, and as quickly as he can he makes haste to see time as essential to the existence of the world and of man. The concept of time, and of time in man (i.e., as his destiny) are the warp and weft of the two worlds' structure, and it is this that joins together society and individuals in the unfolding of the book's narratives.

In the Avesta the fate of the world and even of Ahura Mazda is both explicitly and implicitly involved with man's role, and with the descent of the divine essence, with their becoming "of the world" within our bodies and souls, and with their alliance with God in the battle against Ahriman. It is thought, together with good-speech and deeds, which make the man of God victorious. Mankind and God need one another, and this is especially so in the Zurvan conception of existence in which Ahura Mazda is in thrall to time. But contrary to this, in the thought of Ferdowsi, a Khorasani Muslim of the fourth century Hejri, God has absolute power and knowledge, and absolute self-sufficiency.

According to the Qur'an, over the course of six days God created this world and the world to come out of nothing; as he willed this he said, "Be!" and it was so (19:35).[9] God began the creation of man with mud . . . then he gave him stature, and breathed His own soul into him (32:7–9). Man was created weak (4:28); he is oppressive and ignorant, and oppresses himself. But he is also the noblest of creatures, the representative of God on earth, and for this reason the angels bow down before him, with the exception of Satan who in his arrogance and ambition rejects all constraints. God curses him and drives him away but allows him to remain until the last days, and he says to God, "Since this is the case, I will stay and deceive your slaves and attack them from every side . . ." (32:7, 32:11–18).

I'll summarize, and simply list one or two points, since I assume that the readers of this study are familiar with the Qur'an and know at least the outlines of the creation according to "the word of God," and that they are aware that " . . . all that is in the heavens and all that is on the earth is His . . ." (11:34), that we do not live in vain, and that the jinns and mankind were created to worship God (3:191, 51:56). In the Qur'an, this world and the world to come—like good deeds and sin, heaven and hell, rewards and punishments—derive from the moment existence comes into being. The transient world, that is faithless and worthless, is a dwelling with two doors "through one of which we come, and through the other we leave." Eternal life is in the world to come. Outwardly the world is a place of spectacle and ruin, and inwardly an enticement to sin.

The earth, the "world" of the Avesta, like the world of the Qur'an, is fleeting; it has a lifetime (finite time) and its days come to an end. In the life of this world the turning of heavens and the stars have written our fate, and man, in spite of this—even in Rostam-e Farrokhzad's despair—strives to carve out his own destiny. In the Qur'an too destiny "was formed without our participation," but the pious believer does not rest in his search for the "straight way." In the turnings of fate, we are as bright shadows of good and evil, inextricably caught in bewilderment and increasing perplexity, in hope and despair. But this is a lengthy subject that would keep us from our objective, and so having mentioned these one or two essential points, I shall return to the world of the Shahnameh.

In both Mazdaism[10] and Islam, the fate of the "noblest of creation" in his life in this world is involved with what lies beyond this world; in the one it is with the turning of eternal time, and in the other with the "tablets of fate" on which are written the destinies of mankind until the Day of Judgment. In both faiths man is the assistant of God on earth and answerable to him for good and evil, and in both faiths he is the captive of necessity. In Ferdowsi's worldview man's pain and suffering and misfortune—all that comes to him for good or ill—come to him only from God and according to God's will. And so, for a Muslim like him who cherishes the intellect, accepting that a merciful God visits such suffering on mankind is incomprehensible. And if it doesn't come from Him who does it come from? This is one of the sources of his bewilderment.

As we have seen, according to the concepts of Iranian mythology, time flows like blood in the smallest capillaries of the world; as soon as we say "the world" time is like its body; time has become corporeal and taken on a form. This is why the coming and going of the sun and moon and stars, the revolutions of the heavens, signify the turning of time, and like them it indicates the nature of the world. In its turning the wheel of the heavens brings us here and takes us hence; death is in the nature of the world, and it is born with us and accompanies us, "for no one is born from his mother but for death" (B8:99). And so this world, this living body that is our universe, is also a captive of the turning heavens. The turning of the stars determines the good and evil, the ugliness and beauty, of our lives, and it is this that drives us from youth to old age:

What did that brave speaker say
    When he grew sated with the turning of days
"Would that my mother had not borne me
    That the high heavens had not passed over my head
Encompassed around, and between two points
    What shall I say? There is no alternative but silence."
If you look you see that fate is time
    No man has a cure for this
If the turning heaven seats you on a saddle
    Finally the earth is your pillow

Do not bind your heart to sorrow so much
    And do not trust the high heaven
For it plays with elephants and lions
    Know that it is independent of all things
You will become lifeless and it will long persist
    Speech is long, do not complain so much.

B9:311

The timeworn world is an ancient dwelling place whose inhabitants are caught "between the compass's two points" of day and night, while the two millstones of heaven and earth grind them to dust. In recounting the unmotivated death of the innocent Iraj, Ferdowsi says:

O world, you nourished him in your keeping
    But then gave his soul no refuge
I do not know whom you secretly favor
    But one must weep for what you do openly

V1:121

Where in truth does this smiling, malignant wolf of the world, that provides with one hand and persecutes with the other, come from? Why must Iraj, Sohrab, Seyavash, and Forud die young, and why must the victorious warriors Rostam and Esfandyar know defeat? How can the secret of the injustice suffered by Yazdegerd be explained, if indeed there is an explanation?

We begin with Ahura Mazda who, according to Zurvanite tradition, took existence upon himself in infinite time and who inevitably needed time (finite time) in order to defeat evil (Ahriman). According to this myth, Hormozd himself is time's progeny, and since he cannot be something separate from his own origin and essence, he cannot be "timeless." As a God he commands only what is in time, finite time, and for His war against Ahriman He first creates finite time, and in this time the world and us (who are "this world's divine essences that have taken on bodily form"). We and the world itself have been born in time and come to an end in time, and since we come to an end in time we inexorably travel toward our own time's conclusion.

But we have also already seen, and we know, that we and the world are weapons in the war against Ahriman. In this struggle our role and the world's role are divine. Nature's phenomena, such as the earth, water, fire, plants, beneficial animals, and the man of good thoughts, are sacred. In the Shahnameh, the sacred alliance and coordination between the world's phenomena and man is clear; for example, when the Turanians kill Nozar, the king of Iran, the plants that grow from his corpse's blood "lower their heads in shame before the sun," and the mourners cry out that "the sun in heaven weeps blood upon our grieving" (V1:317). Feraydun and Kay Khosrow are able to reach safety by passing through impassable waters, and Seyavash passes unscathed through fire; when he is killed, the earth will not drink his blood and the leaves of the tree that grows there bear the image of his face.

From the soil that absorbed Seyavash's blood
A green tree rose up to the clouds
Each leaf bore the image of his face
For love of him, musk's scent came constantly
In December (the tree) was as if in spring
A place for mourners to gather and worship

V2:375

Seyavashgerd, which Seyavash built on a mountaintop beyond Turkestan, was a paradise where it was always spring. Feraydun and Zal, raised respectively by a cow and the simorgh, grow in the mountains and are children of nature. Rostam found Kay Qobad in a mountain paradise, and summoned him to assume the sovereignty of Iran.

Opposed to these examples are the agents of another world, such as those that appear in the Seven Trials, a wolf, a dragon, demons and sorcerers, the desert and snow, sleet and intense cold, all of which are enemies to man's soul. Because of its celestial origin the world is sacred, but because of its involvement with the destruction wrought by the turning heavens it too becomes a place of villainy and misfortune. Finally, creation is not only the work of Ahura Mazda, Ahriman too has his creations, although we know that ultimately goodness and the followers of good will be victorious. In time the world, going along its own true way, reaches the last judgment, but there is a long period of expectation to endure before this:

If heaven does not confide its secret to you
    And from its turning you find no respite
It confers the crown and the throne and greatness
    And it confers darkness and humiliation
It remains one for both enemy and friend
    Sometimes you find the kernel, sometimes the shell
If your head presses against the dark clouds
    Finally its place is in the dust.

V1:307

This constant trickery, this untrustworthy enmity and friendship, "since finally you are not of this world" comes from Ahriman, and so, apparently—according to thought and religion—this pain and suffering is not pointless and unnecessary, and neither is the world malignant or criminal. But we feel that it is; we are witnesses to the daily injustice of fate, and we know that one day it will sweep us away, and all that is ours, and hurl us into the abyss of nonexistence. Time, in so far as it is concerned with the world and its inhabitants, devours all things together, because it is stronger than both creations.[11]

In the Shahnameh there is no clear boundary between the world, which exists in finite time, and the cosmos (the heavens and their turning) which we can say reaches fruition in infinite time, and which has itself created and is the instigator of time's revolutions. The mixture of on the one hand an ancient Zurvanite determinism (the unqualified authority of time), and on the other Mazdean freedom (the initial choice, the freedom of the divine essences and their descent to earth, and man's role in life), reached the era of Ferdowsi and survived, at the unconscious level, at the center of the concept of Fate. Perhaps this is one reason, among others, that in the Shahnameh nature's phenomena (the world) are both the friend and the enemy of mankind. Man is victorious over the world's phenomena and in the same moment the world leads him to nothingness; it is an unkind mother, an enemy that nourishes us.

But according to Ferdowsi this oppressor of mankind is created by "the Lord of soul and wisdom," the "generous and kind" fount of wisdom. And so why is it that the heavens, His creation, bring us low in this way, and consign us to the dust? Is He not also "The Lord of Saturn and the turning heavens / the bestower of light on the moon, Venus and the sun"; that is, the God of time and of our fate? Ferdowsi himself often asks this of "the over-arching high heavens," for example at the end of the reign of Eskandar, and complains of the heavens' cruelty. And the heavens answer, "You are knowledgeable and wise, aware of good and evil, but misguidedly unaware that I do not turn except by the will of Him 'who is above all else.'"

The foundation and essence of Ferdowsi's thought is ethical; his way of thinking cannot accept injustice and wrongdoing in what happens and what he perceives, and he suffers in astonishment at what he sees as the way of the world. We are presented with an old erudite recluse in a corner of a village, endless questioning and discussion, and the noblest end of man, which is no more than a lament and a sigh against the eternal heavens! And with all this, death is waiting at the door. One who is intelligent, wise, and mortal is the prisoner of a force that is senseless and immortal! Is this not the unjust world in which Ferdowsi lives, a man who passed his life in despair at his country's history? According to his book, the Arab Zahhak attacked Iran and looted its inhabitants for the first thousand years, and for the next thousand years Afrasyab the Turanian did the same thing. In historical time, after the coming of Eskandar, Iranians were once again subjected to continuous assaults by Turanians and Arabs, until Iran's destiny came to an end, as we know, with the death of Yazdegerd. The memory of this turbulent history was still alive in Ferdowsi's time. From the end of the third century Hejri (ninth century CE) Iranians were once again able to found Persian-speaking states in Sistan (the Safarids) and greater Khorasan (the Samanids), until once again attacks from the northeast began, and the state ruled by Saman's descendants was overthrown; former slaves became kings and princes, and former kings and princes fled to China and eastern Asia, or suffered the same fate as Yazdegerd.

Shall we call what happened to Yazdegerd just
    Or shall we call it the malevolence of the seven heavens?
If one does not know malevolence from justice
    No philosopher has ever answered this question for us
And if he said, "Faith's decrees are closed (to us),"
    The meaning of his answer remains hidden.

v8:368

This is the constant question: "If this is justice, what is injustice, and what is malevolence?" No answer comes from the knowledgeable, no clarifying language from the theologians! This is a hidden enigma, and the search for its answer never lets Ferdowsi go, especially since he saw that his own times and circumstances were not unlike those of which he sang in his poem. It was not only the past of which he sang, but also the living spirit of what he himself had experienced, since he knew

This is the way the ancient heavens turn
    Sometimes as the bow, sometimes as the arrow.

v3:300

The creation of this malicious, oppressive world by a God who is wise and just is a mystery, an unresolvable enigma, one that is apparent at the poem's opening, then with the death of the first king (Kayumars) and then with the death of the last king (Yazdegerd), with which the poem ends. When Ferdowsi says, "In the name of the lord of soul and wisdom / beyond which thought cannot reach . . ." he is speaking of a God who is the bestower of life (soul), and knowledge and the true way to live (wisdom), as well as the bringer into being of place and time (the cosmos and the turning heavens) and the reality of all that is, who is beyond all why and wherefore, and who is inapprehensible by both our sight and our thought. Thought cannot reach to the Creator of thought, as a painting cannot reach to its painter; it might perhaps stir up the dust of His creation, but our understanding remains far from the sight and knowledge of the Creator. The Creator cannot be contained by thought, imagination, or concepts. All that can be known is that He exists, that one should refrain from idle unprofitable talk about Him, that one should worship Him and follow in the way that He has commanded. There is no path for us to the other side of this veil. Such is the unknowable God who has created the world that is incoherent to us, and filled with enmity, and as the poet turns this way and that he can make "neither head nor tail of the world." How can he seek a way from this unknowing and ignorant creation to the subtle secrets of the wisdom and justice of a God who "Has created one with a dark fortune / and created another worthy of the throne"? (V3:250). Why should there be so many contradictions, such a mixing of misfortune and sorrow with happiness and prosperity? Is it that in this blind cul-de-sac we must know and accept that "There is no place for speech beyond this veil / And thought has no path to what is so"? (V1:4). That we must accept and be silent? Is it that "our sage" wishes to say that "Creation's pen has not erred," and can it be that epic is a place for submission and acceptance? That it is not a place for struggle and effort and wrestling with the world?

The attempt to conceive of a creator who is wise and just provokes a constant struggle, an endless questioning and searching, in the poet's mind. The contradictions in Ferdowsi's thought are like the burning and immediate remaking of a living body in the processes of life and death; they destroy his inner world and then refashion it. This conscious and unceasing inner turmoil involves unavoidable bewilderment, and unassuageable pain; the treacherous destinies of Iraj, Sohrab, Seyavash, and the wretched Yazdegerd lead one way, each of their roles as epic characters leads another, and their lives end in the disappointment of their hopes and inevitable death. Only a few individuals, such as Feraydun and Kay Khosrow (or Ardeshir, Bahram Gur, and Anushirvan), through the blessings of their unique fate (destiny) in conjunction with their roles, find their hopes realized. Naturally in an artistically great work like the Shahnameh, this discordant duality is mitigated as it encounters the complexities of life, and the psychology of the book's characters displays an organic unity, rather than dealing in parti-colored individuals who are half dark and half light, or completely good or completely evil. (We shall return to this point more fully in the chapter entitled "Speech.")

And so what is the source of this contradiction between fate (which is Zurvanite) and one's role (which is Mazdean), between the turning heavens that form destinies, and human desires? Is it in the concept of the divine world from which come our luck, our efforts, our pain, and our solace? I feel that in Ferdowsi's thought three notions of God have been brought together as one concept: the first is the absolutely omniscient and mighty God of the Qur'an, the creator of space and time, of jinns and mankind, the lord of all that is and is not, the controller of the world's and man's destinies, from the creation to the last days in both worlds, the Judge of the Last Judgment; the God whose power is unknowable and who is beyond all thought or supposition:

> Know that good and evil come from Him who has no equal
> Whose deeds are without beginning or end
> Who says "Be," and it is so; it is He who exists
> While there is existence, and who is while there is being
>
> B8:288

As we know, God's qualities in the Qur'an are many and various. Like Mowlana and Hafez and everyone else, Ferdowsi worshipped the God he knew and had encountered, the one he saw within the mirror of his own soul. For example, in the whole of the Shahnameh there is no trace of the avenging and tyrannical creator who has set a seal on the hearts of the heathen, who is "the best of sorcerers." Ferdowsi's God is a wise and kind bestower, "a giver of provisions and a guide." The God of his faith and belief is the God of whom he is aware and whom he worships; "He has extracted the pith from the Qur'an."

But apart from this, as we're aware, Ferdowsi was heir to an ancient and deeply rooted culture, one that involved (particularly during the Sasanid era) two conceptions of God mingled together, Ahura Mazda and Zurvan. In the first Yasht of the Avesta, in answering Zoroaster Ahura Mazda says:

> I am the source of knowledge and understanding, I am the provider of flocks and herds, the best of Asha . . . I am wisdom and wise, I am knowledge and knowing, I am mighty . . . I am the creator, I am known to the world as Mazda.[12]

When we look at the Shahnameh, in addition to the features we have already mentioned, we find throughout the whole work this same conception of the nature of God; the name "Ahura Mazda" itself means "the leader of those who know," and in the very first line of the book, the first attribute of the Creator is the giver of life and the bestower of wisdom. From one point of view the Shahnameh can be seen as a "Book of Wisdom" and a "Book of Justice" and considered as an epic that describes the war between the wise who are just against the ignorant who are unjust. The Creator himself is possessed of "knowledge and understanding, wisdom and wise counsel," and if He were not He would not have created the cosmos; and He is just, since if He were not He would have left the world to the injustice of Ahriman. From this point of view the Shahnameh is nothing but an image of the historical battle between good and evil in the Iranian people's life in this world. The concept of the existence of such a God is the warp and weft that binds the world of the Shahnameh together. As far as we know, Ferdowsi did not have a clear, unmediated knowledge of the characteristics of Mazdaism and the God of the Avesta. What has reached him from this source is the remains of long-lasting traditions, an underground culture surviving in the depths of the poet's being, and flowing in the veins of the Shahnameh.

In the letter from Kay Khosrow to Fariborz (or at the opening of the tale of Kamus-e Kashani) we can see how two different strands, derived from the Islamic and Mazdean concepts of God, have been woven together to form a new cloth:

> The letter began with praise,
> As was customary and appropriate
> In the name of the lord of the sun and moon
> Who gave agency to good and evil
> It is He who has made victory, from Him comes defeat
> For good or evil, from Him comes fulfillment
> He created the world and place and time
> He created the ant's foot and the massive mountain
> He bestowed wisdom and soul and a mighty body
> Greatness and sovereignty and good fortune
> There is no escaping His chains
> To one there is given glory and a throne
> To another He gives a bitter fate
> He gives need and sorrow and pain and difficulty
> From the shining sun to the dark earth
> I see all that comes from the pure God is just.[13]

Here, as throughout the Shahnameh, the God of the sun and moon, the giver of good (not of Ahriman's evil) and victory, the creator of space and time, the bestower of wisdom, the soul and a capable body, the God of justice in the heavens and on earth is, as well as all this of Islam, the one God who is all-powerful and all-knowing, who cannot be qualified, from whom all things proceed; time and place, good and evil, defeat and victory, sorrow and misfortune and happiness and good fortune, being and non-being, and so on, and so on!

On the other hand, in finite time, Ahura Mazda is involved in a battle with Ahriman and at the end of this time he will become "omnipotent," and his divinity will reach fulfillment. But in Islam,

God needs nothing, and existence needs Him. The "cosmos" created by Mazda is like the "world" of Islam's absolute God, in that it is fleeting and transient; but the role of these two is not the same. In the first the cosmos is a weapon in the battle against Ahriman, and in the second the world is a mortal place of trial, a stage on the way to the eternal hereafter.

But Ferdowsi's world—its sky, the turning of the heavens, fate . . . even though in its fleetness and faithlessness it is both of these—finally goes far beyond them. In the Shahnameh it is as though the world is the body of time and time is the soul of the world, and this body turns at the behest of this soul. The existence of the world depends on time, whereas the existence of time depends on itself and nothing more. Time is the inner being of the world, and for this reason the world is transient, and in its revolutions that are constant and subject to no delay it destroys all things, until it remakes itself; the world of the Shahnameh is more "Zurvanite" than the cosmos of the creator Mazda, or the world as it is according to Islam.

We shall return to the Zurvanite mythology later on. Here it's sufficient to point out that Zurvan "gives birth to" twin sons, Ahura Mazda and Ahriman; he is the God of infinite time with neither beginning nor end, and like an eternal entity hidden within the past, the future and the present, he is the "soul" within the world created by his sons, and not a moment can pass by without his presence. The hurrying wheel of this "celestial time," this manifestation of the unseen, is concerned with neither justice nor injustice, and is a stranger to human joys, pains, wishes, and fears; it spins and snaps off the thread of our fate, our destiny and, without our knowing why or how, delivers us to the realm of dust. The belief in positive or negative horoscopes and the influence of the stars on one's fate was universal among our forebears, and many still believe in this influence. But in the Shahnameh we come face to face with time that is arbitrary and willful and is, as the Bondahesh says, "stronger than both gods"; the progress of its turning constitutes our fate and that of the world. This is why, in their battles and banquets kings and great ones, and how much more so astronomers and astrologers, interrogate the face of heaven and the comings and goings of the stars, in order to discover auspicious and inauspicious days and foresee the future. Kavus, in order to understand Sudabeh's secret (V2:229), and Afrasyab in order to know the result of his daughter's union with Seyavash (V2:300) turn to priests and astrologers. We know the fortunate outcome of the union of Zal and Rudabeh, and I have referred to this already.[14] But God keep us from the day on which these "just stars" turn in another fashion, since "Whenever ill-fortune becomes enraged / It turns granite as soft as wax" (V2:185). After he has built the city of Seyavashgerd, Seyavash speaks to Piran about the fate that the "turning high heavens" have fashioned for him, and about his innocence and his death, and in answering Piran's concerns he says, "I give news of the glory of God / I am aware of the secrets of the turning heavens." Here the glory of God and the secret of the heavens are one. After this, Seyavash tells Piran of future war and insurrection, the destruction of Iran and Turan, plundering and killing and burning, and the trampling of the ground beneath horses' hooves; and he ends by saying, "He who holds the world has written thus upon the heavens / At his command there grows what he has sown" (V2:308). At the end of the Sasanian dynasty, Rostam-e Farrokhzad, the commander of Iran's army who "was an astrologer, and very wise," writes to his brother about the coming war with the Arabs:

Destruction comes to us from Mars and Venus
    There is no evading the heavens' turning
Mercury and Saturn are in opposition
    Mercury has entered the sign of Gemini . . .
I see all that must come to be
    And concerning this I choose silence.

B9:321

By the turning of the heavens, through an inauspicious horoscope, an ancient and vast imperial realm crumbles at a touch. But this same commander, in the midst of such turmoil, writes a letter to the Arab commander Sa'd Vaqas:

At the letter's opening he spoke of He who holds the world
And that we should live in fear and dread
Since it is from Him that the turning heavens exist
And all of His realm is justice and light.

V9:321

The unjust heavens are stronger than all else, and the just God maintains this unjust entity as "all powerful." At times this intractable knot is shown to be irresolvable. Is the world of the Shahnameh anything other than this; the utter destruction of that empire referenced in Rostam-e Farrokhzad's letter? And were Ferdowsi's own times any different? In his time it was the fall of the Samanids, an invasion by nomads from the wastelands, and endless religious and worldly struggles in a world of pointless injustice.

Let's go on, and summarize; it's possible that we'll find the poet elsewhere than in this "multitude of thoughts":

Unknowing and ignorant the heavens turn upon themselves in time, and they are the cause of time's turning; the two are one and the same. In the uncertain battle between two brothers (Talkhand and Giv):

From end to end the city was filled with fear
Men's hearts crumbled and split in two
Wondering how the heavens would turn
And which of these two great men time would exalt.

B8:227

The turning heavens are not aware of themselves; in the death of Sohrab we see that they do not know what they are doing:

This is the way of the high heavens
Having in one hand a crown, in the other a noose
When someone sits happily wearing his crown
With its noose it drags him from the throne
If there is any knowledge of the turning heavens
Whose brains have become empty

Know that it is unaware of its turning
    There is no way to go beyond the heavens.
V2:195

This ignorant turning world is heedless of the sorrows and joys of its inhabitants.

If one should put his two eyes to the test
    Sometimes happy, sometimes in anger,
Astonished at this swiftly turning dome
    His heart would be filled with pain and burning
Thus it has always been throughout time
    Don't stay in this astonished state
To one there is all honey and sweetness,
    Ease of body and luxury and good fortune
For one everything goes crookedly
    Sometimes he is raised up, sometimes cast down
Thus the days bring up their progeny
    The thorn's pain outdoes the rose's color.
V4:174

It is ignorant and heedless of us, but it has authority over our souls:

The sharp claws of the dragon overcome him
    Who can escape by his manliness and knowledge?
Surely all that is must be
    The knowledgeable man does not escape from time.
V5:298

But isn't this oppressive and absurd figure, inflicting its undeserved sorrows on us, our nourishing and benevolent God? Wasn't it the Creator of the turning heavens who ordered these heavens to give Seyavash to be murdered?[15]

The knowledgeable, mighty, and just Creator is the Creator both of the senseless and ignorant world that is nevertheless permanent and of man with his wisdom and knowledge who is mortal. This senseless, ignorant, and permanent entity is the lord of time, of fortune, and of the lives of those who are wise and intelligent but mortal. The dominion of powerful ignorance over what is knowledgeable but incapable is the "injustice" within creation, and is fundamental to the existence of what is created. What do we conclude from this, that the Creator is unjust?—which is an impossible supposition—or that the unjust heavens turn contrary to their Creator's will?—which is also impossible. The result of all this is bewilderment, an impasse of thought. "Zurvan" is both time and our fate (destiny), and these two are outside of us, not within us; time is a "horizon," and with our birth and death we are pitched into this horizon, this place we don't know; it assigns us our time and place and fixes our destiny. And so, over against our lives in which inward finite time constructs our fate, is infinite time, within the two limits of the past and future, and it is within this arena, whether we wish to be there or not, that we struggle.

One of the sources of the poet's inward creative tension lies in his view of the dual nature of God (Ahura-Zurvan), in that he attempts to reconcile them together as one entity. One is the creator of fate, destiny, of our time on earth and the turning of the world; and the other (Ahura) is the guide to our role in the world; how can we reconcile ourselves to the one and the other to our will, as such a world is not subject to our will or even to that of Ahura Mazda? "From this thread nothing can be spun/ And from this thread no understanding can be woven." This is why it's said that "There is no way beyond the turning heavens"; it is a secret, a riddle; one must take a deep breath, and acknowledge that there is a being that is wise and all-knowing, and that's it! The poet did not know Zurvan, "Time as God," but he saw that time, day and night, gnaws like an indefatigable termite, and from the moment that Ahriman (or Satan?) found his way in, it has been turning the world to dust. He couldn't embrace the notion that such an unbridled tyrant could be considered as wise.

O welcomer of speech's pith
  Detach your heart from this ancient inn

Since it has seen many like you and like me
    And it will make peace with no one
Whether you are a prince or a servant
    You are transient and it is permanent
Whether you suffer, or you've a crown and throne
    You must, at last, pack your belongings and go
If you are iron the heavens will melt you down
    When you are old they will not pamper you
The lovely cypress must bow down
    Sadly narcissus eyes must weep and wail
The face like red-bud blossoms becomes saffron
    The happy sprightly youth grows heavy
Whether you are a prince or an underling
    You will find no other resting place than the black earth . . .
Where are those great ancestors of ours?
    Where are the brave and the pure that were ours?
All of them have earth as their pillow
    Fortunate is he who has sown none but good seeds.

B7:185

In the passing world of Mazdaism, and the transient world of Islam, evil, darkness, and death are not merely born along with good, light, and life; they are stronger than them. Deliverance remains in the eternal celestial realm or at the end of days. Literature, especially Persian classical poetry, generally sees the world in this way; as the blind poet Rudaki saw:

Live happily, with black-eyed beauties, happily
    For the world is nothing but a tale, and wind
One must not be anxious over what is to come
    Or remember what has gone by . . .
Wind and cloud are what this world is, and regret,
    Bring wine, may whatever's to come come.

History

THE SHAHNAMEH is the history of our forebears, and is to all intents and purposes an account of the footsteps left by time in Iran's past. The Shahnameh was written in the fourth century Hejri (tenth–eleventh centuries CE), four hundred years after the Arab conquest of Iran; this was a time when, in opposition to the Caliphate in Baghdad, the Iranians of Khorasan were trying to utilize new conditions to rebuild their own political fate and culture. Iranian dynasties had been formed some time previous to this, and their language, Persian, had been accepted as a religious and administrative language and as the foundation of our distinctive culture, and spread as such throughout Islamic civilization. It was in such a time that Ferdowsi composed his "History." In the Shahnameh he gave shape to both the language and the history together; the form of both was established, and their extent was specified.

Buildings turn to ruin
    From rain and the heat of the sun
In verse I have founded a great palace
    Which will not be harmed by wind and rain
Lives will pass by, and still this book
    Will be read by whoever is wise

V4:173

By founding this palace in "verse," he is the "versifier and organizer" from the beginning, the one who sets this material in order, who draws together the scattered fragments (of "prose") and saves the material from being dispersed and disconnected. The language is founded and built on an ordered structure (i.e., verse), in the form of a "great palace." It is clear that the poet has a great and "architectural" conception of his work; a conception that involves having a plan, laying a foundation, raising doors and walls and roofs that will remain unharmed by wind and rain; of taking refuge in a house of language, of living in language.[1]

And so after the fall of the Sasanids and a long subsequent interval, in the last years of the reign of the Samanids, the history of Iran is once again set on a firm footing; this time not by a king like Ardeshir, but by a poet like Ferdowsi, and in the form of the great and splendid palace mentioned above. For this reason he chooses some of the stories that he sees as "kingly," and sets others aside, and constructs a history worthy of Iran.

The Shahnameh says that by dividing the world between his sons, Feraydun established three countries, Iran, Turan, and Rum. After this, out of ambition and greed two of the brothers became envious of the youngest brother and killed him; and so it was with fratricide, with the shedding of Iraj's blood, that our epic history (heroic epic) begins, and it ends with another fratricide, the killing of Rostam through a trick perpetrated by his brother. The ancient struggle between Iran and Turan is based on fratricide, and the two peoples share a single genealogy, since both are descendants of Feraydun. The structure of this history—in its beginning, throughout its course, and in its end—is as it were an unconscious repetition of an initial pattern; the structure, appearance, and past of Iran represent in this fashion the creation and destiny of the world.

As far as we know, from the time of the Achaemenids, the priestly Zurvanite tradition had existed in western Iran. In the Sasanian period, Mazdean texts and beliefs became so mixed in with the teachings and convictions of this religion that it can be called "a kind of Zurvanite Zoroastrianism."[2] And so we can consider how Zurvanite mythology treats the creation and the history of the world, and compare this with the epic version of Iran's history:

> Before anything existed, neither heaven nor earth, nor any created thing in the heavens and earth, one named Zurvan, which means fortune or glory, existed. He struggled for a thousand years to produce a son named Hormozd who would create the heavens and the earth and whatever is in them. After a thousand years of struggle, Zurvan thought to himself, "What are my struggles and prayers leading to? My son Hormozd must be born, or my efforts are in vain," and as he was thinking this the seed that would produce Hormozd and Ahriman lodged itself within their mother's womb, Hormozd from the blessing conferred by his struggle, Ahriman from his doubt as to its efficacy. When Zurvan knew this he said, "I will make the first of these two to emerge from their mother's womb king." Hormozd knew his father's thoughts and told them to Ahriman . . . when he heard this Ahriman ripped open his mother's womb and emerged from it and presented himself to his father. When Zurvan saw him he did not know who he was, and asked, "Who are you?" and he said, "I am your son." Zurvan said to him, "My son is fragrant and shining, but you are dark and evil-smelling." As they were speaking the time came for Hormozd to be born; he emerged shining and sweet-smelling, and showed himself to Zurvan. And when Zurvan saw him he knew that he was his son Hormozd, for whom he had sacrificed and struggled so long, and for whom he held the branches of the barsom in his hand . . . he gave this to him and said, "Until now I have struggled that you should be born, and from now on you will struggle on my behalf," and he blessed him. Then Ahriman said to Zurvan, "But didn't you say that you would give sovereignty to whichever of your two sons presented himself to you first?" And in order not to break his oath, Zurvan said to Ahriman, "O evil liar, you will have 9,000 years of sovereignty and authority over Hormozd, and after 9,000 years sovereignty will belong to Hormozd and he shall do whatever he pleases."

In this myth, infinite time (Zurvan) is the source of good and evil (Hormozd and Ahriman). And since unwilled by him evil and good appeared as twins, Zurvan brought into being from himself finite time—the era of war between good and evil—so that Ahriman's life would come to an end. In this way Zurvan plans the fate (destiny) of the world without he himself being it, apart from the fact that Zurvan is time and everyone experiences his share of fortune through the passage of time. Perhaps it is for this reason that in the passing of time and the apportioning of fortune they were thought to be one and the same, although Zurvan cannot control even his own fate; otherwise, Ahriman would not have been born from him, and he would not have been forced to find some way that this unwanted son's life could be brought to an end.

Zurvan is not the God who creates the world; this is the role of his sons. This is why he struggles for his son's birth and praises him, or in other words why he adds the world of good in opposition to that of evil. In the view of our own myths, the creation comes about through struggle and sacrifice (and thought, a subject to which we shall return). For example, we see elsewhere that Hormozd created man and metal from the death of Kayumars, whose own name means "mortal life." Forty years after the passing of Kayumars (a sacrifice) and the spilling of his seed on the ground, Mashi and Mashyaneh grow up from the ground:

> with a stem for body, a pillar (stalk) and fifteen leaves . . . and then the form of each of them changed from that of plants to that of men . . . Hormozd said to Mashi and Mashyaneh, "You are men, the father and mother of mankind. I have created you possessed of the highest intelligence and judgment . . . think good thoughts, speak good speech, perform good deeds, do not praise demons."[3] In this way, as the *Minoy i Khrad* (Celestial Wisdom) puts it, mankind, "Male and female were created from his body and . . . metal also was created from his body."[4]

In the Avesta too, the creator is Ahura Mazda. When Ahriman emerges from the depths of darkness and sees the light and its goodness, he desires it and attacks the heavens in order to seize it; Ahura Mazda creates the world of goodness, and in opposition to this Ahriman creates the world of evil. And so the long war between good and evil, based on this contest, begins its course. Ahura Mazda sees the just end of the world, and the outcome of the contest, while Ahriman does not see this.

> In Zoroastrian tradition the life of the world lasts for twelve thousand years. In the first three thousand years Hormozd creates celestial beings (invisible, impalpable, and immaterial). At the end of this era Ahriman attempts to invade Hormozd's realm. But he is driven back and for three thousand years remains unconscious and unmoving. In this three thousand years, the second era of the world's existence, Hormozd creates earthly beings (visible, palpable, and material). At the end of this era Ahriman attacks, and the era of the interaction of good and evil—i.e., of the present world—begins, and the second six thousand years is initiated. Zoroaster appears half way through this period, at the beginning of the last three thousand years.[5]

The surviving remnants of Pahlavi literature indicate just how far during the Sasanid period—that is, at the time of the composition and compilation of the Khoda-i nameh (Royal Chronicles)—Zurvanite mythology and thought had become intermingled with Zoroastrian literature, customs, and beliefs. And so, as we have seen, in Iranian mythology (whether Zurvanite or Zoroastrian), the world has a beginning and as a result a lifespan; the worldview of Iranian mythology is historical, and the Shahnameh reproduces the "historical" mythology of epic heroes of the Sasanid era. This means that the Shahnameh's connection with Iranian mythology can be seen from various points of view; among others, for example, we can discover the thousands of years of the interaction of good and evil, and their war with one another, in the accounts of the lengthy reigns of Jamshid, Zahhak, and Afrasyab, and the stories associated with them.[6]

Myth, epic narrative, history, legend, tales, and reality are woven together in the Shahnameh. As a work of literature, the Shahnameh is an epic in which three sections are recognizable:

mythical, legendary, and historical; mythical epic, legendary epic and historical epic. The first section is the mythical past of fabulous stories and mythical individuals. The next is the epic "history" of Iran, incidents of derring-do, and the battles of champions and kings (this in particular is the epic and heroic portion of the book), and the last section is the era of historical "history." Of course, this division into sections is both brief and approximate, and sometimes a clear demarcation does not exist, especially between the first two sections, in which notable characters such as Feraydun, Afrasyab, and Kay Khosrow are the dramatis personae.

In the Shahnameh the history of the world is a reflection of celestial history; the earth takes its course from the way of the heavens, and reality from the way of myth. If we consider the epic portion of the book from the reign of Feraydun—the division of the world into three countries shared out between three brothers—until the death of Rostam, we can see that mythical notions and a reflection of celestial time are the fundamental warp and weft in imitation of which the heroic history of Iran is woven. With the birth of his sons, Zurvan set in motion the world's destiny, and this destiny is the narrative and history of the world. Feraydun too, with his division of the world between his sons, lays the foundation for the history of Iran and Turan (and Rum, the west). Zurvan did not want Ahriman's war with Hormozd, and Feraydun too could not bear Salm's and Tur's enmity towards Iraj, and when he learned that they had killed their brother, "Feraydun fell from his horse into the dust." In order to bring about the defeat and death of Ahriman, Zurvan created finite time out of himself, and Feraydun too urged Manuchehr to avenge Iraj's death, and did not rest until the fratricides had been killed.

When this was accomplished, his days and destiny declined
    The leaf withered on the Kayanid tree
Feraydun departed, his name remained
    And so his long days came to an end

v1:156

After the destruction of the unjust Zahhak, and now the killing of Salm and Tur, the role of Feraydun the Just is over, and his time on earth is at an end.

According to Zoroastrian tradition, Zurvan and Hormozd are not masters of their own destiny; in the legends of both of them, the existence of Ahriman was unwanted. Feraydun too, who was known as one "whose goodness was inclined to justice and generosity" before the birth of Iraj, became a father to sons whose nature was unjust and greedy, the complete opposite of his own. The only difference is that the twins Hormozd and Ahriman—who are manifestations of the dualism of our worldview—here become three; Feraydun had three sons: the wise and heaven-blessed Iraj, Tur who is quarrelsome and quick to anger, and Salm whose essence is earthly and wants only peace and quiet.[7] In our epic history too the Turanians are restless and belligerent, and the inhabitants of Rum, the land of Salm, stay out of the wars of Turan and Iran. These two opponents (Iran and Turan), have merged as the fundamental constituents of our view of world history. But in all cases the good come after the evil; Cain precedes Abel. After Feraydun the wars between the descendants of Iraj and Tur—with their inner dualist meaning of a war between good and evil—fill the greater part of the legendary section of the Shahnameh, up to the death of Rostam. This is like the continual war between Hormozd and Ahriman which stretches out to the end of the world, but with this difference that world history ends with victory and salvation, while the legendary section of the Shahnameh ends with calamitous rule of Bahman and Eskandar, and its historical section with the defeat of the Iranians and the victory of the Arabs. And so our "history" takes place in the "mixed" period when Ahriman is at work, and evil is at large in the warp and weft of the world.

Iranian mythology is essentially dualist. In our conception existence is not a combination of good and evil, but rather, as with the passage of night and day, the alternation of two separate entities that are joined together; light and darkness, good and evil, beauty and ugliness. And we have known (or know) that these two sources of existence will last in constant struggle with one another until the distant Day of Judgment. This is the reason that our view of the world and the afterlife is in essence ethical; everything is either good or evil. And good and evil are necessarily incompatible and struggle against one another. And so finally, this ethical worldview is also epic. Celestial history, from the Creation until the Last Judgment, began with wars between gods and demons, and so it will end. In the world the wars of kings and heroes are the vehicle of this history; on the one side there are Feraydun, Seyavash and Kay Khosrow, Rostam, Gudarz and Giv, and on the other Zahhak, Afrasyab, and Garsivaz.

But the earth is not a complete mirror of the heavens, and in actuality the world's history goes forward in our lives not according to our desires but according to human experience, and filtered by reality. Reality lays its own inimical designs on our dreams, and even though the Shahnameh's heroes (who live out their lives in the "mixed" period of the world's existence) destroy Zahhak and Afrasyab, or Garsivaz and Sudabeh, they too come to sad ends. Iraj and Seyavash, Sohrab and Forud, Esfandyar and Bahman and so on . . . all these heroes die young, while Zal and Rostam, Gudarz, Piran, and Farangis are finally disappointed in their hopes. The dynasties of kings fare no better; the dynasty of the earliest kings comes to an end with Jamshid—whose sovereignty over the world was his own soul's enemy—and the victory of the snake-shouldered Zahhak. The reign of Lohrasp's family ends with the victory of the accursed Alexander, and from its beginning with Ardeshir's dream we know that time destroys all that the Sasanids achieved. "Whether you are a prince or a servant / You are transient, and it is permanent" (B7:185). Perhaps it is for this reason that conceptions of deliverance and return have been and are so powerful in our worldview. In any case, only one family is exempt from such an end; the Kayanids begin with a deliverer from whom the whole family derives

(Feraydun), and end with another deliverer, a once and future king, who leaves in order to return (Kay Khosrow). Apart from this the Shahnameh is an epic of defeat and historical failure. But only from one point of view, because the defeat of these great men and women is not the defeat of greatness, it is the defeat of great ideals that have fallen into the noose of reality and become defeated but remain unappeased; these stubborn wishes stay unappeased through all the twists and turns of history as it inches forward!

The root of this historical failure of Iran in the Shahnameh can be found in the inevitable tension between ideal and reality, and the way that fate does not second and support heroic deeds. By "fate" is meant that twelve-thousand-year destiny, the preordained world, that like a river sweeps everyone along towards its end, and by "deeds" is meant heroic and historic acts that derive from a mighty will and both appear within history and form it.

The fate of a wise benevolent Turanian like Piran finally renders his deeds ineffectual, since he must act within the historical and geographical reality of the land of Turan, alongside Garsivaz and Afrasyab. And so when he was brought into the world at such a time and in such a place, fate had already mapped out his life's disappointments, and rendered his peaceful ideals null and void; and it is here that we see the connection between fate and time (and place and time), and perhaps their identity with one another, in the Shahnameh.

Idealism, which incites memorable and heroic deeds and leads them into history, is what drives the Shahnameh forward, and history flows inevitably within the limited space of social reality (as well as that of the predestined turning of the heavens). I'll give a few examples of this constant struggle between freedom (idealism) and necessity (reality) in the lives of idealistic men and women in their encounters with reality's opposition and at times destructiveness:

Feraydun	faced with the reality of sovereignty establishes countries (Iran and Turan) and history,
Zal and Rostam	faced with Kavus
Sohrab	faced with Rostam

Seyavash	faced with Kavus and Sudabeh; faced with Garsivaz and Afrasyab
Piran and Farangis	faced with Afrasyab
Kay Khosrow	faced with the personal satisfactions and temptations of power (his fear of Jamshid's pride, Kavus's foolishness, and the filicide of Goshtasp).
Esfandyar	faced with Goshtasp
Rostam and Zal	faced with Esfandyar, a cantankerous proselytizer

I shall leave aside other examples such as Forud who faces Tus, and so forth, and point out that most of these idealists are, as they must be, young people, and reality is the battlefield where mature wolves attack them—that is Rostam, Kavus, and Afrasyab—as an old man. And victory more often favors reality than idealism.

The victory of the old over the young in the Shahnameh, Rostam over Sohrab, Kavus over Seyavash, Goshtasp over Esfandyar and so on, has attracted the attention of some critics and led them to consider this, when compared with western literatures, as a demonstration of the importance of both royal power and paternal authority as the bases of society,[8] both of which from one point of view appear to be the case. But at the same time we should remember that during two one-thousand-year-long eras controlled by Ahriman, the most unjust rulers of all, Zahhak and Afrasyab, are defeated by two glorious young heroes who are watched over by the heavens. All three of the sons of Zoroaster, who bring about the resurrection at the end of time, are young, and at the age of thirty are given the task of renewing the world. The knot of sacred and secular time is undone with the help of the good fortune of the young, who open up the paths of both kinds of history (time). The proselytizer for the "good faith" (Zoroastrianism) who wishes to open the path of righteousness, is the young hero Esfandyar, not the old king Goshtasp, and the seed of his downfall lies in that moment when his desire for sovereignty blinds his wisdom; before this, as a young man he had been successful, and in middle age the old man who kills him has only a short-lived victory, since he himself is killed a year later. And in the tale of Rostam and Sohrab the victorious old man longs in his wretchedness for "his name to be stricken from among the heroes." Apart from these instances most of the failures of the young, when they are defeated by the bitter realities of life, arise from the clash between political conditions (sovereignty and authority), and the restrictions of social and individual life on the one hand and their noble ideals on the other.

Perhaps it goes without saying that the clash between ideals and reality within historical characters is not a simple matter of action and reaction, but something complex, interwoven and with its own form, and that for each case it's necessary to delve into their "history" in order to discover their specific characteristics. For example, in his dividing of the world and the creation of history—that is, in the area of reality—Feraydun suffers defeat, and with the revenge for the death of Iraj he is victorious in the area of ideals (the destruction of injustice), but at the price of losing all three of his sons and of the long-drawn-out wars between Iran and Turan; that is, at the price of defeat in reality. Kay Khosrow's victory in the world (reality) and in the world to come is complete, but on condition that he forsakes the world; his victory over reality depends upon his resolve to put it behind him. Piran's ideal (the reconciliation of two countries) is destroyed in the area of reality. In his battle with Gudarz at the end of his life, even though he doesn't cease to fight, he knows very well that faced with "the turning of fate" (destiny) nothing will come of his vehemence and valor:

> Piran looked at how things now stood
> He knew that this outcome was the will of God
> But out of valor he fought on
> Striving against the turning of fate
>
> V4:128

And Kay Khosrow says of his death:

For ill luck is a fierce dragon
Trapping a ferocious lion in a moment
No one escapes from him through valor
When this sharp-clawed dragon strikes
v4:156

And so, "Now fate was accomplished and Piran passed / All his deeds and achievements became as wind." But as compensation for these failures, in the infinite area of the ideal—particularly at the moment of death—Piran's victory is all the higher and greater over the "turning of fate." On the threshold of defeat, when they say to him, "Take refuge in Iran, take yourself and your people and everything you wish," he says, "To me, death is better than such a life / that I who am a commander should become a slave." He has more faith in death than in life, in not-being than in being, and in his ideals than in reality.

None of the heroes of epic, or a number of the kings, are without ideals, and they are not satisfied merely with the quotidian passing of time. An epic narrative is not the equivalent of a journey across a safe plain; it is mountainous, a cliff, a plummeting down and subsequent rising up, and the high flight of a hunting hawk. This road of defeat and victory cannot be traveled without some impelling force, and an unbreakable idealism. Even those who are unjust, like Zahhak, Afrasyab, and Goshtasp, have within them an impelling force (greed) and an ideal (authority) that are so strong that they form both their nature and their fate. A man without ideals is not a "warrior" on the field of battle so much as a "mere presence," one who can achieve nothing.

According to our mythology and epic tradition, freedom is both man's desire, and a destiny that time has decreed for him—it is predestined and chosen, and as with life and death, Ahriman and Ahura Mazda, the two are inseparable. We also see this same ancient understanding in the Shahnameh. This book is not a cerebral or philosophical work in which we can find a "solution" to the conundrum as to whether the world is the place of man's predestination or free-will. In the Shahnameh the flight of the ideals of the free, and the arbitrary turning of the heavens, exist together with and within one another, and the heroes "Strive against the turning of the heavens / If time and fate appear before them."

In heroic epics it is the kings and heroes who are able to give a reality to their desires, not the mass of people, about whom little is said. It is they who create history, and history goes forward according to their royal deeds. They are world rulers and world conquerors, the accomplices of peace and war and good and evil in the world, and as Bozorgmehr has said in answer to one who questioned him concerning someone who has no share of wisdom, knowledge, or heroism, "It is better that death / Should place a dark helmet on his head" (V8:130). The ideals and ethical values of epic—fame and shame—became firmly rooted in popular culture, and turned into an ethical model for everyone; Ferdowsi himself is a great constructor of this culture, and his book is a "history" of the civilization of free men (the aristocracy) in Iran, and of the noble and elevated progress of their aspirations. Distance and separation, reality and the ideal, fill the lives of these great men with struggle and labor, and lead them to painful ends. And finally it is not only those who make history that come to a sorrowful end, but also history itself.

As it happens the Shahnameh itself is the result of defeat and disappointment; occupation by the Arabs over a number of centuries,[9] the decline of the Samanid dynasty, and the various setbacks of Iran's history. When weakness in the face of historical reality becomes apparent, the need for tradition, for taking refuge in the historic past, comes to the fore; Abu Mansur Abdul Razzaq, the performers of shahnamehs, and Ferdowsi himself turn their faces away from the unpleasant realities of their own time to the reassuring past, not as an impossible escape from the era in which they lived, but rather so that "The terror of events does not sweep away their foundations." The Shahnameh represents a search for a sound footing in the past in order to stand firm in the present, and its appearance arises from Iranians' profound need to remain alive, to "continue as themselves." This book is the victory of the word over the deed; if we are defeated in the vicissitudes of historical action, which is the work of man, we are victorious in speech, which is the masterwork of man.

In the thought of Ferdowsi and his era, man's social history was not separate from the deeds of kings, and incidents on earth were connected to the movement of the heavens. The basis of the mythical worldview of Iran presents itself as dualist. It is in terms of this dualism of reality that our view of kings, the last judgment, ethics, aesthetics, and our nature is structured. In the passage of "epic history" we also find other narratives that are the reflex of this dualism, although not merely as reverse images but with such differences as may be imagined: we can see this dualism by comparing Iran with Turan, Feraydun with Zahhak, Seyavash and Kay Khosrow with Garsivaz and Afrasyab, Rostam with Afrasyab, Farangis with Sudabeh . . . and it is also apparent in the poem's momentous conflicts, the hand-to-hand clashes between Rostam and Sohrab, Piran and Gudarz, Rostam and Esfandyar, Rostam and the White Demon, the heroes and the sorcerers of the Seven Trials, and in various other places. This is even the case in the love stories, such as those between Zal and Rudabeh, or Bizhan and Manizheh, in which two countries are ruled over by two incompatible kings. This worldview finds its expression in the legends and historical narratives of the poem, and leads them to their conclusions.

The greatest example of this incompatibility is the long-drawn-out war between Iran and Turan, led by Rostam and then by Kay Khosrow on the one side, and by Afrasyab on the other. Their prolonged struggle, which takes up almost all of the legendary section of the Shahnameh, is not primarily concerned with lineage; face to face with Esfandyar, Rostam—the prop and champion of the Iranians—boasts that through his mother he is descended from Zahhak, the enemy of Iranians:

My mother was the daughter of Mehrab
In whose reign the land of India flourished
And who was a fifth generation descendant of Zahhak
Who lifted his head above the kings of the world.

V5:347

Rudabeh and Tahmineh, like kind Manizheh, are foreigners from other lands. But the most poignant of all is Kay Khosrow whose celestial nature derives from his father Seyavash and Kavus on the one hand, and Farangis and Afrasyab on the other.

The conflicts and preoccupations of Iranian epic, beginning with the battles against wolves and demons and sorcerers (the seven trials, Rostam and the White Demon or the Akvan Demon) up to the wars between Iran and Turan, and various other adventures, each of which has its own pathos, specificity, and appearance—all of these together, in their hard struggle with nature and what lies beyond it, make up the history of Iran.

- This "history" (which is similar to a mythology) is epic because its being derives from warfare.
- It is ethical because good and evil are opposed to one another.
- Unlike a mythology, it is national, since it is not gods and demons or kings or heroes that are fighting with each other, but two countries.
- The origin of the war lies in a close relationship between two countries (Iran and Turan).
- The stimulus to war is "justice" (the desire for revenge).

To this list of general characteristics we must also add personal stimuli to do with sentiment, psychology, and the individual. It is these individual stimuli that give color and a particular spirit to the battles, and prevent them from becoming a monotonous and soulless repetition of one another. Each battle has its own circumstantial reality. The general characteristics and the aforementioned individual stimuli are woven together into one figure, and to separate them would be like cutting up bodies, like cutting into the living body that we call the Shahnameh, the better to see the circulation of its blood and the beating of its heart.

From the childhood of Feraydun up to the death of Rostam, the epic history of the Shahnameh begins, develops, and ends with war. The combatants on both sides are, as in all epic conflicts, brave and famous heroes. But the Shahnameh is a history of Iran, not a history of warring combatants, even though we also find described there the adventures of such combatants. History and the makers of history are bound together as one, and they are so involved with one another that in reading "history" we are plunged into the circumstances of those who make history, and as we consider the details of their deeds and qualities, we are swimming, whether we wish to be or not, in the current of "history" (except in the case of a few interspersed stories). Due to the brilliance of the poet's art, this consonance of form and content is sometimes like the inseparable union of body and soul; each is both of them and both are each of them.

War in the Shahnameh has an ethical quality to it, since the kings' wars are like those of Ahura Mazda and Ahriman, in that they are fought for the victory of good over evil and of justice over injustice. In the "prehistoric" period, during which men, demons, and celestial beings exist together, when demons kill Kayumars's son Siamak, he gathers together an army of "animals and birds and celestial beings" in order to avenge his son's death, and entrusts it to his grandson Hushang, who fights against the demons and cleaves his father's murderer in two.

> When his desire for revenge was fulfilled
> The days of Kayumars came to an end.
>
> V1:25

Similarly, during the epic era after the downfall of the sorcerer Zahhak, the endless wars between Iran and Turan in order to avenge Iraj and Seyavash begin, and they persist until the victory of Kay Khosrow and "the cleansing of evil from the world." In these wars each hero has the banner of his own clan, but the banner of the "clan" of all the Iranians is always the scrap of blacksmith's leather (the Kaviani banner), as a symbol of the desire for justice. Raising such a banner is a reminder of the most unjust of rulers, and a sign of the desire for justice on the part of warriors who are following the way of Kaveh in his opposition to snake-shouldered Zahhak.

This is true not only of Iranians, but also among the Turanians there are people like the wise Piran, and Aghriras, who do not fan the flames of war. Only Afrasyab and Garsivaz, and among the Iranians Kavus, for obvious reasons do not desire peace. The Iranians' war is basically defensive, like Ahura Mazda's battles against Ahriman. Both in the heavens and on earth, unprovoked invasion, the unjust deed of those who follow Ahriman, is the fundamental reason for their defeat. During the reign of Kay Khosrow, in the war between the forces of Iran and Turan:

The brave warriors of Turan, and their champions,
With maces and arrows and swords
If a mountain were before them on the day of battle
They would not hesitate to flatten it
All their arms hung down uselessly
Bound by the power of God
They were caught in the snare of disaster
For they had unjustly shed much blood
Their horses were rooted to the spot
You'd say that their legs had been bound
All that was good was lost to them
The day was against them, they had no will to fight
This was the desire of the World Creator
And you'd say that the earth had swallowed up these warriors

V4:117

If the stimulus to war is ethical, as with every other ethical phenomenon it involves principles and values that have corollaries that the combatants acknowledge, such as loyalty to one's birthplace, or chivalry vis-à-vis one's enemies and friends. Initiating a war, seeking revenge, and spilling blood needlessly are as unjust as breaking an oath, and in the end they lead to nothing but defeat. As soon as an unjust king like Kavus wants to break a treaty, to kill his hostages and attack the land of an enemy who is looking for peace, the only result he achieves is Rostam's anger and disapproval, the death of a son like Seyavash, and the loss of a wife whom he loves. And Esfandyar, who for the sake of sovereignty and his religion wishes to take Rostam, who is innocent, to Goshtasp in chains, ensures that both he and Rostam will be killed. But we know that out of their sense of martial magnanimity these two warriors extravagantly praise one another even as they are locked in combat. In war, combatants are chivalrous to their enemies, as can be seen in the hand-to-hand combat of Gudarz and Piran, and the ultimate death of one at the hands of the other on the summit of a mountain, which is a sublime example of the noble compassion of hand-to-hand combatants fighting to the death. Kay Khosrow, in the last and greatest war between Iran and Turan, puts these ethical principles into words that always apply, whether in friendship or in enmity:

> Wise Kay Khosrow spoke thus:
> "Whatever does not please me,
> I will not reproach anyone with this evil
> No matter how much it makes me desire vengeance."
> V4:262[10]

War has a role as a maker of history: for example, the war with the sorcerer Zahhak, the desire for revenge for the deaths of Iraj and Seyavash, and Esfandyar's refractoriness and stubborn rejection of injustice. In the era of Zahhak, the shedding of Iranian blood and the invasion of the land of Iran are paired together. In the same way the battles of Iranian heroes spring from two causes, their desire for justice and their love of Iran are not separate, and the defense of the land of Iran is itself a mission for justice. Certainly the "desire for justice" is the inmost soul of the Shahnameh, but each time a hero espouses this it takes its form and expression from the structure of the particular story, or the details of combat. For example, in the long struggle against Afrasyab, Seyavash and Kay Khosrow, Rostam, Giv and Gudarz, or Farangis and Piran, all desire justice and strive for it, but each according to his own motives and place in the narrative, and each time this involves a specific narrative.

From another perspective, the heroes—whether of Iran or Turan—do not wage war because of a single cause (justice or injustice, defense of a country or conquest beyond a country's borders). "Name" (reputation / fame) has a lofty status, as do nobility, bodily and spiritual lineage, and individual strength, all of which drive a man to face the enemy on the field of battle, without fear of death. And so the "deeds and struggles" of the celebrated epic heroes have both individual and communal causes, and since their glorious ethical battles take place in the realm of two countries and two sovereignties, they have in reality a political nature. In the Shahnameh, the universal battle between Ahura Mazda and Ahriman, and the struggle between good and evil that is in the nature of the world, come into being as a way from war to human society; the unique spiritual world descends to earthly and daily life. The causes and circumstances, the good and evil of the wars of defense or invasion, the conventions and rituals of reconciliation, the practice of chivalry, the behavior of combatants towards one another, the mustering of armies, the use of weapons, the descriptions of armies' maneuvers and of the battlefield, and many other things concerning war, are abundantly present throughout the Shahnameh, and are each deserving of separate consideration. Here we can only refer to a few basic points, so that our investigation is not unduly interrupted, or does not stray too far from its course.

In the Avesta we can find signs of a pastoral and nomadic culture; for example, the first bull, and the preservation of its seed in the moon, sheep and other domesticated animals, Mehr the possessor of broad pastures, the God Bahram whose body is the rushing wind, the beautiful ox with golden horns, the white horse, the maddened camel, the male boar, the horned ram of the open plains, hunting birds, and the fifteen-year-old youth. But in the Shahnameh the inhabitants of Turan are nomadic, whereas the Iranians are a settled people whose roots go deep into the soil, and throughout every era they remain firmly attached to their homeland, which makes the national quality of our epic even more clear. Similarly, in the Sasanid era nomads continuously invade the country and Iranians fight "for their country and clan"; that the land comes first and foremost is beyond discussion, and the war is between the people of two countries. We see that the civilization of the legendary and historical eras of the Shahnameh has the appearance of being centered mainly on a local petty aristocracy (referred to as *dehqan*). This is why when contrasted with Turks, Arabs, or Westerners, *dehqan* means "Iranian" (B9:307), which can be taken as an indication of the particular nature of this civilization. The clans of the legendary era, the Gudarzian, Nozarian, or Sistanian (the name of Sam's, Nariman's, and Rostam's clan), or that of Piran Viseh, are like the seven families "of free men" of the Parthians and Sasanids, in that each has its own homeland. Before his journey to the other world, Kay Khosrow bestows the charter of Nimruz on Rostam, that of Qom and Isfahan on Gudarz of the Keshvadegan, and the charter of Khorasan on Tus of the Nozarian. These have their own armies, and are the kings' support and refuge of their own free will. In wartime, something that demonstrates the ethical nature of these independent chieftains' behavior, in my opinion, is that their support is given of their own free will, a free will that we see in its noblest embodiment in hand-to-hand combat. They risk their lives, not merely with their physical strength but with all their being, and exert their will to life's limit, to death itself. Not only in the give-and-take of battle, but in all activities, good or bad, to do with the world's course, whatever can save or destroy mankind and the world, is worthy of immense effort on the part of these same free agents; it is not the business of slaves of the powerful who become caught up in the daily round of events.

Manifestations of this civilization of "free agents" can be found in our epic. Here I want to pause for a moment and refer to the nature of the composition of this kind of epic poetry. The poetry of the Shahnameh, and of narrative poems to do with love and mysticism—that is, *masnavis*—is composed in a different manner from the kind of poetry we find in the Persian *qasideh*, the appearance and purpose of which are borrowed from Arabic literature, and which is basically praise of aristocrats and rulers, and occasionally advice and wisdom-literature. *Qasideh* poetry represents the aristocratic culture of a court, and our poetry of this nature is court poetry composed with an eye to Baghdad, and its conventions are derived from this fact. The poetry and culture of national and local Iranian courts (at least during the Safarid and Samanid periods) do not remain uninfluenced by formal Arab poetry and the power of the Caliphate. Sa'di's *qasideh* lamenting the fall of the caliphate and the death of Al-Musta'sem is perhaps an example of this genre.

In contrast to this, the Shahnameh is the product of another aristocratic culture, and its origin is not in Baghdad, or in the desert lamenting "over ruins and traces of campsites," but is native, and concerned with the land and history of Iran. And since it is concerned with courts and poetries that have no connection with Baghdad, from a time of poets gone by, the Shahnameh sings of a former nobility, even if this is done within the conventions of the praise poetry of the time, albeit in another form; it summons up past ideals to its own era, and with this admixture fosters the national desires of its own time and bequeaths them to the future. Ferdowsi's task is to renew what is old.

> These tales have grown old from their origin
> The ancient days shall be renewed
>
> V2:202

In contrast to epics like the *Mahabharata*, the *Iliad* and the *Odyssey*, the *Nibelungenlied* and so on, which have other motivations and purposes, the Shahnameh is a "national" epic, and this is not only because it celebrates or praises the war and peace experienced by the nation of Iran. Apart from, and before, Ferdowsi's poem there were khoda-i namehs, ancient "chronicles," and other shahnamehs, but they have not survived, because they had no trace of this quality. Ferdowsi's genius is to have knitted together such various stories and historical accounts that his narrative includes the whole of

Iranian cultural—not political—history and geography. Ferdowsi chose what he considered to be worthwhile, and which pleased him, from Abu Mansur's Shahnameh and other sources and put them together to fashion the national history of Iran in the way that we see. Rostam and Sohrab, and "the story of Rostam and Esfandyar, like a number of other stories such as Ardeshir-e Papakan, Bizhan and Manizheh, and similar tales, are independent stories that have been added to the Shahnameh."[11] All this was manifested in the mirror of language, and we know that it was in the greatness of this Persian tongue that a firm and widespread—national—identity was found.

In this way, apart from the concern with the present and the future, history took on another aspect; the "national" stories of those who had gone before became splendid images of a future national identity, and the epic past of the earliest heroes became a way forward for those yet to be born. Ferdowsi consciously looks back in order to find the difficult way ahead. When he said, "Over this book, many lives will pass / and whoever has wisdom will read it," it is as if he is speaking of the future for those who are wise, for those who are aware and attentive. In the Shahnameh, world history is written in terms of a celestial paradigm; Ahura Mazda's battle against Ahriman drives the "history" of the world towards its victorious judgment day, and Ferdowsi uses the history of Iran in its war with Turan to indicate what is to come. But the history of the world is also driven towards an ignominious defeat, for despite the Shahnameh's outwardly legendary appearance it is a book concerned with reality, and the reality of Iran's history was that it arrived at the bitter truth of defeat.

The subject of epic is not simply the struggles and clashes of heroes—the conquerors and the conquered—with one another. The hero lives out his life in the world, and although the world nurtures him, it is his own will that controls the specificity of his victory in the world, and his accomplishment of this. It is the strength of this will that directs the hero's impossible striving towards victory and defeat, as in the cases of Sohrab, Esfandyar, Bizhan and Bahram, or Afrasyab who does not shrink from fire and water in his striving for royal glory. Rostam's end, accomplished at the price of his life in his victory over Esfandyar, is a telling example of the hero's destiny, in that he willingly chooses death rather than the loss of his fame and reputation:

He knocks at death's door
He mounts his horse and urges it forward

The Shahnameh is the history of victory in defeat or, to put it another way, of the victory of defeat. When face to face with death, choice comes into play, and it is the strength of the hero's will, in its instinct for eternity, that impels him. And in the history that Ferdowsi has compiled, when face to face with defeat, choice is victorious; the Shahnameh is a history of the ideal, as we have conceived it and longed for it, and in the choices that Ferdowsi makes he brings this ideal to fruition. Did Ferdowsi put the Shahnameh together as it is according to the conception he had of history and cast the lives of our forebears according to this narrative? Did he really consider the tale of the Akvan Div to be a part of our history? We know that he didn't consider it as such. In the introduction to his narratives, after an allusion to vain philosophies in which he remarks that the opinions of whoever does not look with the eyes of the mind will not comport with wisdom, he says, "I do not travel along your road, the world is full of wonders, and we have no way of assessing them." But

When a wise man hears these tales
With knowledge, he will not incline to this
But if you understand the meaning
You will be at peace, and there will be no more argument
V3:289

If you look with the eyes of knowledge, if you perceive things intelligently, rather than "incline to this," that is, to the tale's surface, you will see and comprehend the tale's meaning. This was also said by his predecessors. In the introduction to Abu Mansur's Shahnameh, it is said that

> . . . this was called the Shahnameh so that those who had knowledge would look at it and find in this book the ways of kings and aristocrats and the wise, the kings' deeds and their characters and behavior, the practice of justice and judgment, plans and their execution, the drawing up of armies, warfare and the conquest of cities, the desire for revenge, attacks by night, contentment and ambition; all these things will be found in this book. And things are related here that will be of great importance to the reader, and from which everyone can benefit. And they will find in this book things that seem dreadful, and this is good, and if you consider the inner meaning, you will see the matter correctly and it will be pleasing to you. For example, Arash's show of strength, or the stone that Feraydun stopped with his foot, or the snakes that grew out of Zahhak's shoulders. The meaning of all these events will be clear to knowledgeable and wise people, and one who is an enemy to knowledge will change this into something ugly, and there are many wonders in the world . . . [12]

The battle with the White Demon, and the wonders of the two Seven Trials, are among those wonders that readers call "dreadful." Nevertheless the poet has included stories of this kind in his book, and excluded others, such as the deeds of Garshasp and the archer Arash. And so at least some of the sections that we see in the Shahnameh are Ferdowsi's own work and the result of his own choice, that "victorious" choice!

Why? When he is someone who has said, "If even one story should be omitted / this would sadden my soul," how can he boast to himself that "I have built a high palace from verse"? With the choices among different stories that Ferdowsi himself had made, was the Shahnameh in his opinion the true history of Iran, and did he really think that snake-shouldered Zahhak had come from the sands of Arabia, and that for a thousand years he had ruled over us unjustly until his departure? Or that a demon had flung the sleeping Rostam from the skies into the sea? And that such stories as these had once happened in, for example, Khorasan and Fars, and that people had recorded for future generations the things that they had seen and experienced?

From another point of view, we see that for all his concern with the faithlessness of life, and the transitory nature of men's deeds, the poet is still obsessed with the heritage of those who have gone before, whether it be small or great or epoch-making, and whether it be historical or unhistorical. The Sasanid period is full of long stories, such as the successive scenes of hunting, love, and merrymaking of Bahram Gur, or as Ferdowsi himself says "tales within tales" (B9:220), or long conversations between nobles and sages, Bozorgmehr and Anushirvan, to the point that the poor poet says, "Thank God I've found release from all this":

Thanks be to the Lord of the sun and moon
    That I have escaped from Bozorgmehr and the king
Because this matter was discouraging for me
    (As if) you have to talk about playing chess

B8:206

Similarly at the end of the unpleasant Eskandar narrative, the poet breathes a sigh of relief and says, "I'm done with this barrier built by Eskandar."

It seems that in Ferdowsi's thought there is a difference between epic history (in the legendary, heroic period) and "real" history, since one involves him adding and excluding characters, but the other, even when the matter is lengthy and unpleasant, must be versified without any cutting or abbreviation. Can it be that Ferdowsi believed that the events of the epic period were concerned with the inner truth of history; that is, that these legendary stories were not descriptions of actual events but illustrative metaphors, and that what happened in the periods of Eskandar and the Sasanids was "real" history; that this is what actually happened at the time? And that this is why he neither adds anything to nor excludes anything from these accounts? And this is so to the extent that we are confronted with two Eskandars in the Shahnameh, one of Iranian origin and a friend to Iran, and the other a foreigner and accursed enemy, and the "historian" versifies both as he finds them to be? If this is a writer who is attentive to his important task, who in his concern to pack a long narrative into a short space sometimes adds new stories and raises them to another level, and who cuts nothing from distressing stories and so makes his work more valuable within this space, then certainly a conscious, shaping spirit is involved.

Before the beginning of the new period, in the religious sense there is no clear dividing line between divine and sacred history on the one hand and the natural word and the world to come on the other. In the same way that the faithful believed in the miracles performed by prophets and other religious figures, events that flew in the face of experience and the usual course of life were also seen as possible. In such a case the course of history is neither logical nor divine, but dependent on a divine will filled with the secrets of the other world, even though much of it is incomprehensible; but in another way we know this much, that the world is the place where God's omniscience and omnipotence are manifested, and it is impossible that any otiose deed should proceed from him. These days we know that any representation that is unreal is a "falsehood," and we believe it to be a poet's invention or fable. We accept the tale of Rostam and Esfandyar, Dante's strange journey to hell and paradise, or the astonishing histories of Oedipus and Faust, as "fictitious" truths. Our forebears believed much more strongly in the spiritual truth of history's divine fables, and the least of their uses was as ancient stories that could be of admonitory use for future generations. The Israiliyyat and the stories in the Qur'an were clear historical examples of this, a mixture of anecdote and reality, advice and admonition and conclusion, as well as being a path to salvation. Similarly with the tales of 'Ad and Thamud, Abraham and the fire, Nimrod, Pharaoh and Moses, or the beauty of Joseph and Zuleikha's love for him. All these are not simply true and self-evident like any historical narrative; because of their spiritual nature they contain various double truths—heavenly and earthly, divine and human—and the double nature of this truth forms one whole; dividing it into two separate aspects is pointless.[13]

But the historical method of tracing hadith was based on oral tradition. Throughout the period of pre-Islamic Arab culture, poetry and literature, genealogy, and "daily" history and so on were not written down (nor could they be); and in the beginning the culture of Islam reached future generations orally, passed on from individual to individual: "reported by so-and-so who had it from so-and-so." The sayings of the prophet and the imams (hadith), as well as the biography of the prophet (which were later written down) were passed down through confidence in this oral transmission. This is how the science of hadith was established, by the effort to know which accounts were trustworthy and reliable from the mass of accounts that had been passed down. This science as a way of establishing a narrative was at first a paradigm for Muslim historians, and was used by Tabari among others.

Tabari, who was certainly one of the first and greatest of Muslim historians, lived around the time of Ferdowsi, and his work became well-known at that time and was translated into Persian, so that we have two observers of history from one and the same culture and period, but with differing ends, methods, and interests. For this reason, I think that reference to these two contemporary savants in order to become better acquainted with Ferdowsi's historical thought, in its similarities to and differences from Tabari's, will not come amiss. Tabari, who was also a prominent commentator on Islamic law and an expert in hadith, reviewed the history of the world from the creation of man until his own time. The opening sections of his book inevitably depend heavily on the "creation myth" and the teachings of religious texts; the history of the life of the prophet, and the appearance and spread of Islam, contained the truest information that this author knew of. But when dealing with the Sasanid era, Tabari sometimes sets various and contradictory accounts side by side within the one narrative. It's as if he cannot attest to one version and choose this to the exclusion of others.

At times in his *History of Prophets and Kings* he gives equal weight to prophets and kings, heavenly and earthly events, seeing them as equally "true." But his narrative in both cases is based on stories and information that have come down to him from the past, and the divine truth of events taken from religious texts is self-evident to him. However, when it comes to secular matters the historian is seeking historical truth—in a new sense—and this is not an intellectual inquiry (and to him the "intellect" meant something different from our conception nowadays) so much as an attempt to find reliable information, with an eye to what seems true and what seems false, in ancient accounts.

Now we return to the Shahnameh, in a section of which myth and history and truth and legend are joined together: Jamshid, and Zahhak and his snakes, and reigns of six hundred or a thousand years, and Afrasyab's sorcery, and the cow which brought up Feraydun, and Kay Khosrow who went to the other world without dying.

And so the Shahnameh is not a history of prophets, it is a history only of kings, and as a result it has nothing to do with the ideas and beliefs of the faithful, in which there is no room for doubt or uncertainty. A Muslim historian who has taken his history of the prophets from a religious text might, by referring to other divinely inspired texts, add some extra leaves and branches to his narrative, but nothing more than this. But the writer of the Shahnameh is the "editor" of his history, he omits and adds and compiles, and has a choice in the matter. Above and beyond this, he himself knows that it is his making and molding that constitutes the why and wherefore of his work, and so he says, "The wise man who hears this tale / Will turn to knowledge, he will not turn to (the surface of) the tale." He leaves it to the wise who have such knowledge to help in solving the secrets of the narratives in this "history," and so to discovering their meaning. Here he is like Tabari in that he calls on the like-mindedness and help of the reader if his text is to be understood.[14]

If Ferdowsi turns to the knowledge of the wise to go beyond his stories' surface and penetrate to their meaning, this is because in his time the mythology of Iran was no longer the foundation and "history" of his readers' religion and worldview; the stories can be thought about and their secrets can be uncovered, so that his history becomes a text that involves both exclusion and inclusion. The Shahnameh is not a history of prophets and kings in which divine and secular events occur side by side. There could not be any appearance of prophets here, except for one (the appearance of Zoroaster, in Daqiqi's verses), and this one comes and departs in the midst of the history of kings. The Shahnameh's mythology is concerned with earthly and social activity; Jamshid and Zahhak and Afrasyab, Feraydun and Seyavash and so on, along with the tales and adventures in which they are involved, all exist for the destruction of injustice and the placing of a just sovereign on the throne.

In contrast to Tabari's *History*, which extends from the creation of the world and man until the time of the author, the Shahnameh begins with someone (like Sohrab and Seyavash) from whose youth's wondrous perfection "there shone the royal glory / like the full moon above a tall cypress tree" (V1:22). Kayumars established in the first human community "the customs of the throne and crown," the sovereignty of the world, the ways and manners of kings and their authority, as well as stability and social organization. For this reason the Shahnameh, from the descent of this "wearer of leopard skins" from the mountains until Rostam-e Farrokhzad's letter, is also fundamentally a work that is political, in the widest sense of the word. Here the vehicle of history is not the appearance of heaven and Adam and Eve, but rather it is set in motion by the appearance of the arts of living, the struggle against demons, instructions concerning food and clothing, and it continues with the conquests of a royal clan and the kingly actions of great households.

In contrast to contemporary histories, throughout its legendary section the Shahnameh is only concerned with worldly events, and with those who are involved in promoting and acting in these, not with God or angels or the mass of men whose will plays no part in the unfolding of history. It does not deal with agricultural matters, the ceremonies of court life, relations between kings and nobles, the means and customs of making war . . . or the connections between justice and force and the passage of people's daily lives, or if it does so this is only in an indirect and mediated way. In the Shahnameh's historical section, however, we find references to such matters, as in other histories.

Like Tabari, Ferdowsi is also a Muslim, with everything that this entails. In Tabari's worldview, the one God has created the world, and from the creation until the end of time He directs its course according to His divine will. Tabari's book is an exposition of stages along this path. But the Shahnameh is firmly founded on a tradition based on dualism; it is a tapestry woven from a warp and weft of black and white threads, with the brightness of "Ahura—Asha—justice" and the darkness of "Ahriman—the lie—injustice" in an era of mingled realities. This ancient dualism lying at the base of stories and events, and which sleeps in our "collective unconscious," exists deep within the unconscious of the great poet, and finds its expression in his self-awareness; that is, in his poetry. There is a contradiction between absolute sole power on the one hand and dualism and its manifestations on the other, and as a result we see the poet's bewilderment, confusion, and perplexity in his book. It is this dualism, as we have said before, that gives the heroic and ethical quality to Ferdowsi's "history," a quality that Tabari's and similar histories should not and could not have possessed.

In reality, the poet selects what he wishes from the stories and historical events that have come down to him, and rejects those he does not wish to use; in fact, he constructs a new history out of ancient tradition, and then remains faithful to whatever version he has chosen. He himself does not say that he has fitted together and versified whatever he has come across; instead he says, "If there were one word missing from a story / that tale would cause me grief"; that is, nothing has been omitted from the tales and stories which he has selected and included in his narrative. But, as far as we know, he has added some stories to Iran's "history" (Rostam and Sohrab, Bizhan and Manizheh . . .), and has omitted some, as well as retaining portions of some very lengthy narratives (in the Sasanid era), in spite of himself.

And now we return to our first question, which was, "What is the motive for this adding and omitting?" Why does he tell a tale he does not believe in, and then say, "Ignore the surface of the story and find its inner meaning?" And why retain those that had no inner secret to them? Ferdowsi is a poet, not a historian, a poet in the sense that he possesses an "informed intelligence" deep within him, as the basis of his being, a faculty that he does not even know of or consider, an ability to perceive the essence and meaning of the culture into which he has been born and which he has experienced in his soul. He sees beyond those unseen things at which we look but do not see, and he says those things that we have in our hearts but are unable to express. Mowlana, the "Discoverer of Secrets," says that "what cannot be found" is the thing he desires, and Hafez, the "Tongue of the Unseen," writes of what is "hidden from view." If the collective unconscious of our culture has given such a quality to our poets—one that it has given to no lord or champion—and if the Shahnameh has been called "the Qur'an of the Persians" (the Qur'an which itself is the word of God), it is because "the great poets" are the most potent of speakers and that in the ranks of truth they are beyond quotidian reality; their concern is with something greater than mere profit and loss.

The introduction to the tale of "Rostam and the Akvan Div" is evidence of the poet having such a conception of his own work: he is at a loss as to how he can praise "the Creator of the soul and wisdom / the knowledge of the clear-souled wise." He must unconditionally accept He who "is and is one." Then he says to "one who is eloquent and who knows philosophy":

O eloquent philosopher,
    I tread a road you have told me not to tread

Whatever speech is not one with the being of unity
　　It is one whether it is spoken or unspoken
Whatever does not meet your eyes
　　Is not stored in your heart with wisdom
Though you have weighed up the way of weighing up
　　This back and forth will never come to an end . . .
The world is full of wonders if you look
　　No man has the means to judge (such things)

V3:288

The poet attacks the philosopher's reasoning intelligence that will not accept the reality of anything (including God) that his eyes do not see, ignoring the fact that the world is full of wonders that we have no means of judging or evaluating. How can such marvelous wonders as the world Creator, the turning heavens, time that day by day passes through us, that day when we shall with one breath be released from it, be understood by means of the petty whys and wherefores of a philosopher? And so in reciting such stories as that of the Akvan Div, Ferdowsi is not of the same mind as the philosopher, unless he too is a wise man who discovers inner meaning.

But isn't the secret or key to Ferdowsi's understanding of the history of Iran the conception that it is a reflection of the universal past on earth? Can we not once again see the war between Ahura Mazda and Ahriman, the resurrection of the Saoshyants, and the appearance of the just savior Kay Khosrow? And aren't the meanings of this "secret" present in the battle between the just and the unjust, and of man's role in this process? A wise man will consciously and unconsciously perceive this in the Shahnameh, as it is the distilled essence of the experience of history present in the book, and I think that this is also what the poet consciously and unconsciously wanted, among other things; precisely this continuous and endless battle, this abounding hope from the past ages, from the ancient days, that has taken its place within our cognizance and in its formless form entered our collective unconscious. In his choices Ferdowsi did not become the prisoner of events; it was this historical secret that Ferdowsi chose in his exemplary stories, and in so doing wrote the poem of our collective unconscious.

The collective unconscious is a new concept in our understanding of the psychology of history and society; one that, like many other cultural discoveries, whether or not it was known by this name, nevertheless existed in the mind of a poet like Ferdowsi. This is why I refer to his "conscious and unconscious" mind, since an artist, and especially a poet, whether he wishes to or not, consciously or unconsciously experiences the cultural reality of his society within his mind, or in Ferdowsi's words, within his "wise soul." How can he express this? Both the word and the meaning of "experience" are inexpressible. Perhaps we can say that in such a case the collective unconscious is the intuitive knowledge that sleeps but is nevertheless active within the poet's mind, like the coming of spring within a tree, or flight for a bird, until he can bring this "historico-cultural" reality into the world in an appropriate form. Knowledge exists within the poet in the same way that his poetic gift does, the gift that bore fruit after a thirty-year struggle. By "poetic gift" I don't mean a talent for arranging words according to meter and rhyme, but rather a poetic nature, that gift which is apparent in the creator's imagination when knowledge and feeling become one with the music of words, like the glimmer of light in the dawn, heralding the sun.

Ferdowsi had such a gift, and his mind and spirit possessed the potential for him to have the essence and soul of Iranian history within himself; with immense labor he organized and elaborated this, and brought it into existence in such a way that the Shahnameh is the template of our collective unconscious expressed in verse that is accomplished, attractive, understandable, and "beautiful." The collective unconscious consists of primeval, ancient experience residing more in the unconscious than in mankind's conscious mind, like a tree putting down roots or like a stream flowing in the depths, so that it is invisible, diffuse, scattered, and formless. Ferdowsi does not utilize this whole unknown mass, but chooses only those parts that are congruent with the spirit of his time, giving them order and form with his verse. In the moment at which Ferdowsi lived, the spirit of the time was the national awakening of Iran, utilizing in particular the foundation of language and history in order to create a national identity.[15] This is why the Shahnameh appears as a national epic commemorating Iranians' resistance to outside invasions and the crises of history. But this is not simply a celebration based on the collective unconscious of one time, since if it were it would have been forgotten in subsequent times. It is a creation that is more exalted than this since it also involves the spirit of other times, a subject that we shall refer to in a moment.

The Shahnameh is a formal expression of the collective unconscious made beautiful by the blessing of language. I use the word "beautiful" in the artistic and aesthetic sense, in that it is a manifestation of a transcendent truth by means of a unity of form and content, a form that gives its predetermined content meaning, and a content that could have taken no other form than that which Ferdowsi chose. The transcendent truth is what is beautiful. If it were merely simple and mechanical, an unmotivated reflex, we would not see it as truth, we would experience it as something we already have; in this case truth is merely a human imperative, something which is within us. Simple outward truth can be inferred from reality, from something's existence or nonexistence, from good or bad behavior, or from for example a correct or mistaken inquiry into something, and so on . . . but transcendent truth is our inference from the truth of truth. As I am unable to express this easily and clearly, I have to give an example of what I mean: the afterlife, hell and heaven, are real for a person of faith, as they are the recompense he receives for what he has done in the world. And so the imaginary journey of Dante through hell, purgatory, and heaven, following the guidance of Virgil and Beatrice, despite the fact that it is imaginary, is derived from a preexisting truth, and the way it appears in the *Divine Comedy* is the "form" in which other truths are disclosed and brought to light; its transcendence and beauty leave the realm of preexisting truth (which exists only for the faithful) and, as it finds its way through the medium of poetry, utilizes both belief and disbelief. Transcendent truth, which goes beyond philosophy, ethics, knowledge, awareness and every other source, is not more compelling than "beauty" (in the aesthetic sense of the word). But in poetry—and perhaps in the arts generally—transcendent truth *is* "beauty," since it is not only intelligence but intelligence together with sensation that raises us up and bestows transcendence upon us. This truth is not present in the *characters* of Rostam and Sohrab, Seyavash, and Kay Khosrow, or for example Rostam and Esfandyar, but finds its reality in the *tales* of Rostam and Sohrab, and of the others, and so comes into being. The individuals comprised in this truth are characters whom the poet has recreated and given life in their interactions with one another.

According to mythology, religion, and history, Feraydun, Zahhak, Rostam and Sohrab, Seyavash, Kay Khosrow, Rostam, and Esfandyar were considered by our ancestors to be real historical people, not characters in tales. Then the poet's creative imagination, and his poetic voice in recounting their tales, breathed new life into them, and gave them a further meaning, making them into examples of transcendent and beautiful truth. Through the blessing of language, great poets are the prophets of such a truth. With the magic of words, which can be like love, they give meaning to the nonsense of the world and the unsupportable conditions of life.

As has been said before, the Shahnameh is not simply a selective versification of an era's collective unconscious based on the soul of that period. In works " . . . like Rostam and Sohrab, Seyavash, or Rostam and Esfandyar . . . language is concerned with the fundamentals that make up human life, with the connections and divisions between people, with their compassion and vengefulness, with their nature and greatness when faced with life and death, with the causes of world events in general and the exposition of man's deepest sufferings that have occurred throughout time's vicissitudes until now . . ."[16] When a poet like Ferdowsi takes up a story and versifies it, everything is transformed, and history is not merely history but an expression of the "soul of that period" for times to come. And the poet is well aware of this since he says:

I have refreshed the world so that it is like paradise
No one has sown more seeds of speech than this

This is a remarkable conception of "speech," that it influences not only man, but also things outside of ourselves; the poet sees it in nature, transforming the world, making it congruent to our wishes and giving reality to a heavenly ideal.

When the collective unconscious is versified as "history," its sleeping past is awakened to a transcendent aesthetic reality, and this awakening is as a dawning light for us. Through the blessing of the poet's speech, within this give-and-take, two things are brought to life: one is a historical consciousness within us, and the other is we ourselves within this historical consciousness. This is the reason that the constancy of our national identity, and outside of this narrow circle the identity of all Persian speakers, is so indebted to, among other things, the Shahnameh.

In reading the stories of the Shahnameh, whenever we encounter within our own souls this transcendent aesthetic truth, which is the defining characteristic of every great work of art, this kind of recognition from the collective unconscious happens together with that overriding joy that the experience of beauty naturally gives us. And the pleasure that derives from this joy, even though it comes from the past, is also fundamental to what we are, and will persist after us. It is in this sense, and with this strength, that Ferdowsi has extracted the past from beneath the weight of ancient days, and given it the means to fly like a bird towards the heavens of the future.

Whatever else is true, it is also this pleasure, this overriding joy, which is the cause of the Shahnameh's widespread diffusion, the way that it is read and repeated by everyone, to the extent that it was considered unnecessary to repeat its tales in other works, since everyone knew and recognized them:

> . . . And Kay Kavus had a wife . . . and when this wife saw Seyavash she fell in love with him, and so it turned out that Seyavash went to Turkestan, since he was afraid of his father, and was

> killed there, as the famous story about him tells us, and it would take too long to repeat it . . . and when Gudarz caught up with Afrasyab's army great battles ensued, as the well-known story recounts . . . [17]

And elsewhere:

> He told King Eskandar the whole story of the murder of Iraj up to the reign of Manuchehr, exactly as it has been versified in Ferdowsi's Shahnameh, and is well-known to most readers . . . then the wise man repeated the stories to the king as they are recorded in the Shahnameh; it would take too long to repeat them here, and most people are aware of them having read them in the Shahnameh . . . then the wise man repeated the story of Goshtasp . . . and the details of Esfandyar's seven trials and his journey to the brazen castle . . . he repeated as it is written in the Shahnameh . . . and during the four months that the king was in the brazen castle he heard all these stories . . . [18]

In *Rostam al-tavarikh*[19] we see that even at the courts of Mohammad Hasan Khan Qajar and Alimardan Khan Zand, neither of whom knew Persian as his mother tongue, the Shahnameh was read, at first continuously throughout, and then from time to time. Countless imitations by anyone and everyone, appropriate and inappropriate epic compositions, conflicting days-long arguments about this or that aspect of the poem in the nooks and crannies of Iran, India, and Turkey, ridiculous tales about it, and even more ridiculous "poems"—all this is another story, whose details can be found in Dr. Safa's *Hemaseh sarai dar iran*,[20] as well as in other places. The *Shahanshahnameh-ye Fathali Shah*, by Saba-ye Kashani, describing the glorious victories of Fathali Shah Qajar, is one of the last examples of this tradition, and one hopes that with Nobakht's Shahnameh on the first Pahlavi monarch it has come to an end.

The legends that were later invented and circulated about Ferdowsi are an indication of the image that everyone had of this great and noble soul. Everyone knows Nezami 'Aruzi's story in the *Chahar*

Maqaleh,[21] of Ferdowsi giving the paltry fee he had received for his poem to a bath attendant and a beer-seller. But another story can be mentioned that shows the poet's independence and courage, even when he was face to face with a splendid king like Mahmoud:

> The story of Rostam is among those which Abolqasem Ferdowsi versified in the Shahnameh for Sultan Mahmoud, and which he read over a few days. Sultan Mahmoud said, "The whole Shahnameh is nothing but the story of Rostam, and there are a thousand men like Rostam in my army." Abolqasem said, "May the sovereign's life be long; I do not know how many men like Rostam there may be in his army, but this I do know, that the great God has not created another of His slaves like Rostam." He said this, kissed the ground, and left. King Mahmoud said to his vizier, "This wretch implied that I am a liar." His vizier said, "He must be killed," but no matter how much they searched he could not be found. Because he had spoken in this way, and given vent to his anger, he left without receiving payment, and went into exile.[22]

Throughout our artistic history, from the time of the Turki-speaking Gorgani and Safavid dynasties, no book has been the subject of as many illustrations by miniaturists and painters as the Shahnameh. When it comes to images in coffeehouses I don't know if the makers of religious images and illustrated narratives can compete with the illustrators and tile makers that represented scenes from the Shahnameh. And we also know about the activity of professional storytellers, which continued until quite recently, in diffusing this material among the people. It appears that the time of such artistic endeavors for the promotion of the Shahnameh—through illustrations in books, or on tiles, and through oral recitations—is now over, and that this book which once held the "history" of Iran within it has entered another phase in the development of its own history. During the last hundred years or so, first Western scholars of Persian culture, and then Iranian scholars, through historical, literary, and philological researches, as well as manuscript comparison and evaluation, have turned to a consideration of the

Shahnameh according to scientific criteria, and in so doing have reached enlightening conclusions. These valuable efforts are still going on. In this research, the "book," like every other object of scientific inquiry, is looked at from outside, and delved into with the tools of knowledge—what is given and what can be derived from this—until a logical, searched-for, unbiased result can be revealed. I think that for some time now we have reached the moment that, simultaneously with this scientific inquiry, writers on literature can also consider a work's inner reality and plunge into it in order to find the soul, the intellectual, artistic, and cultural spirit, of this beautiful artifact. So far most research on the Shahnameh has been carried out by historians and philologists rather than by literary critics, and if, along with such research, intellectuals and literary scholars would enthusiastically turn their attention to this matter, the work would be known more fully, and our understanding of it would be greatly enriched. The time has come that the Shahnameh should not merely be known, but also intellectually internalized so that in this way it will remain alive.

So far the Shahnameh has been a living history, and so has been able to preserve national feeling, but this is not the formal history of pre-Islamic and Islamic Iran, which has been newly understood through the work of various investigators and research conducted by the finest scholars, and not by the mass of people. If we consider the Shahnameh in terms of formal ("classic") histories, most of it can be seen as no more than the record of the rise and fall of dynasties, and representations of war and violence. In contrast to this view, the Shahnameh is the continuous history of a people through three ruling dynasties—the Pishdadian, Kayanid, and Sasanid dynasties (with a short interval between the second and third)—and the clash of battle and heroic, tribal self-sacrifice in pursuit of human and national ideals. Seen as such a tapestry, the Shahnameh is, within our souls, a truer history than the real or political history of Iran, the Achaemenids, the lost Ashkanids, and the Sasanids, or for example the Samanids, Taherids, Ziyarids, Seljuks, Il-Khanids, and Timurids, and so on and so forth. These dynasties ruled in various places, in the mountains, in Isfahan, Ray, Tabaristan, Khorasan, Fars, Daylam, Kerman or Sistan . . . and the times (their dynasties) and places where they ruled are over and done with.

In its historical section, as well being an expression of our collective unconscious the Shahnameh also provides us with a representation of the courtly protocol and political philosophy of the Sasanids, and this has become a part of our age-old image of the way the world's business is carried on. From this point of view, the study of the Shahnameh is a search involving heaven and earth, the relations between human society and the world of the Gods, between earth and heaven.

However abbreviated and scattered our formal history might be, our collective unconscious by contrast—through epic history and by the blessing of the Persian language—has deep and strong roots in the ancient depths of our being. We know that as fate would have it Ferdowsi's portrait occupies nothing less than a historic position in the development of our language, and for history to remain, to progress and "become," it needs a language. The river of history has no better riverbed than language. But from another point of view a language, like all living entities, is inevitably maintained and exalted in tradition and the past; the single word "history" is the guardian, as far as is possible, of the whole past of a tribe or a nation. Ferdowsi is the poet who has brought history and language together in the secure castle of the Shahnameh, and so made time live again in language.

Sovereignty

AT THE END of the legendary section of the Shahnameh, the structure of epic-mythological time also comes to an end. When we reach the historical section we necessarily have another notion of this "inapprehensible apprehension." Mythological time gives rise to notions of gods and devils, of the creation of the heavens and the world and of resurrection, and epic time to the confrontation of mankind from all sides with the world and worldly creation, with natural phenomena and their power, along with man himself, as well as with demons and other supernatural beings. In both mythological and epic time, time is something exalted and lofty, and on some occasions it is even beyond and higher than the reach and power of the gods, so that it is only in the further flights of his imagination that man can conceive of it (as for example in the mythology of Zurvanism, in which the existence of time is conceived of as preceding the appearance of Ahura Mazda).

But historical time comes out of the daily experience of our social life, and is measured against this; it is with the passing of night and day, and the shortness and irreversible progress of our lives, that our existence is woven out of the fabric of society. Time passes on earth, even if it comes from heaven and its destiny is pre-ordained. In such conditions, there is no place for a king who lives for a thousand years, or for a six-hundred-year-old hero, or for the marvel of the simorgh, or Afrasyab's recourse to magic. Even though such time takes its origin and nature from the heavens, it has another aspect, and a book concerned with this historical time also has another aspect.

Historical time passes on earth, and Iran's history passes within Iran (or as Ferdowsi calls it, "Shahr-e Iran"), and takes place in the "heart" of the country.

The land's mythological image is a reflection of the society of the Amesha Spentas, along with their customs and organization. As we know, there are six Amesha Spentas,[1] each with a different being; these are emblems of Good Thought, Just Order, Ideal Kingship, Fruitful Devotion, Health, and the Eternal Life of Ahura Mazda, respectively. And they are gathered in a circle around Ahura Mazda like six petals of a water lily. Ahura Mazda is their center and perimeter, the completion of the Amesha Spentas, as well as being beyond them, more fulfilled than their fulfillment. They are so joined together that not only do they think as one, but they also perceive one another's souls. Ahura Mazda finds the greater part of himself within them, and they find their own unity within him.

In our mythological geography, the "appearance" of the earth is a reflection of this heavenly image, and the heavens are the model for the earth. In the Gathas (Yasna 32, 3) and Yasht-ha (Tir Yasht 40, and Mehr Yasht 15) the world is described as having seven countries, and the earth, that is the world, is one of the Amesha Spentas (Esfandarmaz), just as the existence of the seven forms of the Amesha Spentas corresponds to the seven regions of the world; one in the west, one in the east, two in the north, two in the south and the land called "Xwanirah" in the midst of all the others. And "Iran-Vij" is in the midst of this midmost entity.

> When Tishtar made the rain that formed the seas, all the earth became damp, and separated into seven sections . . . the section that was half of the area of the whole was in the center, and the other six sections were gathered around it. These six sections were together equal in area to the central section, which was named Xwanirah. They had names, and there were boundaries between

> them; one section was the area of Khorasan, one was the land of Arzah, which lies to the east, one was the land of Sawah, two named Fradadafsh and Widadafsh made up the area of Nimruz, and two, named Worubarsht and Worujarsht, lay to the west. The area that was in the center, and was the size of all the others put together, was named Xwanirah. Of the seven lands, greater virtue was created in Xwanirah than in the others. Because he saw this as a threat, Ahriman fought against Xwanirah more than against the others, and created more evil there, and for this reason kings and heroes were created in Xwanirah. The Mazdean religion was also created in Xwanirah, and then taken to other countries. The birthplace of Saoshyant, who is created in order to destroy Ahriman and bring about the last days, is also in Xwanirah.[2]

Apart from this, the heavens and the earth are linked by means of the stars: (1) The sage asked the Divine Wisdom (2) What are the deeds and dispositions of the innumerable stars we see in the sky? (3) And what is the nature of the movement of the sun and moon and stars? (4) The Divine Wisdom answered, (5) Of all the sky's stars, the greatest and best, the most worthy and the most glorious, is considered to be Tishtar, (6) and all the world's good fortune and well-being is due to Tishtar, (7) and the star in charge of water nurtures the waters, (8) and the star in charge of earth nurtures the earth, (9) and the star in charge of vegetation nurtures vegetation, (10) and the star in charge of sheep nurtures sheep, (11) and the stars in charge of water, vegetation, and sheep have been created to nurture the race of mankind.[3]

Also, the introduction to the Shahnameh of Abu Mansouri states:

> Wherever men dwelt in the world, from end to end of the four directions, the land was given to them and divided into seven areas, and each area was named as a country. The first was called Arzah, the second was called Sout, the third was called Fradadafsh, the fourth was called Widadafsh, the fifth was called

> Worubarsht, the sixth was called Worujarsht, the seventh, which was in the world's center, was called the plateau of Xwanirah.
>
> And Xwanirah is that plateau in the midst of which we live, and which its kings call Iranshahr . . . and Iranshahr stretches from the River Oxus to the River Nile, and the other countries surround it, and Iranshahr is the greatest of these countries in all ways . . . [4]

In this way, the appearance of the earth can be perceived together with its reflection in the heavens, as though the earth and heavens are mirroring one another.

> The heavens with their stars are marvelous and beautiful
> And what is above appears below
> If this lower appearance should by the ladder of gnosis
> Mount up, it will be one with its inmost being[5]

The division of the world into seven areas was passed down from the Sasanids to Islamic Iran, and to the Arab geographers. "Yaqut compiled his *Mo'ajam Albaladan* in the 7th century Hejri, and for centuries before this there had been a steady transfer of the basic concept of seven lands to Arab-Islamic sources; one can say that during this time virtually the only significant organizing principle was the Iranian one; at all events the fundamental concept for all of them (court scribes, astrologers, and mathematicians) was this basic Iranian division of the world into seven areas."[6]

We see this same sevenfold division of the earth in the Shahnameh. For example, when Zahhak dreams of his inauspicious fate, and wakes in terrified confusion, Arnavaz asks him what he is afraid of, since "The seven countries of the world are yours to command / Animals, demons and men are your sentinels." When, after seven years of searching for Kay Khosrow, Giv finally finds him, he says, "In seeing you my heart rejoices more than it would in seeing heaven or in ruling over the seven lands," and Khosrow sees these same seven lands in the world-revealing goblet.

The similarity of the earth to the heavens is not simply external; the Amesha Spentas have become incarnate, bodily; their being is this world, and their form is Esfandarmaz, and Esfandarmaz (the earth) is itself a materialization of this maternal munificence, of the blessings of Ahura Mazda, and it is also one of the beautiful manifestations that Ahura Mazda takes upon himself, since he appears as among other things the most beautiful and most splendid of the Amesha Spentas (Farvardin Yasht, section 81). "In Zoroastrianism, the earth, like the heavens, is sacred. Both are designated in the same part of the Avesta, as in Tishtar Yasht, section 8, and Mehr Yasht, section 95, and Farvardin Yasht, section 13 and elsewhere. Much of the world and the heavens has been assigned to protect the earth and sky. . . ."[7] With the aid of Sorush, the Amesha Spentas came to the seven countries of the earth (Yasna, 57, 23). The Amesha Spentas are the lords of the earth's seven countries.[8] The earth is "heavenly," and its kings' justice and injustice on the earth are that which Asha and Druvand (The Lie) enact throughout the world.

In the Shahnameh, nature has a hostile aspect, as in the two sets of seven trials undergone by Rostam and Esfandyar, the snow and sleet that Afrasyab's magic causes to assail the Iranians, the drought and ruin brought about by tyrannical kings, all of which are attacks by Ahriman's followers against the earth and all that is on it. But apart from these occasional intrusions, in general in the Shahnameh, as in the Avesta, the ancient invisible connection between the elements of nature and divine and celestial forces remains unbroken; water, fire, and vegetation are manifestations of purity and growth. Water does not save sinners such as Jamshid and Afrasyab when they are hidden away in the depths of distant seas, and is not darkened by anything except possibly the existence of Afrasyab. After the women of Zahhak's harem are released they bathe themselves in water in order to cleanse their souls, as does Goshtasp after his victory over a dragon. Fire does not harm the innocent Seyavash, and from his blood, which the earth rejects, new shoots of Seyavash emerge. When the prince's head is ignominiously severed from his body, "The plants of that region / hang their heads in shame before the sun," and the heavens weep for his death (V1:317); the nightingale laments not because of separation from the rose but for the death of Esfandyar. The heavens and earth are in sympathy with mankind, and it is for man that at the request of heaven the earth is released from its bonds: one night Sorush appears to Gudarz in a dream to give him the good tidings that Kay Khosrow, the son of Seyavash, is in Turan, and that of all the heroes of Iran only Gudarz's son, Giv, can find him and bring him to Iran. Then Gudarz says to Giv:

> The high heavens have so disposed matters that
> Through you the bonds of grief will be loosened
> You have sought fame in the army's ranks
> Now eternal fame is in your hands
> While men and speech are in the world
> Such fame will never grow old
> Truly the high heavens through your hands
> Will loosen the bonds of the earth.
>
> V2:414

In short, sovereignty over Iran, over this land that is the Iranians' dwelling place, must be possessed of that harmony with which Ahura Mazda rules the world and its inhabitants. For this reason, in order to be acquainted with the soundest manner of ruling over a country according to Ahura Mazda's practice, and in order to understand the nature of kings' role in the Shahnameh, we have to return to the role of the "king" of creation, and look at the earliest section of the Avesta, in the chapter concerned with Ahura Mazda's sovereignty over heaven and earth, and its implications for sovereignty over the land of Iran. In the very first section of the first Gatha (Avesta, Yasna 28, 1) the manner of the alliance between the Amesha Spentas, and the nature of Ahura Mazda's sovereignty, as well as of the guidance of Righteous Being toward the last days, is evident:

O Mazda, o divine clarity!
I come before you in prayer, a suppliant seeking my well-being
and repose.
May I satisfy Gushurvan[9] by the deeds of the Asha, and with
wisdom and good nature.

Zarathustra, whose prophetic mission is the will of Ahura Mazda, longs to satisfy Gushurvan—the soul of the fertile and fruitful world (which can be explained as the symbol of productive Being);[10] that is, the fulfillment of Being with the aid of wisdom and good nature. The Avesta's wisdom—to think correctly, to recognize good and evil, to choose one rather than the other—is to be Ahura Mazda (the lord of wisdom) in one's inmost being. Since "wisdom" is the necessary and unavoidable condition of His existence, God without wisdom is not God, and He bestows no greater blessing than wisdom. Through the blessing of the existence of wisdom, He literally gives Himself as a gift to mankind.

"Asha" is the system of righteousness, or that righteous law that gives order to creation;[11] by means of this law Ahura Mazda preserves Good Creation, leading it against the injustice of Ahriman to ultimate victory, and the deliverance of creation. And so this "law" of the heavenly and earthly worlds is not only true, righteous, and just but is itself righteousness, and is identical with "justice" itself; and justice is not merely order and righteousness but is itself virtually the law, and in this way the justice (law) of the world is able to know the Asha. This Amesha Spenta is Ahura Mazda's son, whom he has created from his own wisdom (Avesta 30, sections 7 and 8; 45, section 4; 47, section 2). For this reason, Asha (whose symbol in the world is luminous fire) like his father and creator is shining and resplendent, and his father (Mazda) can be seen in the radiant light of his son (Asha) (Avesta 45, section 8).

Asha is the healing grace of the world, the friend of Good, the goddess of the earth (Esfandarmaz), the world's nourishment, the ground of eternal existence, the body's health, and the joy and vigor of life (Avesta 31, sections 19 and 20; 32, section 2; 33, sections 7, 10 and 11; 34, section 13). Wherever "Ashavan" (the follower of Asha) steps is the happiest place in the world. And happier still is when such a man builds his house in such a place, keeping herds of cattle, planting wheat, crops, and trees . . . (Vendidad, chapter 3).

From the perspective of truth and righteousness, Asha is the demonstrable existence of ethical behavior (good speech, thought, and deeds), and from that of the law it is the presence of justice and the orderly administration of the world (and the world itself is the worldly manifestation of Ahura Mazda).

Over against Asha, the lie, the practice of wrongdoing and untruth, of lawlessness and anarchy—injustice (the lack of justice)—exists in the world (see for example 44, 14–46, 4, 5, and so on . . .). In both worlds Asha's follower (Ashavan) is successful and is saved, while the follower of the lie (Druvand) is ineffective and worthless.

But the Amesha Spentas' alliance and cooperation, which we see in the second section of the first hymn (and also in sections 3, 5, 6, 8, 9, and 10), and which is repeated throughout the Gathas, is such that every success of the lie is a failure not only for Asha but for all the Amesha Spentas and their manifestations. But harm to the body of Esfandarmaz—that is, to mother earth—is perhaps the most dreadful of all, since the earth is the refuge (Gushurvan) of mankind and all domesticated creatures, and the site of "fire and water and vegetation" (that is, the three Amesha Spentas of the world and this earth's existence, Asha, Haurvatat, and Amurdad). Gushurvan cries out from injustice, and says to the Creator, "Why have you created me? I am wholly encompassed by anger and pillaging and malignancy and over-reaching and rapine." Then the Creator asks Asha, "What kind commander do you know who is benevolent and strong—stronger than all others—who does not act unjustly and who is worthy of the world's sovereignty, who can defeat the rapacious denizens of the lie and anger and send them on their way? In truth my desire is for a capable commander. When will that time come in which a powerful ally such as this will assist me?"[12]

From the point of view of our epic mythology, both capability and strength are necessary in battle. Among the Amesha Spentas,

Shahrivar (Khashatra), as the representative of the sovereignty of Ahura Mazda, is the sign of heavenly capability and a peaceable monarchy. And so it is on earth, among mankind; a king—by following the heavenly king—must act justly and do away with injustice in his country (*keshvar*, a word that derives from Khashatra-Shahrivar). Among other things, justice means that structure or law by which Ahura Mazda directs and guides the world—that is, physical and corporeal existence. And so the world's activities are Ahura Mazda's implementation of justice vis-à-vis his own "body." Seen in this way, just rule within a country takes as its model Ahura Mazda's rule over the world, and the opposite of this, royal injustice, is a duplicate of the disorder and lawlessness of Ahriman who strives to disturb the justice (Asha) that makes the land prosper, and so to weaken the world. Seeing the world's affairs from such a perspective means that a king's injustice not only destroys men's lives, but also confounds the natural order of fire and water, of creatures with souls and those without.

From a world-king's injustice
    All that is good becomes hidden
The wild ass of the plains does not give birth on time
    The crow's squabs become blind
The milk in wild animals' teats dries up
    Water at its source turns to pitch
The world's streams run dry
    The musk deer's navel contains no scent
Righteousness flees from crooked-dealing
    Decay is apparent on all sides.

V2:253

From a king's injustice (as from the victory of "the lie") righteousness disappears, and endless "crooked-dealing and decay" and distress, as well as chaos and confusion in everything, appear everywhere and from every quarter. A king's injustice, oppression such as that practiced by Nozar, means the obliteration of former customs, the love of treasure and wealth, mankind's humiliation, peasants turning into warriors and champions seeking sovereignty, and chaos and confusion throughout the world.

When a loud cry rose up from the face of the earth
From end to end the world became filled with confusion
V1:285

In the primitive societies of the past (founded on rank and status), justice (rectitude) was seen as consisting of everything being in its own place. The world was seen as a composite, like a face in which everything "was good in its rightful place"; just as Ahura Mazda maintained the world in its order with the help of "Asha," so the kings in the Shahnameh, with the help of "justice," were required to be the guardians of Iran and the Iranian people. The first act of Feraydun's reign (as with Kay Khosrow's) was to go about the country binding the arms of injustice and setting justice free; in this way, through the power of his good fortune, "the land became a garden and the time was filled with radiance."

Zal said to his chieftains and champions that a king must possess lineage and good fortune, that he should be glorious and wise, as well as knowledgeable (V1:323). Ahura Mazda created Asha from his own wisdom. A king too has only his wisdom's resources to distinguish between good and evil so that he can act justly. But wisdom is not part of a king's essence. How many foolish kings there have been who have brought harm to the world and to their own souls! But those who are wise fulfill their roles, and the role of a king is to administer justice. Because of their role, just kings like Feraydun and Kay Khosrow possess a God-given glory that makes them worthy of authority, and as a result good fortune is theirs. Kings who act unjustly are without wisdom and neither fortune nor lineage will avail them, and it becomes clear that mental abilities are of more importance than lineage; God-given glory flees from kings such as these, for example, Jamshid and Kavus. And tyrants like Zahhak and Afrasyab never benefit from such God-given glory.

God-given glory, like Asha, and like fire that represents it, is a shining radiance. And so a connection can be seen between the justice (Asha) of resplendent Ahura Mazda in the heavens and the justice of a king possessed of God-given glory on earth. "Since such glory is the radiance of God it must necessarily be thought of as pertaining only to such kings as are God-fearing, virtuous, just, and compassionate."[13]

To summarize what has been said:

The earth has the same appearance as the heavens. But this is not merely a matter of appearance, it also has the same nature as the heavens. In this way, both of them have the same form and structure. Asha (justice) is the law of this structure, its ordering and harmony. Ahura Mazda controls this order on the earth. He has created Asha from his own wisdom. And so this order is born from the essential being of this father and the heart of this "mother." Ideal sovereignty comes from this authority and is made strong in such wisdom.

Ideal sovereignty in the Shahnameh can be seen as imitating, unconsciously, the divine example, and following in the way of God, as is indicated in the Gathas:

> [May it be that] good, benign and knowledgeable sovereigns rule
> over us in the radiance of Armiti
> May it not happen that evil sovereigns rule [over us].
> One must strive for [the improvement of] the world, and
> maintain it with righteousness and lead it towards the light.[14]

In the Shahnameh, God-given glory, like good fortune, comes from "The lord of Saturn and of the turning heavens" and thought cannot encompass it. We do not know why or how the Homa of prosperity indicates one rather than another, and lights upon Kay Qobad who dwells in the mountains, or upon the unknown warrior Lohrasp, or in the form of a ram that follows Babak's fleeing son. But this we do know, that a lack of wisdom is the source of injustice and makes God-given glory forsake kings. The reason that God-given glory fled from Jamshid is that he thought himself (a man) to be God, and in so doing he upset the natural order of things, and as a result disturbed the organization of the world's affairs (Asha); he acted unjustly, and Kay Khosrow, who possessed God-given glory, saved the order of sovereignty so that he would not share Jamshid's fate. From this we can deduce that through the blessing of this God-given glory a just king is "favored by" God, and is "simultaneously a king, a priest, and a champion / (He is) indeed the shadow of God on earth" (B9:217).

> God created sovereignty from justice
> As well as from ability and lineage
> He gives it to one who is more worthy (than others),
> More wise, more compassionate.
>
> B9:28

Whoever is "more wise, more compassionate, more just"; the source of the "virtue, good deeds, and understanding" of such a king lies in wisdom, and in the Shahnameh praise of wisdom precedes praise of everything else, apart from the creator of wisdom. Unlike works that are contemporary with it, the Shahnameh does not begin with praise of the God as the world's creator, of the Prophet, or of the era's king, but after referring to God as the creator of "the soul and wisdom" the poet praises speech. Next come accounts of the creation of the world, the creation of mankind, and the creation of the sun and moon, then praise of the Prophet, an account of the assembling of the Shahnameh, the story of Abu Mansur Daqiqi, the story of the good friend, and praise of Amir Mansur. After all this, the introduction comes to an end with praise of Sultan Mahmoud.[15] Avestan wisdom, which is the inner being of Ahura Mazda, is here God's first creation, His most precious blessing, an auspicious and all-encompassing gift:[16]

> O sage, wisdom has great fame
> Wisdom leads a king to accomplish his desires

One calls it light, another loyalty
    When wisdom is absent, suffering and tyranny remain
The eloquent call it righteousness
    Those favored by fortune know it as sagacity
Sometimes it is humble, sometimes a keeper of secrets
    And speech becomes trustworthy when joined with it
So widely known is the name of wisdom
    It spreads beyond all computation
Do not consider anything higher than wisdom
    Wisdom exceeds everything that is good
Wisdom seeks out all the accumulated secrets of the world,
    Hidden things, which our eyes do not see.

B7:405

These various designations show the different aspects and roles that wisdom has in Ferdowsi's thought; praise of wisdom as the light of the soul and the spirit's guide, and as the understanding of good and evil and the connection of this understanding with knowledge, can be seen throughout the Shahnameh. "Wisdom is like water, and knowledge like earth / understand that neither is separate from the other" (B7:202).

In contrast with mankind, since demons have no share of wisdom, "in their eyes evil and good are one" (B8:197). The connections between wisdom, justice, knowledge, and religion in the Shahnameh, and their complex intertwined relationships, are worthy of a separate study. Here I will simply point this out and move on to the fact that demons are not without a share of knowledge; for example, they know how to write, how to build houses, and how to whirl themselves up into the sky and fly there. But because they have no share of divine wisdom in them, their knowledge is used to stir up wind and sleet and snow, as we see in the story of Afrasyab, and in the two sets of Seven Trials when they turn an angelic face into one that is "full of wrinkles, formless and ugly" (V5:237). Demons' knowledge is used to change the nature of reality, and to seek to exploit this change, it is something that brings down destruction on the natural world, but—to use a modern word—does not go beyond "technological" limits; their knowledge is a tool in the hands of those who are destructive, and is a stranger to that wisdom which is man's guide "in both worlds."

If "justice" consists of putting each thing in its proper place and maintaining it there, and as a result to know and be concerned with what is appropriate, "to praise wisdom by means of justice"—that is, to praise God's noblest gift, as is said in the Shahnameh's exordium—indicates that what is appropriate to wisdom is praise. "Justice" has incorporated this kind of wisdom within itself, and we give justice to wisdom, or in other words we have given wisdom its due, raising it to the level of "the soul's eye," the guardian of "eye, ear, and tongue," so that it is a sentinel guarding our sight, hearing, and speech, keeping them safe from the errors of "injustice."

And so wisdom and justice are twin forces for good, and injustice results from a lack of wisdom. Just as unjust monarchs are the cause of the world's ruin, so in the reign of a just sovereign not only is the peace of mankind assured, but also the soul of the natural world is revived. There are many examples of this throughout the Shahnameh, but I shall have to content myself with two or three examples. First, there is Feraydun:

The world seeker possessed the *farr* of Jamshid
    His actions were like the shining sun
Like rain he bestowed what was necessary on the world
    And on the soul what was appropriate, like knowledge;
He grew in stature like a straight cypress tree
    The imperial *farr* radiated from him

V1:62

It's as if a just king were fashioned from the sun, water, and plants so that through his existence the reality of the world could be manifested in another way (V3:4), or he is like Kay Khosrow who seems made from an essence that cleans away sorrow from hearts and produces green spring from the world's parched autumn:

He made every ruined place flourish
    He freed the hearts of sorrowing people from sorrow
Moisture rained down from spring clouds
    The face of the earth was cleansed of sorrow
The world became filled with streams and rivers
    The heads of those who sorrowed slept
The earth was adorned like paradise
    Filled by justice and benevolence with wealth

V3:4

From the time of Feraydun, the first "historical" king, until Yazdegerd, the last king in the Shahnameh, the Kaviani banner, that legendary piece of leather belonging to Kaveh the seeker of justice, has been the sign of our sovereignty and the banner of all Iranians. When the blacksmith who said to his king, "If you are king of seven countries / Why is our portion suffering and hardship?" left Zahhak's court

He cried out and shouted
    Summoning all the world to (seek) justice
He went forward with a lance in his hand,
    Shouting, "O famous God-fearing people
Anyone who sides with Feraydun
    Who lifts his head out of Zahhak's chains
Search him out, for this man (Zahhak) is Ahriman's nobleman
    In his heart he is the enemy of the world creator.

V1:69

A superficial glance at the Shahnameh shows that "justice" and "injustice" have a much wider sense than I have drawn attention to here. For example, the birth of a hero like Rostam (V1:46) is justice, as is seeking revenge for the death of an innocent like Seyavash (V3:27, V3:146, and V4:306) and breaking an oath is injustice (V3:276). Cannibalism is extreme injustice and the name of the cannibals' city is "Injustice" (V3:255).

In contradistinction to the first model of good sovereignty (Shahrivar), Ahriman is the type and model of an evil king. The cannibal Zahhak is mentored by Eblis, and foolhardy Kavus is his dupe. These "Ahrimans" are not rare in our history, and neither are there few of them in the Shahnameh; the examples stretch from the fratricides Salm and Tur to Afrasyab and the filicide Goshtasp, and the parricide Shirui.

One day Bahram Gur wanted to learn about the condition of his people, and to know whether "there is justice in the world" or not. Little by little he rode on until it was late in the day and he had lost the path; he was exhausted and drowsy and in need of water, repose, and sleep, when he reached a village. He asked an old peasant woman if he could rest a while in her house. The old woman said, "Consider this house as your own," and told her husband to see to their visitor's horse, while she swept the house clean and spread a mat and placed a cushion there, and prepared a dish of "herbs, vinegar, bread and yoghurt." Bahram was sick; he ate a little and slept. The next morning when the woman awoke she said to her husband, "You fool, for a horseman like this—who looks for all the world just like Bahram Gur—you should have roasted a lamb. What good are vinegar and bread?" Her husband said, "You're not responsible for the house's upkeep, its salt and firewood and bread; suppose you'd killed that lamb, and he'd eaten it and gone, and you were left here in the 'cold of winter with the howling wind'"!

But for all her husband said, in the end the woman killed a lamb and served it up with gruel and eggs and herbs. Bahram was sick and unable to sleep; the woman brought squash and powdered mountain ash to break his fever. The king told the woman not to be afraid but to ask him for whatever her heart desired. The woman said, "This village lies in the path of lots of horsemen and courtiers and government people. Sometimes they get greedy for our property and steal things and ruin someone's life, and sometimes it's a virtuous woman they ruin. This is our complaint against the king." Bahram was annoyed and thought to himself, "These people don't appreciate justice and security; they should go through some real suffering so that they'd appreciate their good fortune." The king slept, and "all night his heart was filled with cruel thoughts." The next morning when the woman wanted to milk their cow, she saw that there was no milk in its teats. She said to her husband, "Last night the king had evil thoughts; he became a tyrant." Her husband said, "What do you know about such things? Why are you tempting fate like this?"

This is how the woman answered: Oh my dear husband
　　These words of mine are not pointless
When the world-possessing king becomes unjust
　　The moon does not shine as it should in the heavens
In breasts the milk dries up
　　And musk does not give its scent in the musk-deer's navel
Adultery and hypocrisy appear openly
　　The kind heart becomes as hard as granite
In the plains wolves eat men
　　The wise man flees from the unwise
The eggs beneath the broody hen are addled
　　Whenever the king becomes unjust.

B7:383

A little earlier we saw that that there is a relationship between a king's injustice and worldly corruption, and here we see that even unjust thoughts can cause milk to dry up in teats, and man-eating wolves to attack the lives of the innocent. A king's oppression causes subordinates and powerful men alike to flee the country and scatter, the world is quickly turned upside down, and "after death he will be cursed / he will be called the king with no religion" (B7:255). At the death of Yazdegerd the Unjust the great men of the country said, "We do not want an unjust man on the throne."

Since God created the world
　　No one ever saw a sovereign like this
There was nothing but killing, misery, pain, and suffering
　　Piling up wealth from the goods of the poor

No one has ever seen a more impure king than this
Nor heard of one among former nobles.
B7:285–86

The birth of a king like Yazdegerd is an injustice, and his death is justice: "I see his life as oppression, and his death as justice." Iranians cannot tolerate tyrannical kings like Zahhak and Nozar and they rise up in revolt against them. Towards the end of Jamshid's reign the soldiers even turned to others outside the country, and placed a foreign king on the throne.

The clear-souled Qobad spoke thus
Since the king's heart turns away from justice
The turning heavens darken his right to rule
The stars no longer call him a king
Tyranny gives license to remove a king
Since it causes the hearts of the innocent to suffer.
B7:114

Rostam's insults to Kay Kavus and his disobedience of Goshtasp are examples of heroes' behavior towards foolish and unjust kings, since the sovereign who

Does not incline to justice is not a king
He is unworthy of the royal crown
He has blackened the charter of kingship
And divine glory is no longer his
Know this, that the unjust king
Is a ravening lion in the pastures
B7:183–84

Khosrow Parviz is such a king: Bahram Chubin, Hormoz's military commander, was a man from Ray. He rebelled against Hormoz the Sasanian, and began a widespread insurrection. During the reign of Parviz, Hormoz's son Bahram was finally killed by a trick, and the uprising was suppressed. According to the Divan-e Balkh Parviz then decided to take revenge on the people of Ray and to appoint as their ruler "a wicked man of evil lineage, one who was ignorant and foul-mouthed"

Khosrow spoke at length and said, I want
A red-haired man born under an evil star
Red-bodied, squint eyed, with an ugly face
A face from hell, far from heaven,
A man with an evil heart, mean-spirited, devoid of splendor
His head filled with spite, his mouth with lies
With both eyes green and squinting, with huge teeth,
Going in crooked ways, like a wolf

They searched and found someone like this and he was appointed as the ruler of Ray:

When this noxious man arrived in Ray, he washed
His heart and eyes of all shame before God
He ordered that the gutters on the roofs
Be removed, and he rejoiced to see it done
Then he killed all the cats
The landlords' hearts were angry at him . . .
He said, If you see any gutters in place
Or any cats in this town
I shall burn that roof down
And stone (the cats) to death
He searched out places where one coin was saved
And made its owner grieve
Every house was overrun with mice
The inhabitants despaired of their town . . .
From that ugly, malignant, ill-omened wretch
Who had come from Khosrow's court to Ray
The whole flourishing town was destroyed
While the sun shone down upon it
From end to end the town was filled with grief and pain
And no one in the world remembered its inhabitants

B9:191–92

This is the destiny of man's soul, his wealth, his cities and his undoing, decreed by his ruler; an army commander says to him, "All the cities of Iran are your enemies / they are all heart and soul ready to fight you" (B9:252). As long as a king keeps faith with the divine gift and society's strengths, the king is stronger than all others, presiding over them like a shepherd over the good and evil that befalls his flock. Bahram Gur said, "If I wear the crown in this era / I am responsible for whatever is good or base (in it)," precisely because he is the king of the era:

> He is the source of what is good and the instigator of evil
> In knowledge and struggles wisdom is his
> All is wholly on the king's shoulders
> Since whatever is crooked or straight comes from him
>
> B7:408 AND B7:412

The history recounted in the Shahnameh was a mirror reflecting all the desires of Iranian society, from the centuries before the poet's own time, and after it. The ideal king of such a history must be the most knowledgeable of the knowledgeable in both religious and worldly matters, anxious for what is ethically right or wrong behavior, concerned for the improvement of everyone's well-being. Perhaps this is why, among other reasons, some of the final volumes of the Shahnameh, particularly those that concentrate on the reign of Anushirvan, overflow with concepts, descriptions, pieces of advice and guidance, all of which can be seen played out in the book itself. These diverse matters are intertwined with one another, but appear as separate moments of "practical wisdom" that can be looked at and studied from various points of view. I must be brief here, but will point out just two matters that are fundamental to the political thought and social outlook of the time. Why is it that in the Shahnameh the injustice of tyrants returns against themselves? Before all others, and to a greater extent, unwise kings do harm to their own bodies and souls; this happened to Jamshid, and Farangis warned her father when he killed Seyavash, "You are the oppressor of your own body." And why is it that a man's injustice is injurious to the body of the natural world, to water, soil, and air, to the plains and plants, and to animals whether wild or domesticated?

In the language of Ferdowsi, "The Just," or at times, "The Just Creator," is one of the names of God; God is the being that acts justly. And this, as we have seen, and now see in a different guise, was an ancient concept that had come down from the past to the poet of the Shahnameh:

- Ahura Mazda created Asha (= the law, the world's justice) out of his own wisdom.
- Justice and "Vahman" (= good-thought) are one as a manifestation of Ahura Mazda.
- Ahura Mazda created the world, and man, from his own body.
- Ahura Mazda preserves and organizes this "body" as equivalent to that thought (wisdom, and its law)
- Following on from Asha—in ethics: truth, righteousness; in religion: good deeds, and in society: justice.
- Evil thought (= Akuman, the lie), is Ahriman and the source of injustice.
- Following on from the lie—in ethics: untruthfulness, unrighteousness; in religion: the sinful; and in society: the unjust.
- Among "evil thoughts" the demon Greed is the worst enemy of Asha (= Truth).
- Unjust thought is injustice and makes its way from the unjust into the world.

Greed is a sign of confusion and aggression, covetousness and lawlessness; it is the manifestation of injustice. The greedy person is never satisfied with a limit, a stopping place, he is always wanting and cannot be sated; he wants everything, devours everything, and if he can find nothing else he will feed on himself. "Greed is a demon that devours all things, and if it cannot reach to anything else it eats its own body. Even when all the wealth of the world is given to it, it is a need that remains unfilled and unsatisfied. It is said that the eye of greed is a plain that has no limit."[17] In the *Pahlavi*

Narrative it is said that in the last days, when the demons shall come to an end, Greed will first devour the bloody banner of Anger, and after that the demons of Winter, Death, and Old Age, until apart from Greed and Ahriman no other demons will be left. Then "the demon Greed will say to 'Gana Minu' (Ahriman), 'O fool, now I shall devour you too,'"[18] and when there is nothing left of Ahriman, Greed will tear apart and devour itself.

Such is the demon Greed. In the same way that justice and wisdom are waters from one source, so injustice and ignorance are chained in the one prison. What is greedy is always needy, and Greed and Need are twin-born demons. In the Shahnameh we frequently encounter these two incurable ills together, especially among sovereigns and chieftains. When Khosrow Anushirvan asks Bozorgmehr for the names of demons that are enemies to the soul and to wisdom:

> Thus he answered, Greed and Need
> 　　Are two demons who are strong and proud . . .
> He said to him, Of this harmful evil
> 　　Which is Ahriman the mighty?
> He answered Khosrow, Greed
> 　　Has long been a cruel demon
> For nothing satisfies him
> 　　He is always seeking more
> Need is that which brings grief and pain
> 　　Making men blind and yellow-faced
>
> B8:196

Since man is himself a creation of God the nurturer, an unjust man is violating the process of creation, and also harming the organization of his own body and soul. The unjust in the Shahnameh do not have a happier destiny than the ill-fated end of their prototype, the demon Greed; an unjust man is a facilitator of injustice. Jamshid, the first victim of greed in the Shahnameh, boasted that he was divine, which was a major injustice (and sin); Salm, Tur, and Kavus are other examples, as are Sohrab and Esfandyar who are the Shahnameh's "sinless" examples of overweening greed. All of these inflicted harm on their own bodies before anyone else did. This is because as soon as an unjust person thinks of injustice (which is born from evil thought), injustice enters into his actions and takes on a reality outside of him. In the story of Bahram Gur and the peasant woman we see these two states existing as one. If creation is, according to the above explanation, the visible manifestation of Ahura Mazda, the oppressor of himself (man) is also the oppressor of the Creator (the world). In its enmity with Asha, Greed is injustice complete and entire, the ultimate extent of injustice, since it attacks the just, true order of the world (Asha and fire, which are its body) in order to destroy anything and everything—even its own body. Injustice and Greed are of one nature and flourish within one another. And so the unjust man is not sufficient unto himself, especially if he has authority over men and the earth. In that case his reign disturbs and disrupts anyone and everything, and the performance of injustice is not merely something appertaining to the king and Ahura Mazda, but involves everyone. Man's justice and injustice—a microcosm of the world and creation as acted upon by God—return to act upon both instigator and recipient, and above all upon the body and soul of a man himself, and so he should consider his own body as Ahura Mazda considers his "body." It is as if man is also responsible for the "body" of God. The obscure bases of this conception can frequently be found throughout the whole of the Shahnameh.

Ardeshir says, "Your heart finds peace in four things": fearing God and being grateful to Him, doing justice to one's own body, being truthful, and finally, as regards the king of the world, "If you look justly upon your protector / You feel the same benevolence towards him as to your own soul" (B7:183). And in another place, in answer to a wise man who asked, "What shall we do to obtain a good name / In the beginning to have a good end?" Bozorgmehr says that he should stay far from sin, and "Desire for all the world what you desire for your own body" (B8:123).

If a man feels gratitude towards God, avoids injustice, and maintains the order of His creation (Asha), he inevitably acts justly towards his own body. The ways of God and man, what is lawful in the act of creation and for man, are not separate from one another; the two are one, and this "one" consists of truth and righteousness (the ethical manifestations of Asha). It is due to this insight or concept—although unconscious—of the Creator and creation, that the Shahnameh says, through the words of Ardeshir and Bozorgmehr, that you should love the command of God, the king, and the world as one loves one's own body, and a king should love the world and you its inhabitants as he loves his own body. Given this analogy, the man who is unjust to his body, his soul, the world, and the heavens destroys himself. "Whoever thinks evil / in the end does evil to his own body" (B8:53). And if we take this into account, the king has a better or worse fate than everyone else, since "All evils come from the king, and good is from the king" (B8:120). When in order to keep the crown and throne for himself, Goshtasp sent Esfandyar to fight against Rostam, knowing he was sending him to his death, his other son, Pashutan, addressed his father:

> He cried out, O chief of all chieftains
> The sign has come of your fortune's reversal
> By this act you have done evil to your own body
> You have boasted so much about (possessing) Iran
>
> V5:429

What we have discussed so far has been concerned with the ideal virtuous king, and the reality of the reverse of this, authoritarian and tyrannically destructive kings. But of course the Shahnameh is much more than this view suggests; in practice the book is also a great examination of politics, if we consider politics in its widest possible sense as the organization and implementation of the life of a society, stretching from the earliest times when a king dressed in leopard skins descended from the mountains, unaware of the practice of war, with an army consisting of "wild and domesticated animals, birds, and angelic beings," and who fought naked against demons, until the construction of social entities and the founding of an empire—from Feraydun until Anushirvan the Just—and finally the fall of Iran and the transformation of the world, of being and of life, in accordance with another world order.

During the Shahnameh's mythical era man, with the subsequent help of nature, extricates himself from his slavery to nature, and establishes the first foundations of communal life, a central authority (kingship), and a social structure; this is the epic of origins. The period of warrior champions is the epic of world conquest; the appearance, and search for, and discovery of a world apart from their own, and the molding of it according to their wishes; the seven trials of Rostam and of Esfandyar, the entrapment and pacification of malignant forces and of the stubbornness of nature, Rostam's leading an army to Mazanderan and his slaying of the White Demon, Sohrab's arrival in Iran and Esfandyar's expedition to the Brazen Castle can be mentioned as a few examples of this. The construction of Seyavashgerd by the stranger-prince in a distant country, "He made a city like paradise / He planted roses, hyacinths and tulips in the plains" (V2:314) is a similar moment. Of course facing the world simultaneously involves knowing oneself as a child vis-à-vis the world, and the victory of one's will over it. And strength of will in battle—more naked, more victorious, more furious than elsewhere—makes for stubbornness, and bursts its bonds. Battle is both one with the turning heavens, and what impels the epic of warrior-champions.

The Shahnameh's view of the world and its phenomena is epic. This is in contradistinction to the work of a lyric poet, who views the world in the workshop of his own imagination and paints a picture based on his inner state, as does Hafez when he says, "In the meadows each page is a record of a different state"; but in epic poetry the world of the narrative is formed by the sensitivity to the outer world of the poet's intelligence. A narrative that involves a wide varied arc such as the historical era of the Shahnameh is inevitably an encyclopedia of the civilization and culture of an ancient, tried and tested people, and as such it is concerned with "the world and whatever is in it."

> In this book of former princes
> Of former nobles and warring horsemen
> All battles and banquets and opinions and speeches
> The passing of many ancient days
> Of that knowledge and faith and restraint and reasoning
> Of that guidance to the other world.[19]
>
> V5:441

The historical era is the epic of kingship and sovereignty and the satisfactions of the world of power over others. In the Sasanian era the linking of sovereignty with religion, the rituals of the court and the splendors of regal governance, enthronement, the exercise of authority and that of giving audience, are all repeatedly spelled out in great detail during coronation addresses from the throne, or in conversations with priests, sages, viziers, and advisors. In this era we can find various indications of daily and social life, such as the payment and collection of taxes, land reclamation, oppression by the powerful, popular uprisings, relations between the king and the army and the peasantry, agriculture and livestock and methods of accumulating wealth, generous hospitality and miserliness, enmity and friendship . . . and war and peace. Here we witness battles and banquets, hunting and the pleasures of feasting, drinking, and making love—"Wine and feasting and entertainers and drinking to excess" (V2:316)—games like chess and backgammon, knowledge and discussions, culture and polite society, education and instruction, advice and guidance.

The historical era opens with the tumultuous story of Alexander and a few lines concerning the Ashkanians, of whom the poet "has heard nothing but the name," but in reality it is with the Sasanid dynasty that a new epoch begins.[20] Like Jamshid and Feraydun before him, Ardeshir was a king who inaugurated a new administrative regime in a new era. Even so the foundation stone of leadership and sovereignty, namely a belief in the justice of this era, without which no other stone could be erected, was still firmly in place. When he was enthroned and placed the crown on his head, he said:

"In this world justice is my treasure
    The world lives through my good fortune, my efforts,
No one can take this treasure from me
    Evil will come to men from evil deeds . . .
From end to end the world is under my protection
    My way is to choose justice . . .
This court is open to everyone
    Both to the malignant and the benevolent"
All the company praised him
    Saying, "May the land flourish through your justice."

B7:155

Above and beyond this, because of the association and mingling together of religion and the state (religion became state-centered, and the state became a religious entity) the nature of kingship and, as a result of this, sovereignty over the country, was transformed. In the Shahnameh, this association appears during the reign of Ardeshir. The advice given on his deathbed by Ardeshir to his son the crown prince is a significant indicator of this new era. He first says, "With the sword of justice I have made the world as it should be," and then, after referring to his struggles and the deceptive turning of the heavens, he adds:

When the king respects and extols religion
    Sovereignty and religion become brothers
Religion is not stable without the king's throne
    Nor can sovereignty survive without religion
They are two silks woven one with the other
    And their mingling together brings forth wisdom
Religion is not independent of the king
    There is no praise for a king without religion . . .

Since the king is the guardian of religion
Do not call them anything but brothers . . .
Do not consider as religious any man
Who speaks against a just king
What did that praised speaker say?
"When you look, (you see that) religion is the pith of justice."
B7:187

Such a conclusion indicates that kingship and religion are two brothers and that "religion is the pith of justice." Since kingship, even if it could survive without religion, is unstable without justice, kingship has no desire to abandon religion, in the same way that religion requires the king's "sword of justice"; the two are knitted together and both have similar functions; sovereignty must spread a heavenly religion on earth, and religion must make earthly sovereignty a heavenly entity. In this era, on the one side there is the "national" belief of Iranians, Mazdaism, and on the other the Sasanid imperial dynasty, wielding its "sword of justice," is the preserver of this belief throughout Iran. Evidence of such a view of kingship, and of its persecution of other religions and their beliefs—and of the injustices of this justice—can also be found in the Shahnameh. In the heroic section of the poem, Rostam had his own religion and Esfandyar had his, but concerning the religion of Sam the son of Nariman, of the warrior Sohrab, of Sindokht, Rudabeh, Tahmineh, Sudabeh, and Farangis, or of the tolerance of others, we had no information; we only knew that from the time of Feraydun to that of Kay Qobad, there was "observance of the way of God" (B9:79), and battles between the good followers of God and the evil followers of Ahriman. But with the partnership of kingship and religion, the Sasanids brought into being a unified and centralized state of a kind that had not been known before, neither among the earliest kings and the Kayanids, nor among the Ashkanians. With the absolute authority of the court and the priesthood, which included this world and the world to come, and in which men were confined to their own social stratum and prisoners of their "caste," and those who professed an evil religion were worthy of death and all opposition was silenced, the time of the legendary struggles and extraordinary feats of free men came to an end. This is because society was now closed, with each social group confined within its own limits; transgressing such limits was considered to be an invasion of the realm of the rulers by the ruled, the cause of communal chaos and the destruction of society.

One day Bahram Gur went hunting; he found no prey, the day grew long, and the king became weary. At evening he reached a flourishing village and the peasants came out to watch him but they did not welcome him as they should have done. Bahram was annoyed by this and said to a priest, "May this green and flourishing place become a lair of wild beasts and hunters' prey." The priest understood what the king meant. He went to the village and said, "The king is very pleased with you; may your hearts rejoice, because all of you, women, children, men, servants, hired workers, and landowners, you're all equal, all in authority. No one should obey anyone else or give orders to anyone else." Then,

> Everyone became confused with everyone else
> On all sides blood was spilled
> When this tumult arose among the villagers
> They all suddenly fled from the village . . .
> The whole village began to go to ruin
> The trees turned dry, there was no water in the irrigation channels
> The plain was desolate and the buildings were desolate
> The whole area had neither population nor flocks of animals
>
> B7:327

The famous story of Anushirvan and the cobbler is another indication of how each group was confined to its own limited social and cultural level. During the war against the Romans the cobbler gives three hundred thousand dirhams to the king's empty treasury, in the hope that his son will be educated and be included among officials of the court. Despite Bozorgmehr's intervention on his behalf, the king does not agree to this; he sends the dirhams back and says that if the children of artisans and merchants were to become "skillful and knowledgeable" court officials, this would do nothing but annoy those who are sons of the wise, and "I shall be cursed after my death / Since this was the tradition of this time" (B8:299).

In this era, manifest freedom belonged to the king, and concealed freedom belonged to priests plotting in secret. Their alliance was to some extent one of the causes of the success of imperial rule and the expansion of Iran, but after a while blatant royal corruption and the priests' mental aridity, authoritative religious rulings, persecution of the adherents of other faiths—Nestorian Christians, Manicheans, Buddhists, followers of Mazdak, and so on—led to court intrigues, murders and slaughter and general confusion and, as a result of all this, to the deterioration of both religion and government.[21] A mere glance at the Vendidad, *Shayast Nashayast*, or *Ravayat-e Pahlavi* is enough to show that the authority of arbitrary rulings over daily life, together with the claim of "justice" in thought while "injustice" existed in deed, inevitably ended in a social and cultural impasse. Kay Khosrow, who was the most just of all kings, said that a man who:

> . . . wishes to bring about misfortune
> And sets a worthless person on the throne
> Is devoid of just inquiry, motive, and thought
> With his "justice" the ruled have no security
>
> V4:225

And God is worthy of praise since he "gives wisdom, the soul, and a strong body"; to one He gives "glory and a throne," to another "Misfortune, want, sorrow and pain," and then

> From the shining sun to the dark earth
> Everywhere I see justice come from the pure God
>
> V3:77

And so, given this strange justice and injustice of the heavens, it is not surprising that when Anushirvan asks Bozorgmehr what the strangest thing is "beyond which no assessment can be made," the most knowledgeable of the knowledgeable answers, "All the deeds of heaven are strange."

We see a man with authority
    His crown reaches up to the black clouds
But he does not know his left hand from his right
    From his fortune he knows neither increase nor loss
For one turning of the high heavens
    (who can) Say what stars are, and how many there are?
The guidance of heaven is hard
    Misfortune comes to him because of it

B8:204

Justice as an ideal of kingship was an end towards an "ethical politics," an ancient organizing principle left over from eras that were long gone, and it was not compatible with the structure of Sasanid society; ideals and reality had parted company. The existence of the sun and moon, the heavens' stars, the turning of the seasons, each in its place and performing its own function, this is divine and worldly justice (Asha). Seen in this way, social justice for man, whether ruler or ruled, was for each group to remain in its own place (caste). In a society which—whether it wished to or not—cannot remain in one state, this "justice" attempts to fix each person in the narrow place and time that he is in, and to keep him in that same condition. In the end, this kind of dissonance between thought and deed, between the soul and the body, tears society in two so that justice ends in injustice, which is what happened.[22]

At the end of the Sasanid era, when the last ill-omened king dragged this great dynasty down, we hear this bewilderment and mental confusion in the poet's words:

Shall we call this justice for Yazdegerd?
    Or shall we call it the enmity of the seven heavens?

If he does not know (whether it is) justice or enmity
    The philosopher would not give me an answer
And if he says religion (is to blame), what he has said is closed
    The answer remains hidden.

B9:368

Is the end of the helpless Yazdegerd "justice," or is it the enmity of the vengeful and pitiless heavens? Every answer, whether it be from philosophers or theologians, indicates bewilderment when faced with the struggles and downfall of a civilization.

Similarly, in the Islamic period the concept of "exercising justice" was not socially consistent and was restricted to equality before the law (which we see once in an army review during the reign of Anushirvan, in the increase of the soldiers' pay) (B8:62). Otherwise "justice" would mean that both the sheep and the wolves, each according to their own kind, came to the watering hole and took what they could (B8:154), without any mention of pay being involved. In the Sasanian period this concept of social justice became a matter of "balance," "from the lower orders submission, from the nobility benevolence / to the evil-minded the two are one" (B8:316). After Feraydun (the exemplar of social order for the Sasanids) was seated on the throne of Zahhak, his first act was to get rid of Zahhak's "evil ways":

He ordered that in the court it be proclaimed
    "O wise and renowned advisors
You should not carry weapons of war
    Since this is not the way that men seek fame and fortune
The army should not consort with artisans
    And with one face seek two professions
One man is a peasant, one bears a mace for war
    It is right that each man's business be obvious
If this man seeks that one's task, that man this man's
    From end to end the earth will be filled with unrest."

V1:83

In such a system with traditions like this there is no place for Giv and Gudarz. Within the restraints of such a society these heroes are finally perhaps like Bahram Chubin, appointed to command the emperor's armies. Another example of the ideal hero is Rostam-e Dastan; like Bahram Gur, when a battle is to be fought he has to be sought for throughout the kingdom, since he is a subject whether he likes it or not and it is only his will that is free. And so it is with the prince and hunter Bahram Gur, the man worthy of both battles and banquets, who with one arrow pierces two wild asses, who both with his polo mallet and at target practice, in killing a rhinoceros and a dragon, is his age's unrivalled master, and is also that brave man who snatches a king's crown from between two lions, as well as being the epicurean lover for whom beautiful musicians take up their harps and praise him thus:[23]

Your waist is like a reed, your stature like a cypress tree
    A cypress tree that walks as proudly as a partridge
Your heart a male lion's, your body a mammoth's
    In battle you hurl your javelin two miles
Your cheeks are just like pomegranate blossom
    You would say they had been washed in rose-water
Your upper arms are like camel's thighs
    You are as firm on your feet as Mount Bisotoun
You are such a man whom no one's eyes
    Have seen, or will see on the day of battle

B7:353

And so in Sasanid society, with its centralized government, its administrative apparatus, its country-wide organization, its army and military force spread throughout the nation, and the visibility of its judgments and of the strength of its teachings, and with its people who had no choice but to live within its customs and conventions in which law, stability, and conduct are woven together—in such a society free will belongs only to the king seated on his throne at the apex of the social pyramid. Even Bozorgmehr, the wisest of the wise and the greatest of viziers, finds himself in prison for no rational reason and becomes blind; this is something that a foolish fraud like Kavus could not do to either Rostam or Zal or to any of the tribe of Gudarz; even Khosrow cannot do this, nor wishes to do it, to the arrogant and foolish warrior Tus when he has his (Khosrow's) brother Forud killed. Each of those champions who were "free agents" was the leader of a tribe and possessed of land, villages, an army, weapons, and arbitrary authority, while on the other hand, according to legend, Bozorgmehr was found as a child among plebian people and taken thence to the splendor of a royal court; his greatness and "freedom" were in his knowledge, not in his possessions or personal glory. He himself once said in answer to Anushirvan, "Woe to the days of a wise and noble man who 'is ruled over by a king who is a fool'" (B8:201).

In this era of opulence, sovereignty and kingship took on a new and more splendid appearance, and because of the prosperity derived from ownership and knowledge it looked on the world as a more gorgeous and splendid place. In place of Kay Khosrow, we see Anushirvan the just, with his legendary chain of justice, as the ideal king of the age. The account of this wise and glorious king, together with the peaceable and secure condition of the people in his time, his wise and knowledgeable councilors, and various other matters—which take up a considerable portion of the Shahnameh—are all indications of our former notion of an ideal of sovereignty and kingship which found its way into the Islamic period; it is that notion which we and others called "the king as the shadow of God"; although even when he is the shadow of God a king can survive when he is a heretic, but not when he is oppressive.

After the coronation ceremony, Anushirvan (like Feraydun and Kay Khosrow before him) toured the country, constructed barriers against the attacks of foreigners, and subdued the obduracy of the Alans, as well as insurrections by the inhabitants of Baluchistan, Gilan, and Daylam. The exercise of his justice, especially when it came to decreasing taxes and the improvement of the lot of his subjects, began at this point. But the longest section of the history of his lengthy reign is the account of his conversations with companions, and with wise and knowledgeable courtiers. In the long, repetitive, and wearisome ethical discussions carried on between the king, Bozorgmehr, priests, and philosophers, justice, knowledge, honesty, moderation and, above all, an unhurried thoughtfulness are praised. Conversely, lies, injustice, ignorance, greed, anger, and precipitate harshness are vehemently condemned; also discussed are fortune that is ours but not subject to our will, as well as effort that is ours and is subject to our will, and time that is within us and exists without us, linking together what is and is not.[24]

Both Kay Khosrow and Anushirvan are possessed of God-given glory, and are wise, just, and knowledgeable; both are ideal kings and both are *ensan-e kamel* (perfect human beings) in the Shahnameh, one from the legendary era and the other from the historical era, each with the characteristics specific to their own time. Both derive their glory from God, as is the case with Kay Khosrow's God-given knowledge. This "young stripling," having spent his early years in the company of shepherds, deceived Afrasyab, who was an experienced and intelligent practitioner of magic, when they conversed with one another; Afrasyab thought him mad, and said, "I ask him about his head and his answer's about his feet"![25] Kay Khosrow's wisdom is mainly an understanding of the heart, a divine insight rather than a conflation of knowledge and experience. His advent and his departure are also both celestial events that are connected with the fate of the world; he has to come because a thousand years of injustice is coming to an end, and he leaves without dying, so that he can return at the end of time. Kay Khosrow is outside of time, and there are two indications of this—at his advent (Shahrivar) and at his departure (Soshyans). These signify the Amesha Spenta Shahrivar, who is the emblem of Ahura Mazda's ideal sovereignty, and the last renewing of the world in the name of *Astva Artah*, which means "Asha" or manifest justice.[26] After fifty-seven years in the world Kay Khosrow is an ally of "manifest justice" and its fellow-combatant. He is above history, an ideal king who does not die, through the blessing of whose existence original celestial justice (Shahrivar) and ultimate worldly justice (Soshyans) come together, as if from two sides of time's turning circle, and injustice is no more.

But Anushirvan is a historical king, as a result of which he lives in time and is acquainted with death, although in the hope that his soul is eternal (Anusheh Ravan, meaning "Eternal Soul"). His deeds are those of a mortal who has himself fallen into time's circle, and they do not bring about the end of history; his role is to wield royal authority according to the ways of the world—that is, to exercise justice. In contrast to that of Kay Khosrow, his knowledge is mixed, and comes from speaking with and listening to "seventy men who in eating and sleeping" were always with him; sitting and rising "he adorned his heart" with his courtiers' eloquence. Each of these two individuals is a perfect instance of his own time; the difference between them lies in the nature of their eras, in different ideals and realities, aspirations and deeds.

Now is the time to add a few other points to what has been said. However much Kay Khosrow and Anushirvan are ideal kings, each of whom is also a "perfect man," this state is not restricted only to them; it can be found at different times, in different circumstances, and each time in a new form, throughout the Shahnameh. When Sohrab is at death's door, before he knows who Rostam is, he says to him:

If you become a fish within water
    Or like the night shrouded in darkness
Or if you become like the stars in the heavens
    If you remove all light from the earth
My father will seek revenge from you
    When he knows that the dust is my pillow.
V2:186

Surely every explication and explanation of the splendor of such poetry must fall short; it is enough that we know that the hero who seeks justice will be victorious over the fish who has fled into water, the night shrouded in darkness, and the distant stars. In a similar way, Rostam's answer to Esfandyar, who wants to take him with his hands bound to Goshtasp, comes to mind:

Who tells someone to bind Rostam's arms?
The high heavens cannot bind my arms
And if the heavens tell me not to fight
I will smite its two ears with my heavy mace

V5:354

There are many examples like this throughout the book. Among others we can cite the words and behavior of Piran Viseh when he is face to face with death, or we can recall the stubborn pride of Rostam and Esfandyar, which is not simply arrogant flyting but an affirmation of their bodily strength and the greatness of their souls. From these few brief examples we can see that man at his most noble, for all that he is time's slave, reaches beyond the heavens. Ferdowsi himself is one of these "high flying souls"; in his splendid reproach to the cruelty of the turning heavens, he says that when he leaves this dark earthly abode, "I shall complain of you before the pure God."

The high heavens answered him
"O eloquent and faultless man
Why do you see all good and bad as (coming) from me?
How is this proper for a knowledgeable man?
You are higher than I am in all ways
You nourish your soul with knowledge
I have no way to the things of which you speak
The sun and moon are unaware of such knowledge
Seek your way from Him who created the way
Who created night and day and the sun and moon . . ."

B7:112

Man is God's ideal, the adornment of the world and of time. Concerning Rostam, Esfandyar addresses the Creator as follows, "You created him as You desired / You made him the adornment of the world and of time."[27]

In the Shahnameh the history of the Sasanids is an "epic" of culture and civilization, and here Ferdowsi writes like an informed historian examining each facet of his subject, and celebrating every aspect of wisdom and knowledge. Perhaps Anushirvan's guide and vizier, the sage Bozorgmehr, can be considered as the greatest "hero" of this age on the battlefield of insight and knowledge. Due to his talent for interpreting dreams, which is "a prophetic gift," he was successful from childhood on as someone who was able to see the world's reality in dreams. Among the kingdom's elderly sages he learned every component of knowledge, and "surpassed those philosophers in wisdom," to the extent that when, in an assembly of his sages the "wise king" required each of them to display his knowledge and the young Bozorgmehr stood and received permission to speak, "The young man showed sovereignty in speech / brilliance shone from his words" (B8:117). Before Anushirvan, in seven royal assemblies spread over seven weeks, he answers various questions put to him by knowledgeable courtiers, priests, and astrologers. The sixth time it is the turn of the most preeminent nobles in the realm and the royal vizier and scribe, and in the last session his only questioner is Anushirvan. From Bozorgmehr's words, he wishes to know himself, and says to him, "Tell me truthfully what you know of me" (V8:143), and he answers appropriately, as he must.

And so Bozorgmehr's knowledgeable behavior during the seven trials of knowledge, and his demonstration of his wisdom—like that of Piran—together mean that he attains a noble and unique position at court. In these long questions and longer answers, we discover again knowledge and skill, good and bad ethics and behavior, the ways of life that lead to an honorable reputation, and the customs of sovereignty and civility. His discourses, which are an example of the highest didactic principles of the Sasanid era, meant that "Among the nobles the fortune of Bozorgmehr / Was like the shining of the sun in the heavens" (B8:119). Only a king possessed of the divine glory could rise higher than this. Anushirvan was an enquiring king who sought knowledge, and by the end of his reign he had solved the knotty problems that preoccupied his priests, reaching a stage of knowledge and eloquence that surpassed that of all other sages, and so made him worthy of sovereignty.

We know Ferdowsi's Piran through his actions, not through his words. We see this general, vizier, and counselor from a former age on the one hand through the give-and-take of battle, the successes and failures of the struggle between Iran and Turan and his loyalty to Afrasyab, and on the other through his kindness to Seyavash, Farangis, and Kay Khosrow, as a renowned man in the whirlwind of an event-filled life shackled both by his land and by his tribe and people, and caught up in an unwanted and inevitable war while searching for a way to deliverance, righteousness, and justice.

But we come to know the world of Bozorgmehr and his exalted mind and beliefs mainly through either his own words or the words of others. Everything that is in legendary epic—the might and battles of free men—manifests itself as action; in historical epic, action flowers and is brought to fruition in speech, especially in the field of sovereignty, administration (justice and injustice), and practical wisdom. Finding the correct answer and uncovering the secrets of things is not the only way to eminence and honor; there are also the debates of the king's messengers—which are sometimes like victories and sometimes like defeats in battle—in which the participants must inevitably accept the more knowledgeable as the winner and submit to his judgment. In the story of the appearance of chess, a messenger from the king of India arrives with jewels and many fine items of tribute, plus a chessboard and its pieces and "a letter written on silk," saying that if "your" (Anushirvan's) wise men can discover the secret of "this excellent game":

I shall gladly send the taxes and tribute
    Commanded by the king to his court
And if the assembled knowledgeable men of Iran
    Are baffled in their attempt to understand (this game)
When their knowledge cannot compete with ours
    They should not demand taxes and tribute from this country

They should undertake to pay the taxes
Since knowledge is the best of glorious things.

Kasra says to Bozorgmehr, "It's up to you to solve this, and if you can't

It will be a great defeat for our learned men
And for the court and the throne

and the Indians will say that the king has no one who seeks out knowledge." After a day and a night Bozorgmehr had worked out the secrets of the game and the king was so happy that "You would say that Good Fortune had showed him her face." Then in return Bozorgmehr set out the game of backgammon like a battlefield—two armies arranged opposite one another in four corners, ready for combat, and a letter was sent from the Persian king to the Indian king, saying

We have put in place of chess backgammon
Now let battle be simulated in a game

summoning him to "battle" with this game. It becomes apparent that the Indians cannot work out the secret of the game; they are defeated, and are obliged to send even more taxes and tribute.[28] In this way, the competition for a cultural superiority manifested in knowledge and speech replaces the physical combat of legendary heroes. Needless to say the vehemence and violence of battle, the warrior's arrogance and sense of honor as he risks his life for glory, cannot be found in the conversations of wise old men, and no one should expect them to be there.

They should not be expected because legendary epic is an expression of the violent taming of the world and its inhabitants. The great battles between men and the world, and between men one with another, the life and death struggle of heroes, together play out this astonishing conflict. In legendary epic, instead of a mere description of good and evil we see the combatants' souls tested throughout their lives and in their encounters with one another, by the world's ugliness and beauty, by agonies and desires, by instinctive strength, overweening ambition, love of country, and the desire for vengeance, and by justice and injustice. But in the historical era those proud heroes, who longed to hurl Iran and Turan against one another and to assail heaven itself, have placed crowns on their heads and peacefully taken their place on the throne. And so we find ourselves encountering reports of kings' reigns, and of the civilization and culture to which Sasanid imperial rule had brought peace. This history is a description of wisdom, justice, knowledge and the like, or of foolishness, injustice, ignorance, and ruin. And the perception of this, the understanding and recounting of it, comes about only with the help of speech. Speech is the house of wisdom and the "green pasture" which nourishes our understanding and recreates it. It is because of this that speech is so valued, that around the king of kings of this era

> Seventy eloquent men were always present
> In the court, at the times of eating and of sleeping,
> Whenever (the king) rested from his activities,
> From justice and generosity, from wine and drinking
> He asked new questions of each learned man
> And delighted his heart with knowledge.
>
> B8:116

But Anushirvan is not satisfied with this and he sends people to faraway countries in search of knowledge. One day during an imperial audience a doctor named Borzui tells Anushirvan that he has read in an Indian book that in the mountains of that country there is a plant which, if it is gathered by experts and then " . . . scattered over a dead man, certainly / He will immediately begin to speak." The king opens the door of his treasury and gives Borzui three hundred camels laden "With gold coins and brocade, with furs and silks / With seals and crowns, with musk and fine cloth" (B8:248), together with a letter to the sovereign of the Indians, telling him to go and discover the meaning of this mysterious account. Borzui sets off and after extensive searching and suffering he despairs of success, until finally an ancient sage explains the mystery of "the mountain and the plant" to him, saying:

Understand that the plant is speech and knowledge is the
 mountain
 And may splendor always attend both of them
The dead body is like a man without knowledge
 Since a knowledgeable man flourishes in all places
With knowledge certainly a man becomes alive
 Where there is no knowledge don't bother to search
Man is praised because of knowledge
 The plant is like *Kalileh* and knowledge like the mountain
A book shows the way to knowledge
 Come then if you are searching for the king's treasure.
B8:251

Knowledge is a mountain, and when the plant of speech grows on it "its head becomes green, its heart grows strong." Without this plant the mountain is dry and desolate, and knowledge without speech is silent and dead. Speech is the plant which when scattered on the dead brings the dead to life. Finally, after much suffering and having put his soul in danger, Borzui brings the book, which is a form of speaking knowledge, home, and when the king sees this "sea of knowledge" he says: "This book named *Kalileh* has revived my soul." And immediately he tells Borzui to take the treasury key from the treasurer, saying that as a reward for what he has done whatever silver and gold and royal jewels he desired are his. After expressing his gratitude Borzui says:

I have a request that I wish to make of the king
 So that there remain some memorial of me in the world
When Bozorgmehr copies this book
 May it show the face of Borzui's sufferings
May it open with a memorial to me
 Who obeyed the victorious king's command

So that after my death, in the world
My sufferings shall not be unknown to the wise.
B8:253

When *Kalileh* reached Khosrow Anushirvan and the king saw Borzui he said, "Rejoice in your heart and free your mind from troublesome thoughts, because my favor towards you has reached such heights that it has no limit, and you may expect from me more than you can possibly imagine." Then he remembered his promise that he would open his treasury's doors to him so that he could take whatever he wished . . .

When the wise Borzui heard this speech and saw the honor that was being paid to him . . . he made his obeisance and thanked the king in the most elegant manner he could and said, " . . . Since the king has commanded this reward for me and has opened the door of this slave's heart with the hand of happiness, this slave has no choice but to submit to the king's command, especially as it was sworn to as a promise. I wish to ask one request; if it is granted that my business in both worlds is fulfilled, it will be a treasure that nothingness cannot destroy and no event will be able to affect. From all the king's magnanimity I ask but one thing; that your majesty would command Bozorgmehr, when he comes to compile this book, to record my name at the beginning of this great work so that whoever reads it will make my name live again.[29]

Like Ferdowsi, Borzui has sown the seeds of speech, and he has the same wish as Ferdowsi: the survival of his name through language, despite the vicissitudes of time, so that he will live after death. Man does not know the plain and hidden secrets of the world unless he hears the speech of those who are expert in each realm of knowledge, and never ceases from learning. There is a debate between wisdom and knowledge, and the means by which this debate is carried on is speech, since man finds his way to knowledge through speech, and from death to God's eternity, in the splendor of the light that is the "sovereign of the learned" and whose sovereignty is learning itself.

Speech

ANUSHIRVAN WAS TOLD that there is a mountain in India on which a plant grows that can bring the dead back to life. It became clear that the mountain was "knowledge" and the plant "speech": the plant of speech on the mountain of knowledge. Before this we indicated that in the creation of the world, creation occurs by means of thought, and thought becomes manifest in speech (the divine word). In the Old Testament it is written, "In the beginning God created the heavens and the earth. And the earth was without form, and void; and darkness was upon the face of the deep. And the spirit of God moved upon the waters. And God said, Let there be light, and there was light . . . And God called the light day, and the darkness he called night. . . ."[1] And in this naming known as the Creation the recognition of God's deeds began. In the New Testament (the Gospel according to John) it also says, "In the beginning was the word, and the word was with God. All things were made by Him; and without Him was not anything made." And in another place God describes Himself by means of the first and last letters of the Greek alphabet—that is, in terms of the written form of speech—"And He that sat upon the throne said, 'Behold, I make all things new,' and He said unto me, 'Write: for these words are true and faithful.' And He said unto me, 'It is done. I am Alpha and Omega, the beginning and the end.'"[2] Perhaps it is not necessary to mention that in the Qur'an God says, "Be" and it is so. By means of the two letters of the Arabic alphabet that make up the word for "Be," through this "command" the created world came into being.[3] The Qur'an is the word of God, and according to various theologians is "eternal," not created; that is, from the beginning of time and even before the creation it was within God, and at the predestined time was revealed to the Prophet of Islam. In any case, whether it is eternal or created, the word of God, the conveyer of truths that are divine and everlasting, is the manifestation of creation and the connection between the created and its creator through the agency of the Prophets. Be this as it may, in the Qur'an the "verses" (the word of God) are the highest indication of God's existence; they are "signs" of the other world and of the most complete exposition of His will, that at the same time make manifest His glory in language. From this we can deduce that the miraculous nature of Islam's Prophet lies in language (the Qur'an), and not in anything else. Naturally, in all systems of faith the word of God possesses its own meaning and special spirituality. These remarks are only to remind us of the exalted, primary, and celestial nature of language, and nothing more than this.

In our mythological thought too, speech is the greatest of man's acquisitions; it has been bestowed upon him from the heavens so that human beings should not be without some knowledge of God. In the Gathas, the oldest portion of the Avesta, our first prophet and poet, Zoroaster, questions Ahura Mazda:

1. "O Ahura Mazda, O most celestial of beings, O righteous judge of the world, O Ashavan! What is that speech which you have placed in my heart, O Ahura Mazda?

2. "Before the creation of the heavens, of water, of animals, of plants, of the fire of Ahura Mazda, of the Ashavan man, of destroyers and demons and mankind, before all the world's life, before all the descendants of the good Asha?"

3. Then Ahura Mazda said, "O Zoroaster, that speech which I have placed in your heart was 'Ahunvar.'"[4]

In answer to the prophet and poet God replies, "The first thing that I created, before the heavens, the earth, water, and fire, was speech."

The work of the poet, in poetic creation, is to follow the work of God; he too is a creator of language, and in this role he is a creator of things, one who produces knowledge of the world, because the poet as a master of "intelligence" possesses insight (unconsciously) and knowledge (consciously). This dual capacity comes from the sources of his creativity, which is the means by which speech becomes a stable world that our knowledge can also enter into. The world in human terms, the world of men, "our world," is nothing but the distinguishing of our own being from being in general, from all that exists. If there is no one to make this distinction the world is as nothing. In the world of the imagination we can think it is impossible for a world without awareness to exist. Existence for beings that have no awareness is meaningless. Essentially, in the absence of awareness the meaning of "meaning" itself is meaningless.[5] Like the prophet, out of the blessing of his own knowledge (conscious and unconscious) the poet gives his own meaning to the world and its inhabitants; living and dying become meaningful, we know why we exist and why we do not exist, or at the least we know that we do not know why we exist and do not exist, we know our own ignorance and are aware of it.

Let us return to the exchanges between Zoroaster and Ahura Mazda, which have come into being through the blessing of speech, so that in this way man and God become of one mind and one language. In this relationship, this friendship, the poet (Zoroaster) becomes reacquainted with himself and with the world, and since he conveys his "friend's" message to everyone, he becomes his prophet and his messenger to us. The "speech" that Ahura Mazda teaches to Zoroaster is a wonderful invocation (prayer) that has miraculous and magical properties as a means of destroying demons, the lie, and the evil of evildoers. Ahura Mazda expresses this speech (Ahunvar) in language and Ahriman falls into unconsciousness for three thousand years. This blessing is the foundation and essence of religion (and of divine knowledge) and these two—religion and prayer or divine knowledge and speech—are created together and simultaneously.

From infinite light Hormozd created infinite existence, and from that "Ahunvar" came into being, which was " . . . the beginning of creation, and finally created entities appeared from this, and this (is called) religion, since religion was created simultaneously with the creation" (Bahar, Bondahesh, 37). And so first, from infinity (infinite light, infinite substance) finite existence (the beginning and the end) appeared, and then "Ahunvar" and religion—speech and knowledge; and as one with this, the revelation of time, the beginning and the end, came into being. Because the genesis of religion (knowledge) is inevitably in speech (prayer) it cannot be known without speech, since for a knowledge of religion God must be known and there is no other "way" to knowing God apart from speech. He either reveals Himself through speech (as revelation) or a suppliant summons Him through speech. It is as if there is a "magic" in speech that makes visible and discovers—that is, which creates—things that are hidden, invisible, and undiscoverable (things that are "no thing"). It is for this reason that "We who need Him and He who is desirous of us" reach one another through the medium of speech: throughout the Gathas we find this desire between two friends to know, to see, and to speak with one another.[6]

Zarathustra wishes to know God's thought through His speech, since thought has no other body than speech, and this body has no other soul than speech. This is why he asks the creator, "Who is the creator? Who is it who sets the sun and the moon and the stars in their courses, who lifted up this lofty sky, who made the wind, clouds, and water, so that the plants would grow and flourish?" He wishes to know everything, the light and the darkness, sleep and wakefulness, dawn, noon, and night, and the "good nature" that is the essence of man and of the world. Impatient for knowledge, he asks God, "For whom did You create this fruitful, enchantingly delightful world?" He wishes to see both worlds in the mirror of God's sight. The ignorant man who is unaware of his ignorance wants certainty, but God does not free Zoroaster from indecision and doubt as to his own knowledge: "Is it not true that all that I proclaim is good?" (Yasna 44), and by means of speech God shows him creation and eternity, in the form of Ahunvar " . . . from whom in the beginning creation is made manifest and in the end what is created, so that religion (as it is named) should exist, since religion is created simultaneously with the creation." (Bahar, Bondahesh, 37).

The motive and goal of creation is to wage a victorious war against Ahriman, and religion is the means by which this victorious war is fought. Zarathustra sees the world and the way of righteousness in the world together and simultaneously. This is the way in which, with the aid of speech (Ahunvar), he functions within time and place, or in other words his personal (inner) time and place flow into him from the time and place of the external (what is outside of him, and worldly) and his soul takes the outer world into account. At this stage he shares in God's vision of the world, as Kay Khosrow does with the cup that reveals all the times and places of the world.[7] And so he sees God "At the beginning of life's creation . . . until the creation came to an end" (Yasna 43, 5), and when "good nature" asks him, "Who are you, and from which people do you come . . . ?" he says, "I am Zarathustra, the enemy of the lie and the friend of truth (Yasna 43, 7–8). He is from "truth's" family.

This kind of culture and custom, with its deep ancient roots, passed into Islamic Iran, perhaps more by oral means than written, and more by unconscious means than conscious. In the fourth century Hejri this feeling had not only not yet died but—thanks to history, language, religion (Zoroastrianism, and the copying of religious texts), the translation of the knowledge and literature of the past into Arabic and from there into Persian, the persistence of custom and folklore, sociopolitical movements and so on—was beginning to reawaken and revive. For Ferdowsi, who amassed, arranged, and ordered this tradition, and for his book, the first concern was to preserve the tradition, albeit in a different form and configuration. Zoroaster was a prophet who had collected the mythology and beliefs of former times, and out of this mass of material he had fashioned a glorious book and religion. Like Zoroaster, Ferdowsi is an eloquent poet who seeks to know and understand, but unlike him he is not seeking to converse with God, because he is a poet living in historical time, not a prophet of a mythological age. In Zoroaster's thought there is no unbridgeable abyss between the Creator and his creation. If the world is the manifestation in visible (worldly) form of Ahura Mazda, then he—as a man—is present in this world in his own body, and in this way both are on the same level of existence, like the celestial world and the existence of the primordial essences along with Ahura Mazda. From another perspective, Ahura Mazda, with the Amesha Spentas as intermediaries, takes on worldly form as fire, metal, water, plants, and dust (the earth). The existence of the Amesha Spentas is a bridge between the heavens and the earth. It is a two-way connection between the world and the heavens, and as a result it is not impossible for God and man to converse with one another. In particular, the fact of a relationship between the primordial essences (the essence of the heavens and of man, coexistent with the heavens) in the heavens and Ahura Mazda in the world means that as well as God and man being able to converse with one another, they are also contemporaries. At this stage, in his conversations with Ahura Mazda, Zarathustra is in a timeless realm. He is like those who desire to see both the beginning and the end, and to perceive all of time; this is that "spiritual apprehension" that Mowlana and Hafez sometimes experience. In this experience of selflessness and union he is not concerned with the passage of time.

But in Ferdowsi's thought, this is impossible. As is apparent from the opening of the Shahnameh, God cannot be known, there can only be faith that "He" exists and is unlike anything that can be imagined. And if it becomes clear from the book that He is merciful and benevolent, or for example powerful and almighty, this is only so that we can, according to our own capacities, acknowledge His existence. God is such that knowledge of Him is beyond the capabilities of our understanding, never mind our seeing Him, or conversing with Him.[8] Moses was eager to see Him, and the answer came that he could not; in the same way the relationship between the Prophet of Islam and God was a one-way street, through the intercession of Gabriel and revelation. As a serious Muslim Ferdowsi does not think he can converse with God, and as a wise human being living in finite time, which hurries on towards death, he is well aware that living is linked with dying; these two are time's children, and every breath we draw leads us to death. And so his heart is distressed, he is impatient, and since he cannot converse with God, he turns to this eternally hidden entity that according to Zurvan tradition is more powerful than Ahura Mazda and Ahriman; he turns to the turning heavens, to infinite time, to "Fortune." The story of his mental state is that of a complaint against the injustice of time;[9] he wishes to know the unknowable reason for time's (the high heavens') injustice. Why have you reared me, and having reared me why such betrayal? And for all this he knows that his question is pointless, that there is no answer, and that time is a mother who murders her children. But for as long as he has not left this darkness, in order to flee from the pain of death he turns to speech. Ferdowsi, like Zarathustra, is weighed down by the past and like him has much to say, but since it is impossible for his mind to deal with the timeless celestial world, in his awareness of death this poet turns to speech in order to construct a building that will last, that will be a refuge for both the past and the future, that will give life to the dead and assure his own continued life; he will pass through death and put it behind him, like the free heroes of epic, like Seyavash and Kay Khosrow. He dies in the body, and his fame lives on.

"Before the creation Hormozd was not a God"; it is in creating that he is a God and the first thing that he creates is speech. If the Godliness of God lies in creation, then man too is man by means of creation because consciously, not instinctively, he has control over nature, and controlling nature means reconstructing the world around him and creating a home for himself. And in terms of religion, knowledge, love, and so forth, he wishes to create himself as "free" from the depredations of time, to go beyond himself and grasp at the sovereignty of God.[10]

Because Ahura Mazda has knowledge, he is a creator, since it is due to this that from the beginning he knows the end and creates the world for the battle against Ahriman. Creation originates in knowledge. Man too, because of wisdom (knowledge), is a creator. Man is not the creator of wisdom, which is a blessing from God, but he inevitably turns to speech in order to exercise wisdom. Man is the creator of speech, since this is perhaps the only way he can bring forth wisdom (knowledge), give it a form, and realize it in action. Wisdom is a gift from God, and its union with speech generates the celebratory soul that brings man close to God the deliverer and savior. The poet's freedom from the exigencies of being—from the measure of his life and the substance of his body; that is, from his time and place—is a prerequisite for creation, and what creation is nobler than speech? The speech that Ferdowsi articulates does not accept an existence without wisdom; these two are like a bow and an arrow, one useless without the other. "Sound your soul's tocsin in speech / Make wisdom the bow, speech the arrow" (B8:140). It is speech like this that comforts the poet's soul and frees his spirit. "When speech is accompanied by wisdom / the poet's soul knows peace" (V2:201); on the one hand he benefits us by this wisdom and brings us close to God—"the wise man is closer to God" (B7:403)—and on the other, he recreates the immortal knowledge of God, and in this way makes his own "name" immortal through speech; through speech and in speech, since a "name" only survives in speech, speech which derives from wisdom. The judicious poet desires a complementarity between wisdom and speech like that which exists between a bow and an arrow. In the introduction to the Shahnameh we have seen why this wisdom desires to encompass the world, despite the fact that thought has no means of doing this. "If wisdom chooses speech / it chooses it in order to see" (V1:3), it chooses man and the world around him to appropriate and celebrate so that in knowing them he will reveal new deeds and new matters, and make them permanent in speech.

In the composition of his ghazals Sa'di is a great lyric poet, but in his *qasideh*s and in the *Bustan* he is an "epic" poet, in the sense that his thoughts, practical wisdom, and spiritual explorations are apparent in his writings in a subtly concentrated form. Out of his worldly encounters and life experiences he sets out to expound ethical advice and practical wisdom. It happens that the meter of the *Bustan* is the same as that of the Shahnameh, and we know that in the composition of his work Sa'di is aware of the sage of Tus's masterpiece. At the opening of his book Sa'di says:

I have been about the world a great deal
  And spent my days with many people
I have found pleasure in every corner
  I have gleaned something from every harvest
It pains me to come back from all these orchards
  Empty-handed to my friends . . .

"And so I have written a book and in it, I have made ten entrances for instruction" such as The Exercise of Justice, The Fear of God, Civility, Love, Benevolence, and so on. . . . This book is a summing up of his conclusions drawn from observing the outer world, from looking at the "appearance" of the world, from the narratives he had heard and the things he had learned.[11] But when this same unique poet turns to the ghazal he says in an incomparable verse:

In truth I do not know what you resemble in the world
  the world and all that is in it is mere appearances, and you
    are soul.

The lyric poet desires to see the world's soul, and the epic poet, like a pilgrim "through history," to see the customs and manners of the world's geography and its inhabitants; as the poet of the Shahnameh has said:

In this book of former princes
  great nobles and mounted warriors
There is fighting and feasting, counsel and speech,
  the passing of so many ancient days
There is knowledge and faith, forbearance and counsel
  And guidance to the other world

From that which pleased them
there is profit for these days
May those great men be remembered
may their days remain with us

V5:441

Epic poetry takes outer matters as its focus, but it is not simply a description of the outer world, because this "immortal knowledge" (with or without God) has cast its anchor deep within the poet's mind and become something inward. He looks at the outer world from this inwardness, and bestows his own meanings on it, according to the colors he sees and the signs he becomes aware of. And so this outward reality is also something inward, except that now this gaze that looks "into the wounded heart, and its sorrowful tumult" is chiefly focused on the passing of time and our happiness and unhappiness. Given such a perspective on battles and banquets, on the passing of warriors and great men and those who put their stamp on days gone by, the poet internalizes such knowledge, faith, and goodness, and turns his gaze toward his own time and his own great work. For example, he says this about one of Ardeshir's dead warriors:

There was no prince in the world like him
there was no memorial of him after his death
It is I in particular who make his name live
may his end be nothing but good.

B7:178

When he says of Anushirvan, "From my words his justice has become young again" (B8:154) we see the same conception of the work performed by speech. "These stories have become old, from me / the ancient days shall be renewed" (V2:201). The nobles said to Bahram Gur, "You raise all the dead from the ground / with justice and benevolence, with pure speech" (B7:441); but these words of theirs are more applicable to the one who celebrated Bahram's adventures, who wishes to awaken the sleeping past, to foresee the time to come, and to keep his own memory alive within these two boundaries of time, so that his name will outlast death, if it can be outlasted![12] At the beginning of his book Ferdowsi relates how scattered narratives remained from former times. A man who was "a small landowner, brave, great and wise" summoned knowledgeable men from every quarter so that they would collect together these scattered accounts. This man wished to know "How they held the world at the beginning," and what had happened to these famous men that remained for us after they had gone. And when he heard and knew the situation, he collected the accounts, and with good fortune's help they reached a unique poet who would memorialize them:

> When this account fell into my hands
> Within a month I was ready for work
> There was an account from ancient times
> its language was of a truthful nature
> It was old stories, written in prose
> there was nothing extraneous in it
> I took this noble book as a good omen
> and labored over it for many years
> I saw no one who was noble and generous
> no one in a royal position who was splendid
> This speech did not lie easy on my heart
> there was no remedy for this but silence . . .
> I held back from speech for twenty years
> waiting for someone worthy of such trouble
> V5:175–76

When this "account" came into his hands it must have seemed as though he'd landed the biggest fish of all. His only fear was that relentless time was passing too fast, that constant unremitting time that was always flowing onward like a stream in the poet's mind.[13] We can cite many examples of this noble and justifiable fear. Ferdowsi is worried that, God forbid, he should die and his great work remain incomplete. Fortunately he survived, and cultivated his "garden" and grafted his soul with that "pure mine" for a while, so that "this renowned book" reached its conclusion. At the end of his book (B9:230) the old man says:

When sixty-six years had passed
    pitiless men did not act well
When this renowned book comes to an end
    the face of the world will fill with talk of me
From this time forth I shall not die, I am alive
    for I have scattered the seeds of my speech—
Anyone who has intelligence, good judgment, and religion
    shall speak well of me after death.

V9:230

And so this extraordinary, royally bejeweled work became the aging poet's companion and the solace of his soul, a memorial to him that was safe from time's depredations; its language is life-giving, an antidote to death, and Ferdowsi builds it like a great castle, such that "it will be unharmed by wind and rain," and revive the fame and fortune of those whom time has destroyed. This "castle" is an epic that recounts the three eras of Iran's past: the mythological, the legendary, and the historical. The distinguishing feature of the Shahnameh and of its poet's art lies in the meanings and style of the narrative. Up to now, and in the earlier sections of this work, we have mostly been concerned with "meanings." We shall now briefly refer to the poem's style as it is the expression and manifestation of these meanings, the way in which speech confers being on these meanings. This style is simple, noble, and splendid, as everyone has agreed, among them Nezami 'Aruzi who said that Ferdowsi "raised speech to the highest heaven and so that it flowed like bright water, and what temperament has such vigor that it could bring speech to such a level as he has?"[14]

"Flowed like bright water" and "the highest heaven" are expressions referring to facility and simplicity, the nobility and splendor of poetry. Every poetry, as with every great artist, according to its time and the different demands placed on it, brings to the light of day a fresh manifestation of reality, and reveals new meanings; the thinker and the thought (in this case the poet and the poem) are like two phenomena that each have no effect as such, but together are both agent and acted upon, both giving and taking, one with his searching fluid intelligence, and the other gravid with this intelligence, the pregnant recipient of meaning. As a result of this, every aesthetic insight derived from poetry or art is on the one hand individual, specific, and conditioned by time and place, and is therefore historical, and on the other hand it is transformative and relative, relative to the individual and his environment. This phenomenon, so far as it is specific historically and socially, is subject to time and decay, and so far as it is transformative it is relative, evading time and renewing itself; it moves free of a specific moment and reveals new meanings as it conforms to other eras; it becomes a work from a thousand years ago that is relevant to us today, in our own time.

In addition to this we should point out that when it comes to the essence of poetry or art, to that something which suddenly makes language or a work of art an object of lasting value, whatever is said about this, something still remains unsaid. And this is the "something," palpable but unknown, that even Hafez did not know how to express in language. Every sublime artistic creation, in language or another medium, is like a body. Bodies can perhaps be opened up and studied and comprehended, but nothing of their life-giving soul can be grasped or seen or shown or described. This is that essence of beauty that Hafez sensed and could not express; it is that "magic" that is not only present in every part of the poet's generosity of character and disposition, but inheres in the beauty of the words used, as it does in every sublime beauty.

And so after these preliminaries perhaps it can be said that the nobility, simplicity, and splendor of Ferdowsi's language basically derive from three sources:

- from confidence in the noble and unique standing of language
- from the free nature of the nobles and heroes about whom the language is used
- from their fortunes and extraordinary deeds, which are the subject of the language.

These nobles, kings, princes, heroes, and queens have the toughness of "fire, granite, and steel," the strength of "mammoths and lions and crocodiles," the fresh charm of "musk and roses and slender cypresses," and the youthfulness of "spring" (V2:391). They are free, since they can act as they decide to, even at the price of their own souls, and they fashion their life histories, in spite of fate, as they wish. Their fates (or destinies) from Jamshid and Afrasyab to Feraydun, Seyavash, and Kay Khosrow, or those of Sohrab, Rostam, and Esfandyar and others are extraordinary, and their deeds are even more extraordinary. By means of their deeds they break free of their fate; the kings' "deed" is to rule, and the heroes' "deeds" are battles and banquets. Elsewhere (as in *The Shahnameh and History*) it has been said that our epic history comes into being through war, and war is concerned with the soul's bravery, the body's strength, and steadfastness before death. All this can be seen most clearly in the episodes of single combat, which is a great and courageous matter, one in which the combatants "hurl the high heavens to the ground." The "role" of the heroes consists of weighty deeds; their combat is with the turning heavens, and with the earth and time. Putting their struggles into words needs a language that has the simple noble splendor of their deeds; it needs in fact the resplendent style of the Shahnameh. For this reason the style throughout the Shahnameh, even for the speeches and activities of base characters, remains consistent, not in order to elevate them or show them as greater than they are but because their useless lives are inevitably lived out in the patrician world of free heroes. It is clear, and perhaps it goes without saying, that this is still the literary written language, learned and popular, spoken by the literate, the powerful, and the poor in Sa'di's works, or by kings and peasants in Abul-Fazl Bayhaqi's *History*.[15] Going beneath the characters' skin, and having each person speak in his own language—for various reasons, among which are transgressing the ancient limits of literary discourse, widening the scope and changing the sense of culture, as well as recognizing the social worth of individual characters—is a relatively new departure which belongs to more recent times.

There are so many examples of elevated, eloquent language in this great poem that it is difficult to choose among them. It is enough simply to look at the conversations and flyting of Rostam and Esfandyar, the last words of Sohrab before he recognizes his father, Piran's answer to Gudarz when he is on the brink of death, the encounter between Rostam and Ashkabus, and many, many other examples throughout the book. This elevated language is of a piece with the wisdom of the worldview expressed; as Ferdowsi himself says, "I have molded my narrative with wisdom / I have reaped the harvest of the seeds I sowed." It is pointless to praise Ferdowsi's language; how can one praise the sun for its shining, its clarity, its elevated splendor, without derogating it? Perhaps we can say that thanks to the blessings of this poet's genius his language has a singularly expressive quality that is truly pleasing and which without any diminution inevitably finds its way to the reader. By "expressive quality" I mean the inner movement of the poetry; the union of language's sense with a word's connotations—like the oneness of body and soul, or the harmony of the rising and falling of a wave with the sea's tumult and the blowing of the wind—that creates an "expressive quality" overflowing with harshness and softness, sorrow and joy, signs of incurable pain and justified pride, something as simple as Sohrab's youth and the apprehension he feels during his journey.[16] In the tumultuous course of the language, the words are like a beating heart so that sometimes the meaning and meter give the feeling of rain pelting down in the spring, or they open up with the peacefulness of blossoms in a garden. We ascend from one stage to another, so that in reading and hearing the poetry it is as if we are climbing a mountain and gazing into the distance through clear shining air, hovering between possibility and impossibility.

Countless examples of this can be found throughout the book, and out of such a large number I don't know how to reference just one or two. But finally we have to offer instances; one is the conversation between the aged Zal and young Rostam and his choice of a horse, its description and the preparation for war against Afrasyab (V1:330), which overflows with the father's love and concern, the son's pride and stubbornness, and the horse Rakhsh's restless strength. Or another instance, in which the tone of the poetry is calm and regretful, occurs when there is a discussion about old age, weakness, and the games fate plays with our souls and bodies (B8:52). We can compare the strong, sharp, harsh beat of the language in the first example with the drawn-out calmness and sadness of the second, and realize the suitableness of each with the subject that is being presented. These are but a few examples of many.

The nature of such genius cannot be expressed, and neither can this "expressive quality"; both are that Hafezian "something" we mentioned. Ferdowsi is not a poet who makes a show of his art or who uses elaborate language; in his poetry we find no artificial diction or learned expressions, or if we find examples of such things they are present accidentally rather than deliberately. In his language every word has a fixed meaning and every poetic image is used to suggest a particular state, not for the sake of making an artistic display.[17] This poet is like his poetry—"simple," noble, and splendid, and he sees no reason for either himself or his language to make an elaborate display. He was a small landowner from the village of Tabaran near Tus in the Khorasan of the fourth century Hejri (tenth–eleventh centuries CE) at the place and time in which the national and political culture of Iran was being reborn. A new, young life was stirring in Khorasan at that moment; we can see this in, among other examples, Rudaki's "living joyfully" with his "black-eyed beauties," in Farrokhi's love-making, and in Manuchehr's cheerful roistering. All the extraordinariness of this renewal is felt by Ferdowsi, and the Shahnameh is the result of his reflecting on this happening in such a time and such a place, so that even in old age he says of the freshness of this springtime, this youthful passion, this high-flying rebelliousness:

> I have completed the story of Nushirvan
>   the world is old and my thoughts are young
> It's no surprise if my spirit is still sharp
>   that in old age it has become so fiery.

The unadorned simplicity of Ferdowsi's language can be gauged by comparing his passage on Mazanderan, before Kavus travels there, to the verses on the coming of spring which are so full of images and ornamentation in the often very appealing and charming elaborate *qasidehs* of his contemporaries that were written with a sophisticated literary rhetoric suitable to courtly poetry.

The force and influence of Ferdowsi's words derive not only from their noble simplicity, the strength of his imagery, and his poetic capabilities, but also from the complete truthfulness and humanity of his thought. Even so, "truthfulness" by itself without "honesty" is not enough to make words appeal to the heart. Ferdowsi has tested in his heart and soul what he says, and lived it. The uniqueness of his thought, speech, and deeds gives such simplicity of tone to his language that its "beauty" certainly speaks directly to a reader or listener. If we look at the picture of didactic verse in the past we shall realize the influence and effect of this tone more clearly. People looked to verse then not only as a means of teaching life's manners and customs, religion, ethics, compassion, manliness, and so forth, but even as a way not so much to teach as to pass on various kinds of knowledge. Didactic verse of this kind found a ready audience. Like an experienced peacemaker, in his *Golestan* and *Bustan* Sa'di provides a torch to light the way forward. Naser Khosrow is an honest, sympathetic teacher, but he is demanding and at times prone to anger. Even though he knows a great deal, in his *Masnavi* Rumi is fatherly and informal. Without any expectations, Sanai, Attar, and Nezami scatter their "Sufi wealth" before seekers after truth. Among all these, Khayyam takes flight in another world, beyond good and evil. But Ferdowsi's didactic language, which he inserts at the beginning and end of various episodes, or to refer to characters in the course of the narrative, or in their conversations with one another, registers astonishment at the turning of the heavens and the vicissitudes of time and destiny. Sometimes the poet also refers to himself. At all events this language has no feeling of imperatives about it, or of the commands a knowledgeable teacher gives to an ignorant student, and for this reason it is more readily accepted by a reader. He is like Hafez who, when he wishes to teach someone something or to pass on advice, doesn't exclude himself.[18] Because of this, Ferdowsi's "advice" can be more easily accepted than the straightforward sermonizing of Naser Khosrow, as when he says

> Do not blame the blue wheel of the heavens
> empty your head of this wind of astonishment
> Since you yourself make your own star evil
> don't expect a good star from the heavens

As in Iranian mythology, Ferdowsi's image of the world's vicissitudes is "ethical." However, the composer of the Shahnameh is not simply a thinker but also a poet, and even though he is not interested in displays of elaborate language, as a great poet his insight and sensitivity overflow with incomparable images concerning nature and its phenomena; the moon and sun, the break of day, battles and banquets, the limitlessness of man's will and the strength of death, the beauty of lovely women and the tumults of love, the give-and-take of battle and the joy of the victors, the generosity of the wealthy and the injustice of oppressors, the pitiful fate of those who suffer oppression, sorrow and joy and other emotions, as well as many other matters! How often the straightforward, unadorned language of the Shahnameh expresses itself in poetic images. For example, this is how morning breaks: the sun "like a body whose heart is filled with love" shows its face and leads its army across the sky; it pitches its tent of yellow brocade on the dark blue earth; it displays its crown and raises its banner into the sky, and so on in many other images. Images of night also come many times, the difference being that, unlike day, night has a shameful, passive atmosphere.[19] After the victory over the Khaghan of China, and the dispatching of a letter to Kay Khosrow, Rostam

> Made his way from that place to the army
> like dark tresses the two locks of night appeared
> They sat cheerfully with lutes and wine
> on one side were lutes and on the other flutes

They each went to his own rest
  clutching to his breast his heart's desire
When the sun with ornaments and yellow brocade
  overcame the mass of dark blue
At that moment from within the pavilion
  the sound of trumpets arose
Mighty Rostam prepared himself for battle
  and mounted his swift horse.

V3:247

Here we can clearly see that day is the time for work, effort, and battle, and night is the time for rest, pleasure, and sleep. In the poet's mind boldness, fearlessness, ripping aside obstructions are man's sphere, while privacy, calmness, and affection are woman's sphere and this is how the poet perceives the outer world's phenomena; it is how phenomena are seen from the inner perspective of an epic poet, and are represented in language. Rostam is "the sun at dawn" and the sun is a hero flourishing his bow in the high heavens. In epic, nature is the site of battles and banquets and the struggle between "deeds" and fate, not a place in which to sit beside a stream and contemplate life as it passes by.

Epic literature, as has already been said, is narrative, and what it narrates are matters concerning war and peace, friendship and enmity, love and the longing for revenge. And narrative, like our dual worldview—Ahura Mazda and Ahriman, good and evil, light and darkness—has a dual structure, constructed of face-to-face encounters, tension and action together, the making and unmaking of dualities; life and death, battles and banquets, or two tribes, two combatants, two partners together and separated; Iran and Turan, Rostam and Afrasyab, Zahhak and Feraydun, Afrasyab and Kavus, Piran and Gudarz, Zal and Rudabeh, Rostam and the White Demon, Sohrab and Rostam, Rostam and Ashkabus, Rostam and the Akvan Div, Bizhan and Manizheh, Bahram and Arezu, face-to-face combats, the two "Seven Trials" of Rostam and Esfandyar and the encounters of the twelve champions in each of which two combatants face off against each other, and other incidents, such as the proverbial battle between two brothers (Talkhand and Giv).

In the story of Rostam and Esfandyar, in which on the two days of combat each of them is the victor on one day, this dual structure can be seen more clearly: Pashutan and Zal are the wise advisors, one on each side; in opposition to Esfandyar whose brass body makes him invincible, the riddle-solving simorgh comes to Rostam's aid. The single combat between two warriors, each of whom has been tested by his "Seven Trials," and whose flyting before battle, like two equipoised pans of a balance, shows that in greatness, lineage, bravery of body and soul they are equal and worthy of one another. And in the end relentless death waits in ambush for each of them, for one without any delay, and for the other with a delay of one year. In the story of Seyavash the equivalent symmetries are both similar and dissimilar, and we see a more complex situation: Kavus and Afrasyab, Sudabeh and Seyavash, Sudabeh and Farangis, Seyavash and Garsivaz, Rostam and Afrasyab, and so on until the end of the Revenge for the Death of Seyavash at the battle when Sorkheh, Afrasyab's son, becomes the prisoner of Faramarz, Rostam's son. He brings the captured champion to his father:

> Mammoth-bodied Rostam looked at Sorkheh
> who was like a freestanding cypress in a meadow
> His chest like a lion's, his face like the spring
> (his hair's) musk shading his flower-like face
> He ordered that they take him to the desert
> with a dagger, sentries, and a dish
> They bound his arms with a lariat
> they laid his head on the earth as (if he were) a sheep
> They cut his head from his body as (had been done) with Seyavash
> and covered his body with a shroud
>
> V3:391

Sorkheh is a young man who is as handsome and innocent as Seyavash, a freestanding cypress with the strength of a lion and the youthfulness of spring, and "as with Seyavash" his head is severed from his body. In this incident it is Rostam who is eager to avenge Seyavash, since he, not Kavus, had brought him up. In the same way, the warp and weft of the story is woven and worked out on two sides (Iran and Turan), and the overall picture and the images appear as if on a tapestry. Although Fariborz is the son of Kavus and one of the army's leaders, nevertheless it is Rostam's son who lays hands on Afrasyab's son, and in the same way that the hands of Afrasyab and Garsivaz are not stained with Seyavash's blood, and Garsivaz gives his shining dagger to Gerui in order to kill Seyavash, so it is that here neither Rostam nor Faramarz kill Sorkheh, and Rostam's brother Zavareh (like Afrasyab's brother Garsivaz) hands the dagger to Sorkheh's killers.

Perhaps it is not irrelevant to mention that in this dual structure, in terms of the difference of individuals or at the least the opposition of body and soul and the world and the end of days, the worldview of the Abrahamic religions is here less apparent or insisted upon. This is because man's body is his celestial being (his soul) that has become worldly and bodily. There is no essential incompatibility or contrast between the world and heaven, and both are divine, despite the fact that, as in the monotheistic religions, the world is the way to the heavens.

In the heroic section of the Shahnameh this simple symmetry is the binding agent of a great many stories, and their dual nature is both unique and organic. I think the meaning is clear: the story is the "living" body made up of two dual and symmetrical bodies, like the two wings of the simorgh, and it is the poet's genius that endows it with flight. Of course this doesn't mean that the many and various incidents and stories in the Shahnameh should all have this same symmetrical design, or that the poet created them according to a preconceived pattern, but in general terms perhaps we can say that—just as God created us with two eyes, two ears, two arms, two hands, and two legs—Ferdowsi's aesthetic sense, consciously or unconsciously, found strength in this symmetrical opposition of good and evil, beauty and ugliness, not in an unchanging, monotonous fashion but with the elements complexly woven one with another. In many stories, due to a trick of fate or a man's actions, a startling event occurs that at a stroke changes the course and meaning of a narrative, in such a way that nothing remains as it was. I will briefly mention a few examples of when this occurs in the Shahnameh; that day on which all the lords and nobles are trembling for their lives because of Zahhak's extreme cruelty, suddenly "a harmless blacksmith" with a worthless scrap of leather hoisted on a spear stands up and shouts to them that they "are in the clutches of Ahriman," and the throne and good fortune of the snake-shouldered demon are at an end. Similarly, after Iraj is killed by his brothers, Feraydun, who does not know what has happened, has ordered a banquet with "wine and music and entertainers" and is waiting for his son's return. But instead of his son arriving, he is brought his son's head as a present, and the king is so devastated by this that he falls from his horse to the ground, and from that moment on the fate of the fratricides and their countries is set on a new course. Or when Rostam and Sohrab each learned who the other one is, when Seyavash passed unscathed through the fire and in the hope that all would be well entrusted his life to Afrasyab, when the arrow of tamarisk wood struck Esfandyar in the eye, when Rostam fell into Shaghad's pit and died, when Kavus fell from the heavens to the earth and did not die, or when Jamshid who had wished to be God was sawn in two . . . in all these moments, in the twinkling of an eye, a man comes face-to-face with himself in a new way, and with a world that is stranger than he knew. "This unpredictably turning heaven is like a juggler / who produces new outcomes with seventy hands."

The Shahnameh is divided into three eras, the mythological, legendary, and historical, and on this basis it includes three kinds of history. The book's stories, like the tensions and struggles that take place during this "history," have been combined in a symmetrical dual fashion. But truth is not twofold, and the ancient dualism of our traditional thought as it appears in the Shahnameh's stories disappears and changes into unity. Reality, and our understanding of it—that is, "truth"—does not admit of division and is both light and darkness together, as in the twilight of dawn; in every story, whenever these dual agencies are linked to man's nature and role and the turnings of fate, the incidents that occur in the fortunes and misfortunes of the poem's narratives appear in another form, as a singular entity. The stimulus for such "images," and their being made into a single "living" entity in this way, is due only to the poet's self-awareness, as it is in his language that this tense unity of reality replaces the formerly dual worldview.

The real world is not a place in which good and evil are separated; light and darkness are together, and this can clearly be seen in the masterly presentation of the life and death of Piran Viseh. Isn't this because we are drawing to the end of the "mixed" era? The courts of Kavus and Afrasyab are this "mixed" era; a man who is an idealist must either, like Feraydun, throw everything into confusion, or, like Seyavash, give his body to the flames, or, like Kay Khosrow, flee from it altogether. These individuals whose eyes are on the heavenly world are examples of the man of ideals, symbols of goodness and renewal. But given the ineffectiveness of their lives due to the inner and outer stresses and strains put upon them, even these "models of behavior" are not free of such pressures; how much more is this true of the other characters in the Shahnameh who have their place in reality and are thus "real." Afrasyab, who was a demon, a magician, and so on and so forth, wept in agony for his son and felt "that pain for which there is no medicine known to physicians" and did not know how to demonstrate the extent of his grief. We have no greater demon than "the lie," and no greater hero than Rostam, and no greater liar than this filicide, no matter how much the lie of this "support and prop of Iran" can be explained away by saying that had he not lied what else could he have done, as he would have been handing Iran over to Turan? There are few kings with Kavus's greatness and few people who are as wretched as he is. Out of love for his wife, who loves someone else, he gives his son—and what a son—over to be killed; and because of his son's death he does the same to his wife. He is wretched, ashamed, and cursed by everyone as his wife has her head cut off before his eyes. Who has ever seen a more worthless life, and a more abject king? Or a greater, more exalted army commander, and one who endures more agony, than Piran Viseh? I have cited these few examples to show that the characters in the Shahnameh are not composed of a single nature; each of them has his own history and character, his own deeds and behavior, and for all their heady flights and longings they are people living between the frontiers of fear and hope, sorrow and joy, capability and incapability, in a way that is quite contrary to most allegorical figures.

In Iranian literature's allegorical mystical, erotic, and didactic legends and stories there are many mystics and lovers who are examples of complete faith or complete love, but in another fashion. For example, in the midst of the profound and beautiful allegory of the birds' journey to seek the simorgh, and the final arrival of the thirty birds to the simorgh (meaning "thirty birds") which shows the oneness of seeker and sought, the story of Sheikh San'an does not take place in sober awareness of the world, but as a fantastic dream in the boundless spaces of theology.

In such stories the real world is a "sea of metaphor" and has no truth to it. Truth cannot be found in awareness and sobriety but in dreams. For this reason such a story begins with a dream and is propelled forward by other dreams. A dream is outside of the limits and constraints of time and place and whys and wherefores, and is a tale liberated from logic. In this "freedom" what happens is not due to a "poetic exaggeration" meant to arouse the reader's wonder and admiration, it is simply a mystical negation of the reality of the lower world that is a snare of lasciviousness and sin, and of the self that cannot understand "the many things that happen along the way of love"; along such a way whatever one says is possible, and so whatever one desires is said. Since the characters in such stories have left this world behind, they have no part in the uneven vicissitudes of life, in pain and sorrow, kindness and anger, in eagerness for life and confrontation with the cul-de-sac of death, or in life's many other states of mind. They are not involved with the ugliness and beauty of life, but are cut from the whole cloth of idealism, and they feel none of life's irritations since their desire is to pass "like a drop of water from this sea of metaphor into the ocean of truth." These guides to the religion of heavenly love are faceless, as is the case with all impeccably religious figures, or they are like one another in all having one face.[20]

But things are quite different in the Shahnameh; neither the kings nor the heroes nor the battles nor the stories nor the narratives are of one kind. Jamshid, Salm and Tur, Kavus and Afrasyab and Goshtasp, Sohrab and Esfandyar are all greedy and overreaching, but each in his own way. The lies uttered by Sudabeh, Garsivaz, and Rostam (in his combat with Sohrab) and Kavus (in hiding the elixir that will cure all wounds) are not of one kind. Each instance of greed and each lie has its own substance and nature and is a thing unto itself. Each incident has its own arena, structure, and outcome, and is woven in a new specific way. The beauty, heroism, and goodness of Seyavash, Afrasyab's infatuation with him, the jealousy felt by Garsivaz (Afrasyab's brother and the commander of his army) towards the Iranian prince, his malicious machinations that lead to Afrasyab and Seyavash distrusting one another, are all so bound up with the enmity between the two countries that the story can only end in death. Each of the Shahnameh's major narratives is like a body, and its various incidents and sections that seem to be disconnected from one another are like the limbs that together form a living body; this is so in the stories of Rostam and Sohrab, Zal and Rudabeh, Rostam and Esfandyar, Bahram Chubin and Khosrow Parviz, and so on.

Despite the existence of various disparate factors in their make-up, the meta-historical truth of each of these "historical" stories is consistent and complete in itself. "History" is a thread that binds together these various well-knit narratives and brings them out of their scattered state into the book's multitudinous whole; in particular it is in the tales from the book's beginning up to the reign of Ardeshir dealing with major long-lived characters like Jamshid and Zahhak, Feraydun, Afrasyab, Rostam and Kay Khosrow that history is incarnated, since each of them is a "history" unto himself. After the mythological and heroic eras, during the Sasanid period, history takes on its own specific meaning. And so we can say that history appears in three guises in the book, each time with a different meaning and inner reality.

In the introductory comments to stories, and when major episodes come to an end, Ferdowsi draws attention to the lessons of a story, and to its ethical and spiritual implications. As soon as Seyavash is born, one who knows the secrets of fate sees from the child's horoscope the good and evil that he will suffer. In the case of Rostam and Sohrab, Rostam and Esfandyar, and the Sasanian kings Ardeshir and Yazdegerd, we know at the beginning of a narrative what its end will be. This is in contrast to the major western novelists; the author is not outside of the events he describes, so that only the characters within the narrative speak and the author is simply an "impartial" observer who gives shape to what he knows. At its core, our classical literature does not recognize this kind of separation between an anecdote or story and its writer or speaker, and is a stranger to such "impartial observation of reality." The author is within the story, and sometimes he pauses within the flow of the narrative and speaks in his own person. And the readers of these stories are aware of how the business of Sohrab and Seyavash, or Esfandyar and Forud, will end. In the past, when oral storytellers flourished, everyone knew that the night of the 21st of Ramadan was the night of "the killing of Sohrab," the same night that commemorated the death of the first of the Shi'i imams. And each night the storyteller and his listeners came one step closer to the painful end. This means that in stories that everyone knew there was no place for a gradual unfolding of events, for suspense, for the unraveling of a plot's complications; according to his capacity, everyone made the story his own.

If for example the reader of a novel is like someone traveling along a road, so that from moment to moment he has a new perspective on the mountains and valleys and plains of the human soul, in such a novel the reader has from the beginning a mirror before his own soul, in which he sees himself. A more detailed account, one that is beyond the capacity of this book, is required, but we can briefly say that it is relatively recently that, historically, mankind has become preoccupied on the one hand with "individuality" (the rights of the individual, and personal freedoms), and on the other with history as the journey of mankind's transformation and development. Apart from its other characteristics, the classical bourgeois novel is one of the expressions of the experience of individual life within society, as it develops in time and within the arena of history. However, in our classical literature man is the "microcosm" within the "macrocosm," and both are constructed and realized as complete in themselves, so that man's perfection is "vertical," concerned with the celestial spiritual world above; it does not occur in the passage of time "horizontally," in history and society. In this cultural arena, the flight of the soul, like that of the simorgh, is towards the heavens, and if there is to be any grievance or complaint it is of "the turning of the heavens," or sometimes of "the shadow of God," since right and wrong have their place between heaven and earth, and finally of "He who is, and apart from whom nothing exists." The stories of the Shahnameh are a mirror showing the heights and depths of man's body and soul; the harm and destructiveness that come from overweening greed (Salm and Tur, Sohrab, Esfandyar), lies (Sudabeh), pride coming before a fall (Jamshid, Kavus, Goshtasp), demonic and godly sovereignty (Zahhak and Feraydun), fidelity to one's promises to God, oneself and the world (Seyavash), the battle between justice and injustice (Kay Khosrow and Afrasyab), the desire for fame at the expense of one's life, the victory of vigilant man over brute nature (Rostam's and Esfandyar's "Seven Trials"), and many similar motifs. In contrast with the realist novel, these are stories of an idealism that teaches the "eternal wisdom" of an ancient culture and civilization from the days of the Sasanids and their predecessors, numerous straightforward and unadorned examples of which can be found in the speeches of Bozorgmehr, the royal counselors, and Anushirvan, and in the homilies given during kings' coronations. The "idealism" of these stories is not something divorced from reality. Isn't the possession of idealism one of the characteristics of being human? Can one be human and without any kind of idealism? And so the stories of the Shahnameh are finally realistic, but with a "realism" that has been pressed like wine, and filtered through a cultural ideal (wisdom), not a realism that is the direct unmediated echo and reflection of whatever appears in the physical world. In the Shahnameh, myths and legends, the mysterious powers of the heavens, become real, so that what is by nature spiritual descends into the natural world. For example, in the story of Rostam and Esfandyar, the legends of the simorgh and of a brazen impregnable body serve to indicate existential and spiritual realities—Rostam's freedom, Esfandyar's religious allegiances, and the disastrous linking of religion and the state—finally resulting in war and death. In "Rostam and Sohrab," we find human realities—the enmity between two countries, greed and lies—in the form of a story. We know that the myth of Feraydun is concerned with the creation of countries and the division of the world, the coming into being of history and geography. The "real" truth of the story of Zahhak and Kaveh is obvious. There is no need to give other instances; for example, the legendary quality of the passing of both Seyavash and Kay Khosrow, and so on. I think these few indications are enough for us to see how reality, in the realm of the imagination, is something greater than what is quotidian and trivial, and that it presents a more complete truth. And we can say that in this sense the Shahnameh is realistic, even in spite of the poet, since for all the love he has for Iran and Iranians the "end of the Shahnameh" comes with Rostam Farrokhzad, and the Arab victory.

But the stories in the historical section of the Shahnameh are of a different kind. In this section we are dealing with "real," not "ideal," history, and with an unmediated historical representation, not one reflected in the mirror of myth and legend. This means that the stories in this section are perceived and presented in a different way; they appear as reality itself, without any mediator, either celestial or ideal. They take place in the arena of quotidian life, as we see in the account of Ardeshir's deeds and his rise to the throne, in the stories that deal with the battles and banquets and journeys and hunting expeditions of Bahram Gur, or in the story of the appearance of chess, the importation of *Kalileh and Demneh*, or the end of the account of the life of Bahram Chubin, which is precisely the opposite of that of the legend of Sheikh San'an as it is constructed by stringing together realistic adventures one after another—his battle with the Turkish chieftain, his conversations with Saveh Shah and Parmoudeh, Bahram's dream, the magical turn his fortunes take, the turning of fate, the greatness of friends and enemies, wisdom and justice, his foolish king's injustice and the present he sends his victorious general (cotton and a black spindle suitable for an old woman who keeps to her house), Bahram's disillusionment with his king, his chieftains' advice and Gordieh's heartfelt outburst, the similarity of the advice his sister gives Bahram to the advice Katayun gives Esfandyar, Bahram's rebellion and his alliance with the enemy, his striking coins in the name of the king's son (Khosrow), the father's suspicion of his son and his intention to kill him, Khosrow's becoming aware of this and his flight, his alliance with army commanders and soldiers, Hormozd's attempt to solve the crisis, the rebellion of the nobility, the blinding of the king and so on until the victory of Khosrow Parviz and the death of the general Yaghi . . . ;[21] these are all shining examples of narrative storytelling skill, a veritable deluge of Sasanid literary and didactic lore, presented in the poet's incomparable language.

The life-giving soul of the Shahnameh's narratives, in all its facets, even that of erotic love, is action. Action is the stuff of epic, the blood flowing in its veins, and if it were absent each of the battles and banquets would be lifeless and silent. This is clear in the battles themselves; each story is driven forward, step by step, by the heroes' efforts and deeds: a demon deceived a capricious king with his description of Mazanderan's eternal spring. When Kavus heard his words, "His heart decided on battle / He would lead his army to Mazanderan" (V2:5). The more advice this foolish king is given the less he listens; he goes, with the result that he is defeated, imprisoned, and rendered blind. Rostam, who is a man of great deeds and momentous undertakings, hurries to help him, and in order to reach the king and his captive army, chooses the dangerous path of his seven trials.[22] In the world of epic, the timid and the courageous are defined and known by their actions, and what happens in the Seven Trials of Rostam or Esfandyar—whether it be snow and the desert, Rakhsh and the simorgh, a dragon, or a wolf and a sorceress—shows that the world and man are in action, so that the story can begin and proceed to its end. The image of action is apparent in every epic narrative, even in the deeds of lovers. In the Shahnameh delicacy of feeling (sentiment and affection) appears in the flow of "outward" narrative through the effects of action. The love story of Bizhan and Manizheh begins with Bizhan's boar hunt and his heroism, the outdoor banquet of Manizheh, and their seeing one another. Then there is the soporific drug, the taking of Bizhan to Turan, his imprisonment in a well, news of this reaching Iran, the enmity between the two countries, the king's request to Rostam, the army's expedition to Turan, the officers' crossing the border dressed as merchants, Manizheh's cooperation and her delivery of Rostam's message, the warriors' night attack and the battle between Rostam and Afrasyab, and finally the Iranians' victory and the lovers' happiness; all this happens in an eventful love-story, the warp and weft of which are woven by heroic actions. In the story of Zal and Rudabeh, and the brief love encounter between Rostam and Tahmineh, again it is clearly "action" that moves the narratives forward. What is especially notable is that—contrary to the cultural and literary traditions of Persian literature—in many of the events of these love stories it is the women of the Shahnameh who take the first step, and are much more bold than are the men. In the impatience of her love for Zal, Rudabeh opens her heart to the servants who are intimate with her and says,

I am a lover like a stormy sea
    From which waves rise up to heaven

My bright heart is full of Sam's son
In dreams the thought of him never leaves me
Where shame should be there is only love for him
Night and day I think of his face

v1:188

And she adds that they should think of some way to help her, to free "my heart and soul from suffering." They tease her and say that there is no lovelier young woman than her from China to India, and how can such a noble young woman as she is give her heart to a man who was born looking like an old man, and reared in the mountains by a bird? When Rudabeh heard what they had to say, "She was angry and frowned, and shouted: 'I don't want the Faghfur of China or the Emperor of Rome,

"'Zal, Sam's son, is worthy of me
with his lion-like arm, his stature and shoulders
Whether you call him old or young
He is the man I desire, body and soul'".

v1:189

Rudabeh does not sit sighing in purdah hoping that someday her luck will change; she sets things in motion and asks her maids who are her confidantes to help her.

Here is another example of the way that "action" is portrayed in amorous adventures; one day when Bahram Gur was out hunting he heard that a wealthy, hospitable jeweler called "Mahyar" had a daughter called Arezu who was a good singer and musician. Hoping to enjoy some music and singing, Bahram set off for the man's house. After welcoming him, the owner of the house said, "May this be an auspicious night for you; I am ready to sacrifice body and soul for a guest such as yourself" (B7:350). He had a meal prepared, and after dinner was over a pretty serving girl brought a tray and ewer and they washed their hands, and then "red wine, a goblet, roses and fenugreek" were brought in so that "they could refresh their weary souls." The host drinks first and then they rinse the goblet with musk and rosewater and hand it to the guest (B7:351).[23] Bahram, who had introduced himself as a cavalry officer called Goshasp, said, "I've come here to hear some harp music, and I'm keen to do so." The father says,

"There is a wine-server here who plays the harp
She is a singer and a fine performer."
He said to the slender cypress, "Bring the harp,
Come arrayed in your best clothes before Goshasp."

And Arezu addresses the "cavalry officer Goshasp,"

She said to Bahram, "O noble cavalry officer
You resemble a prince in every way
Please understand that this house is here for your enjoyment
My father is the host and your treasurer
May the dark nights be auspicious for you
And your head be raised above the rain clouds

B7:352

And then after praising her father she sings a song for their guest with the beautiful innocence of a young woman who has been smitten at the sight of this tall, splendid man, this young warrior, and she ends by singing

"You are such a man as no man has ever seen
Or heard of on the day of battle
May Arezu's body be the dust beneath your feet
May all her years be lived at your bidding"
The song and her harp
Her appearance and stature and manner
Affected the king in such a way
That you would say his heart was a treasury in tumult

B7:353

Each of them was smitten by the other and the king asked the girl's father for her hand. Instead of answering, the father first said to his daughter, "Look at him and see if you like him." And Arezu answered that she wanted no one but him, "Since it is life itself to sit with him for a moment." Mahyar then turned to Bahram and said, "Look at her carefully, and see whether she pleases you or not." And once he heard Bahram's answer, he asked his daughter again, "Do this man's character and what he says please you?" And his daughter who was growing impatient with her father's hesitations and delay

Said to him, "Yes he pleases me
    My heart and soul are his since I set eyes on him
Do it, and leave the rest to God,
    The heavens are not at war with Mahyar."

Her father said to her, "Now you are his wife, and you should understand that you must go with him" (B7:355). The two lovers were now together, as they desired, and the next day Mahyar realized that the cavalry officer Goshasp was none other than Bahram. Instead of hiding Arezu away from the gaze of strangers at the back of the house, Mahyar had boasted about his daughter's good qualities, and instead of finding a husband for her as he wished and sending her off to her new home, he first insisted on finding out what his daughter really wanted, and only when he was sure that she wanted this man heart and soul did he say, "Now you are companions and confidants of one another, as husband and wife."[24]

It's not out of place to add that it is not only in predicaments concerned with love and lovers that the women of the Shahnameh, such as Sindokht, show themselves to be more capable and courageous than men in their ability to overcome difficult crises. During Bahram Chubin's rebellion, when he has the naive idea of removing Hormozd from the throne and placing himself on it, his sister Gordieh disagrees with his army commanders and warns him that this desire for sovereignty will destroy both him and the noble reputation of his family.[25]

I have strayed a little from my topic, which is the representation of "action" in the structure of narratives concerned with battles and love, and the encounters between combatants and lovers. In contrast with the ghazal and lyric poetry, in which action is not outward but "inward" and takes place in the arena of the soul, in love narratives like the *Vis o Ramin* of Fakhr-aldin Asa'd Gorgani or Nezami's *Khosrow and Shirin*, the lovers' fate, and the warp and weft of their love, is inevitably woven in the outward world. From this point of view, such narrative poems—with all the differences they exhibit—can be considered as belonging to the broad category of "epic." But in mystical stories the incidents take place wholly in a world of symbolic meanings (as in Attar's *Manteq al-Tayr*) or in a visionary dream world (as in Kh'aju's *Homa-i o Homayun*).

In Mowlana's *Masnavi* and Sa'di's *Bustan*—as in the lengthy conversations between the counselors, priests, and kings of the Sasanid period in the Shahnameh—symbolic representations, or the direct speech of the poet or someone else, are there chiefly to explicate a story or incident, and to express its ethical and practical implications. In love narratives the speakers' words express the affections and desires of the lovers, and in a ghazal they are an account of the poets' inner state. We can take as an example the endless conversation between Khosrow and Shirin at the foot of the castle wall, and their longing, sorrow, anger, and reconciliation, while Khosrow is mounted on his horse Shabdiz and Shirin is on the castle roof. The ten sections of Vis's letter and Ramin's reply, and their accounts filled with hopes and complaints of one another's faithlessness, are a similar example. For the ghazal no more eloquent examples can be cited than those by Hafez and, especially, Sa'di, in which the variety of love's expressiveness, like the beauty of the language, is fully developed. In the love ghazal, in which lover and beloved are one in their love, there is no space left for a "conversation" between two participants:

> You came through the door and I left myself
>   You would say I left this world and entered another
> I listened for knowledge of my friend to come from the road,
>   The lord of knowledge came and I became without knowledge

I was like dew that lies before the sun
My love gave up the ghost and I reached the stars[26]

Every monologue or account of a lover's state concerns selflessness, since as has been said, "Lovers are those killed by the beloved / no voice comes from those who are killed"—and if for whatever reason, for example the beloved's faithlessness, that unity of love is absent and "a voice" is heard, it is as a complaint concerning the lover's amorousness and despair.

I said "I grieve because of you," he said "Your grief will end"
I said "Be as the moon to me," he said "If (the moon) rises"
I said "Learn to be faithful from those who truly love,"
he said, "The handsome rarely act like this."

In the ghazal, the words spoken between lover and beloved are naturally of various forms and kinds, and differ from the verbal back and forth of epic which is either absent or, if it is present, is of a different character. Although it is not possible, the poet sometimes wants there to be no "He said" before the answering "He said in return." We know that "Khamush" (silence), and all that this implies, was the pen-name of Mowlana in his *Divan-e Shams*, which is the be-all and end-all as an account of the vicissitudes of love. There, this master of the lover's distracted state transcribes Shams's language, and finds his own language incompetent and incomplete in his quest for "speech without speaking": "Enough, this is the tongue's speech that veils the heart and soul / Would that my heart were unaware of the tongue." But when this same poet comes to tell a tale he wants a mouth "as wide as the heavens" in order to express the pain and longing involved in lovers' separation and reunion. The *Masnavi* is a description of the daily fate of the soul separated from the beloved, replete with anecdotes and tales, stories and complaints, the words and deeds of Sufis, accounts of mystics' mental states, of signs and symbols and didactic moments, and for this reason it inevitably opens, from the very first line, with an account of the pain of love and the sorrow of separation. The *Divan-e Shams* is an overflowing of the soul's longing, and the *Masnavi* is an account of this soul's vicissitudes.

But to return to the Shahnameh. In epic, speech is at the service of action. And action rises like a wave to end in war, and reaches its limits in hand-to-hand combat in which the soul is at stake, because at this stage death too is a combatant who patiently waits and watches. This is why the combatants' preliminary verbal flyting rouses their blood to boiling point until they are ready for action, to risk their lives and fight to the death. Among many examples, we can cite that of the incomparable verbal give-and-take between Rostam on foot and the mounted Ashkabus.[27] Among many such verbal confrontations the haughty boasts of Rostam and Esfandyar are another splendid example, in which each of them praises himself and incites his opponent until they are ready to fight one another, since killing and being killed between two such warriors cannot be undertaken without preparation. It is speech that smooths the way that cannot be retraced to combat. Kaveh's speech, when he is exasperated by Zahhak's injustice and rips up the courtiers' document affirming Zahhak's justice and benevolence (V1:67), is an example of language that inevitably leads to action.

The meetings, and the conversations between the meetings' participants—Rostam and Sohrab, Zal and Rudabeh, Rostam and Kavus, young Kay Khosrow and old Afrasyab, Piran and Rostam, Piran and Gudarz, Giv and Kay Khosrow, Khosrow Parviz and Bahram Chubin, and so on . . . all these are among the finest and most moving sections of the Shahnameh; they are masterpieces of Persian literature, and their equal is to be found in the dramatic works of the great writers of world literature. In our classical literature, the space for "drama" is an empty one (except for Ta'zieh, and this only from the end of the Safavid period). But the conversations in these stories are our closest approximation to dramatic literature, since the flow of events, and their development, depends fundamentally on these tense encounters between the characters involved, and the back and forth of their conversations.

In the Shahnameh, conversations between friends and enemies occur either in the midst of action, or, as with the auspicious meeting between Giv and Kay Khosrow or the ill-omened encounter of Bahram and Khosrow Parviz, they are a prelude to it. When Giv finds Kay Khosrow he is exhausted and despairing after seven years of searching. After the necessary preliminaries of conversation, they go without delay to Seyavashgerd, and then flee to Iran with Farangis. But the bitter taunts exchanged by Khosrow Parviz and Bahram Chubin (B9:19) are another matter. One of these two enemies is optimistically hoping for reconciliation, the other is angry and belligerent; he says, "A mountain will shatter at my cry / a courageous lion will flee." He has come to overthrow the king, and to seize the crown and throne.[28] Khosrow considers Bahram to be "Dark and deceived by demons, angry and ambitious," but he is afraid of how the business will end and thinks of a plan, so he makes a show of magnanimity and offers Bahram the command of his armies. But Bahram has taken command of his own army and risen in rebellion against the king; he has come to fight and cannot retreat and he is not going to be taken in by the king's trick. And so he can only answer:

I shall soon raise a gibbet here
    I'll bind your two arms with a lariat
I'll hang you from that deserved gibbet
    You shall see a bitter fate from me

B9:23

The conversation between the two of them includes mildness and anger; it overflows with insults and harshness, with contempt and sarcasm; it traverses depths and heights and uneven terrain; it leads the two speakers like two arrows released from a bowstring towards the final outcome, which is inevitable battle.

Evidence of the poet's skill in writing conversational exchanges is scattered throughout the book. Here, as a single example from the available harvest, we can refer to the meeting between Rostam and

Piran, two combatants who feel love for one another in their hearts, and who praise each other's greatness and prowess. The meeting begins with Rostam relaying Kay Khosrow's and Farangis's greetings to Piran:

Rostam said to him, O champion
    (I bring) greetings to you from the clear-minded sun
And from his mother, the daughter of Afrasyab
    Who always feels love towards you even in sleep

And in reply:

Piran said to him, O mammoth bodied
    May God's benediction be upon them
May God the provider bless you
    May the heavens turn as your seal commands
Thanks be to God, my refuge is Him,
    That I have seen you living here
Zavareh, Faramarz, the horseman Zal
    Who is a reminder of the ancient kings
Are they well, happy at heart, and honored?
    May the world never not be in need of them!
I shall tell you, if it is not irksome to you,
    How subjects complain of their rulers

V3:406

Where could we find a more noble meeting than this, with its greetings, and blessings, and hopes of good fortune; its gratitude towards God for the health of his opponent, and asking with chivalrous politeness after his people and his family, and "the subjects' complaint against their rulers"? And then there follows a description of the "sorrow and difficulty and pain" that he suffered on behalf of Seyavash, his broken heart and tears of blood at the turnings of fate! Can there be a kinder conversation, and this between two opponents? Without their wishing to, two friends find themselves forced into the position of enemies. They are friends because they are both chivalrous; they don't smother "the behavior due to an enemy" in dust and filth, they acknowledge one another's greatness and magnanimity, and are appropriately "just" to their enemy. This is chivalry, heroism, just dealing, and each desires justice for the other, even though circumstances and fate have cast them in the role of enemies. By the deeds they have done, Garsivaz and Afrasyab have shaped both Piran's fate and Rostam's, have embroiled Sudabeh, Kavus, and Seyavash in death, and have set two countries at one another's throats. Rostam's and Piran's fellow feeling comes from their own characters, from their nature and innate chivalrousness; their enmity comes from their relationship with the tribe and country to which each of them belongs. The enmity between their two countries and their roles as heroes inevitably brings about the sunset of friendship and the onset of darkness. Within the confines of a dangerous road, two just chivalrous men have come face to face. In terms of victory in battle, what Rostam must do is not difficult; the Turanians must either accept his terms or prepare themselves for war. But what Piran must do is difficult: "How can justice result from an unjust act?" The dead-end of fate gives him no way out; he can neither accept Kay Khosrow's message, go to Iran and so be saved, nor can he stay and see Turan destroyed "as Iran's warriors would wish."[29] This is a sickness with no cure, but Piran does not flinch, and he does all that he can do in order to delay a little "the day of reckoning." The Iranian equivalent to Piran, in his wisdom, chivalrousness, and magnanimity, is Gudarz. Piran is killed by his hand; they are the last of the dueling combatants of the "twelve champions." Before this happens, the Turanians have killed more than seventy of Gudarz's sons and family members; now with a broken arm and in hand-to-hand combat, the life of this minister and general of Turan's armies, this "pillar of warriors, and support of Afrasyab" comes to an end. Gudarz says to him:

Fate has turned its face away from you
    This is no time for fighting, don't seek for some way out of this,
Since your affairs are in this state, ask that your life be spared
    So that I shall take you alive to the king

Piran said to him, May this never happen
    May such an evil not come to me at the end (of my life)
That I should live on after this
    That I should think of asking to be spared
Since I was born into the world for death
    I am ready to die in combat with you
I have heard from great men that
    However happy you are in the world
Death is your end, there is no escaping it,
    Set on then, this is no place for idle talk

V4:129

Although Piran wounds Gudarz, in the end it is Piran who is killed. For all his goodness and high-mindedness he finds himself in the dead-end of an inauspicious fate; his life has passed in the unavailing effort to fashion a noble destiny for himself, but he is caught in the heavens' devious turnings, and his "fate" destroys all that he has done. This man's fate and his hopes for himself are incompatible with one another, and there is no cure for Piran's pain. If no language records them, such pains remain with the one who suffers, and in the end are forgotten with him. It is through the blessing of language that we experience in our souls the pain of this benevolent, clear-minded man, and become conscious of his humanity. Language, speech, is the river-bed of consciousness, or to put it another way, "this consciousness" flows in the river-bed of speech and so moves forward. If we linger in the conversations of Piran and Rostam, and especially in this speech, it is thanks to the greatness of the language, and the incomparable skill of the man who wields it.

In considering the conversations in the Shahnameh we can briefly indicate many moments when the characters in a narrative say something appropriate to themselves but which are not the poet's opinion, and are even the opposite of it; for example, we know Ferdowsi's opinion of Iran and Iranians, but in the tale of Bahram's journey to India, we hear from the king of that country, Shangal, that Iran is a desolate place whose inhabitants are two-faced liars, "When was a Persian heart ever faithful to its promise / When he says 'Yes' his thoughts are 'No'" (B7:436–37). But on the other hand, in the same story we see Bahram Gur who has gone to India in disguise using the name "Borzui," where he kills a rhinoceros and a dragon, and displays his skills in other ways. The Emperor of China becomes aware of this and sends a letter summoning "Borzui." Borzui's answer to the Emperor begins by saying that the emperor had begun his letter by referring to himself as the king of the world, whereas he (Borzui) recognized no one but the prince of Iran as king of kings, and that he is sovereign over all other kings. Borzui is his messenger and is in need of neither wealth nor gifts and he therefore excuses himself from visiting the emperor. He says that whatever he has done

> This was performed under the star of Bahram
> Who possess glory, a royal throne, and fame
> Besides, Iranians have such skills, there's no more to say,
> They don't think of a savage rhinoceros as a real opponent.
> B8:431

The first example was the opinion of an enemy concerning Iranians, and this one is an answer praising Iranians and their king, given to a foreign king by a heroic "messenger." Similarly in one place we read that, "The child of a servant is unfit (to rule) / even if his father was a king," and in another place we hear Ardeshir say, "We need a boy, whoever he's born from he will be acceptable / and people will say, "This is the son of a king" (B7:171). Judgments about different people and things, in particular about women, Sudabeh and Farangis and various others, are not of one kind. When Rostam wants to avenge the death of Seyavash, who was innocent, he drags Sudabeh, who is guilty, from Kavus's private apartments and kills her and says to the king:

> A man who is the leader of a community
> A shroud is better for him than obeying a woman

Seyavash was destroyed by a woman's words
An auspicious woman is one not born from her mother
V2:382

This is the opinion of Seyavash's grieving surrogate father concerning one woman, an opinion that at that moment under the pressure of great anger he applies to all women, and the poet indicates his despair in this way; but we have already talked about the nature of women in the Shahnameh, and it's not necessary to repeat that. Concerning the wife of another king (of India) the poet says, "She and her lineage were intelligent / skillful and knowledgeable, and mild in their conduct" (B8:217). In another place, and not in a story but in his own words, Ferdowsi has said what he thinks about women:

If it's a king you've seen or a subject
A pure-hearted God-fearing man
Know that there is no alternative to a spouse
For clothing and eating and somewhere to sleep
If she is noble and thoughtful
A woman is a treasure spread (before you)
Especially if she is tall
The black noose of her hair reaching down to her feet
Wise and sober, circumspect and modest,
Speaking well, with a soft voice.
B8:95

Ferdowsi's thoughts concerning women, and his behavior towards them, can best be seen in the short introduction to the story of Bizhan and Manizheh. On a long exhausting night, the poet is sleepless and restless; his friend, "kind, and tall as a cypress with her face like the moon," brings him "pomegranates, citrons, quinces, wine and a royal goblet," and says to him that if he can't sleep he should drink some wine while she tells him a story "Filled with wiles and love and deceit and war," on condition that after he has heard the tale he will versify it. She says, "I shall tell you the story and be grateful (if you versify it) / Now listen, my knowledgeable friend" (V3:306). This story about two lovers, the product of a friendship between two like-hearted companions who share a common language, is told by a woman who, like other women in the Shahnameh (Sindokht, Rudabeh, Tahmineh, Farangis, Katayun and Gordieh), has remained relatively unnoticed, while the forged, bogus line masquerading as a verse by Ferdowsi, "Woman and a dragon are both best (buried) in the earth / the pure world is better off without these two impurities" is endlessly repeated.

Each remark has its meaning only within the weave of words around it, not taken out of its context. This is self-evident, and to deny it renders the remark meaningless, or changes it to its opposite.[30]

This discussion is necessarily rather protracted. The Shahnameh is a great work, in a political sense as well as in others, and politics is an area that invites misunderstanding and, worse than that, bad faith. Misunderstandings and misconceptions concerning the Shahnameh have gone on from the time of Ferdowsi and his presentation of the poem to Sultan Mahmoud—and his death and the prejudicial behavior of the inhabitants of Tus who would not allow the poet's body to be buried in the Muslim graveyard there—until the present day when ignorant and ill-intentioned people have consciously or unconsciously said whatever they liked, especially concerning women and kingship in the book, and attached whatever meanings they wished to it.[31]

The Shahnameh is the epic of Iran's history and of the inner reality of this history. Considered as a work of literature, epic is concerned with outward events and narrative; it narrates adventures, occurrences, phenomena, stories, and anecdotes, in either verse or prose. In terms of its inner reality, the Shahnameh recreates history in the exploits and experiences of historical personages (mythical, legendary, "real") or in simple events, such as hunting and feasting, traveling to a country and bringing back a book or a trivial game, the bravery of two brothers. Ferdowsi is a great writer not only in the poem's masterly and most striking moments, but also in the presentation of minor events. The meeting of Bahram Gur and Arezu is an account of the encounter between the king and the singer at night, and it indicates the inner wishes both of them harbor, as well as the father's pride in his accomplished daughter. It is a simple narrative without any fabulous or surprising elements or the discovery of some previously unknown detail. But from the beginning and throughout the tale, this smooth and relatively uneventful narrative flows so pleasantly and has such charming language that the enchanted reader—along with the incomparable beauty of the account of the free magnanimity of the father and the freedom of the daughter—is carried along to the end.[32] As I have indicated, epic is a narrative art, and out of all the other narratives in the Shahnameh I have chosen this example so that it is clear what a masterly narrator Ferdowsi is even in a simple story; an alternative instance of the highest expression of the poet's artistic prowess and skill can be found in the letter the commander of the Iranian armies, Rostam-e Farrokhzad, writes to his brother, since this description of the disintegrating fortunes of the Iranians is an unparalleled example of narrative (and "political") poetry.

In studying and evaluating each of the stories, and the beginning, middle, and end of each of them, the poet's expressive art and many other notable features can be seen and appreciated in the way he presents the complicated skein of our existence and our connections with others and with the world in which we live, as well as in the depiction of fate and humankind and the outward expression of the participants' inner conflicts. But so far as concerns the manner in which he composed his stories, and the way in which he worked on them throughout the long years of composition, we know very little. Only in a few lines in the introduction to the story of Seyavash can we perhaps find some hint on the subject, where Ferdowsi says:

Now O speaker whose mind is alert
    Compose a marvelous story
When speech is equal to wisdom
    The poet's soul will be at peace

For a person whose thoughts are not happy
 His ideas are adversely affected by that unhappiness
He crucifies himself
 He is disgraced before the wise
But no one sees his own faults
 You see your character as clear and bright
But if it is right that (what you make) is to come to something
 Perfect it and show it to the knowledgeable
If the knowledgeable are pleased by it, it is pleasing
 It is seen like water flowing in your channel
Now return to the words of the knowledgeable
 See what the poet says.

V2:201

However much wise language is a comfort to the soul, boasting about one's own foolish thoughts and thinking one's faults are virtues is a recipe for making a shameful exhibition of oneself. The important point here is that he says, "If it is right that it come to something"; if it is right that the work (here, writing the story of Seyavash) be undertaken, or to put it another way that the right to accomplish this work is recognized, the work should be written and then shown to those who are knowledgeable; if it pleases them, "the singer's soul will be at peace" and clear water will flow like tears in the channel of his soul. But if it isn't right, seeing the faults in one's own work is not easy and the poet's language will falter and stumble.

Wherever you are with your mind's thoughts
 Compose your language, without others near
If your thoughts are accompanied by effort
 All your days will increase

B7:205

We cannot be sure but, as we have seen, hints can be found in the Shahnameh itself that during those long years Ferdowsi perhaps regarded his work with exactly this self-awareness, thoughtfully and clearly weighing it and testing it, guarding himself against deception and self-importance. He both praised Daqiqi and took him as his guide, and considered his verses to be "weak, feeble, and unsuitable," taking note of what was both good and bad in his work (V5:176). He did exactly the same with his own work, and said that it contained five hundred inferior verses. In the historical portion of the poem he saw how lengthy some of the narratives were, and he didn't hide his weariness in composing them. This man who considered wisdom to be the first and greatest of God's blessings, and knowledge to be a jewel, warned himself as a wise man does that ignorance is limitless, and that he should not boast of his knowledge:

Do not for a moment cease from striving
    Do not abandon knowledge, speculating in your heart,
As when you say, I have acted with wisdom
    I have learned all that is necessary for me to know
Since life plays many games
    And as a teacher leads you forward

B8:146

Life is an unforgiving teacher and Ferdowsi had no doubts about how it acted and the games it played; he well knew that man is limited in his body and his soul and that his perfection lies in striving to go forward along the way of wisdom, not in fighting against life's circumstances. But then lack of wisdom, and as a result ignorance and incompetence, are always waiting in ambush.[33] For this reason I think that because of his concern for perfection he passes language through the sieve of assessment and reflection, in the hope that perfection of thought in language and language in thought will, through the sorcery of words, be the result, exactly in the way that conjurers' ruses bewitch an audience and take them out of themselves. And if this is not the case what difference is there between poetry and any other kind of language?

But let us leave Ferdowsi's poetic style and habits of work and the little we know about them, and turn to what the poet and his poetry actually do and how this enables him to fly beyond the confines of the cage of his own time. Man is the conscious child of time and beyond the brief moment between two darknesses, that of time past and time to come, he sees the presence of death. It is this consciousness of nonexistence that drives him to seek an existence that is permanent, in another world beyond the reach of death. Man's life is brief, and the passage of time overtakes him, but whatever happens he still tries to transcend his own time.[34] In this flight from time's haste, Ferdowsi is faced with two connected threats, poverty and his age; God forbid that his life not be long enough, or if it is that poverty should keep him from composing his poem. At the beginning of the story of Rostam and Esfandyar, he says:

> Now good-tasting wine must be drunk
> Since from flowing wine comes the scent of musk
> The air is full of cries, the earth of confusion
> Fortunate is the man who is happy as he drinks
> Who has cash and sweetmeats and a goblet of wine
> Who is able to have a sheep slaughtered
> I do not have these things; lucky the man who has,
> May he be generous to the poor.
>
> V5:291

And again towards the end of the book he says

> If my income and expenditure had been equal
> Fate would have been like a brother to me
> Hail came this year like death
> Death would have been better for me than hail
> Firewood, wheat, and sheep
> The high heavens withheld all these
> Bring wine, since not many days are left to us
> Thus it is, until a man has no more days.
>
> V9:369

That such a man should wish for death because of a hailstorm! In order to cure this pain—and also so that such a large and costly book could be copied and distributed in a number of manuscripts—the Shahnameh was dedicated to Mahmoud.[35]

Both from the Shahnameh itself and from historical research, we now know that the composition of the book began before the reign of Mahmoud.[36] Ferdowsi was fifty-eight years old when Mahmoud in 387 (997 CE) came to power by killing his brother; in 389 (999 CE) he began his reign in Iran by driving out the last Samanid ruler. The first version of the Shahnameh was completed in 384 (994 CE), a few years before these two dates.[37]

At the time when I was fifty-eight years old
  I became weaker since my youth was over
I heard a great cry rise up from the world
  Saying thought has become keen, and the body without harm
O famous men and nobles
  Who has sought for an auspicious sign of Feraydun?
Feraydun of the awakened heart is alive again
  The earth and time are slaves before him
From when my ears heard this cry
  I paid attention to this splendid sound
I put this book together in his name
  May his destiny be ever better than before . . .

V4:171

Here as a kind of footnote, briefly and in passing, I will refer to a particular point and then return to the other threat—the swift passage of time. The name of Mahmoud and a passage in praise of him were added to the second version of the Shahnameh. But given the sociopolitical structure of the time and the nature of kingship, as well as the poetry and literature of the period and the kind of poetic praise used in the composition of the *qasideh*, Ferdowsi's praise of Sultan Mahmoud is similar to various praise poems by Sa'di, in that—after an introductory passage in the name of the object of praise—it is accompanied by advice to rulers to be aware of the transience of status and worldly glory, and by encouragement to practice justice, so that one is honored and favorably remembered. I shall mention a couple of other instances on the same subject, briefly, so that we don't stray too far from the main argument.[38] In the homily at the opening of the account of the Ashkanian dynasty, after praise of the sultan and the commander of the armies, the poet mentions the just royal command that taxes should not be collected more than once a year. And then he immediately adds: "With this the pact of Anushirvan was renewed / All business was conducted in another way." Then he expresses the wish that because of this just act the Sultan should receive "heaven's cloak of honor," "which never grows old." What can this enduring gift be but the poet's speech, since "Speech remains as a remembrance in the world / Speech is better than royal jewels" (B7:114)? Ferdowsi considers the scope of the Ghaznavid king's (Mahmoud's) justice and nobility to be equivalent to that of a past just king (Anushirvan). The unjust are despised and reviled, and the just live renowned in men's memory. In an unstable world, speech remains stable; praise of the king and his justice, through the poet's praise and the royal jewel of his speech (which is precisely this book which is read and lauded by the wise), are not separate from one another; the king's justice and the poet's praise belong together (B7:114). I shall give one more example and leave it at that. In his "account of Kay Khosrow's great war," before turning to the battle itself, Ferdowsi introduces a passage on the "essence of speech." This passage is concerned with the transience of the world, the extraordinary turnings of fate that are so "filled with remorse and pain," and the end of man's labors, which is to depart and leave behind both trouble and treasure:

Consider the work of Kay Khosrow
    See as present the ancient business of the world
He sought revenge for his father from his grandfather
    With his sword, with plans and magic
He killed his grandfather, and he himself did not remain,
    The world did not confirm his charter either
This is the way of the fleeting world
    Try to stay far away from sorrow

V4:176

And Ferdowsi inserts this passage immediately after his lengthy praise of Sultan Mahmoud as "The lord of benevolence and the lord of treasure / The lord of the sword, of armor, and of sorrow" so that he will read it and know what it's saying. In its use of the example of Kay Khosrow's fate, the homily refers to a "you" that, because of the poetry and the way in which it is presented, can refer to anyone, to this great Sultan and also to a reader with no power at all.

But in the introductory passage in which the Shahnameh is dedicated to Mahmoud, after the praise of the Sultan no advice or ethical instruction is addressed to him. Contrary to the custom of the time, this introduction does not begin with praise of God, the Prophet, and the king. In this book praise of the Sultan comes after everything else; after the mention of God and praise of wisdom, the creation of the world, the creation of man, the creation of the sun and moon, praise of the Prophet, a description of the collecting of the materials for the book, the story of Daqiqi, the story of the kind friend, and praise of the petty king Mansur—only then does the Ghaznavid monarch Mahmoud appear, after an unimportant petty king! After such an introduction, which by itself could have been sufficient to have provoked Mahmoud's anger, this defenseless minor landowner living in a distant village perhaps knew well enough that this was the height of audacity, and so he wisely placed covert and overt advice to the Sultan in other parts of the poem.

Now I shall go back to the poet's other preoccupation, the threat of the relentless passage of time. Throughout the whole book, fear of "the turning of fate," of having to leave the world with his work unfinished, never lets go of the poet; he had before his eyes the untimely death of Daqiqi who "Departed, and this book remained unfinished / his fate which had been awake now slept." And so Ferdowsi took it upon himself "to take the book in hand."

I asked countless people
    I feared the turning of fate,

That if I would not be here long enough
I should entrust the work to someone else

V1:13

This is the fear that from the beginning to the end of all those long years never let go of the poet. In a passage on the old age of Anushirvan, close to his death, the poet once again considers his own situation:

I ask for time from the world's creator
That my heart should remain joyful for a while
For these stories and so many words
Have lasted many years and become old
From the time of the Kayanid kings until Yazdegerd
Through my speech may they be broadcast far and wide
Let me compose them, and make a faultless garden
Let me renew the tales of the great kings
So that my heart will not be troubled
When I must leave this fleeting world[39]

B8:304

The history of Iran is an ancient garden that the poet has reclaimed from weeds run wild, one that he has cultivated with royal language from the time of Kayumars to that of Yazdegerd; he wishes to stay alive so that in his wise words this garden will remain not only as a remembrance but as an act of "justice" to the ancient kings. I shall not here go over again what has already been said concerning the concepts of fame, justice, and creation as they are embodied in such splendid language. I merely mention that to make "alive" the fame of past kings is a worthy act, one that "is clothed in justice" (B8:304) since it praises the just, ennobles the world, and promotes wisdom and truth:

The unjust king brings to his own body
Nothing but the grave and curses
If your heart's trade is truth
Know then that you ennoble the world

If you wish for praise after death
    Wisdom must be your crown and helmet
Just as after the death of Anushirvan
    His justice lives again through my words

B9:154

Ferdowsi says the same thing about Ardeshir, except that here fate and the poet act together in preserving the memory of the just:

When the king had departed from the world
    There was no memory of him after death
I am the means by which his name lives again
    God forbid his reputation should be anything but good.

B7:178

When a king is a partner with justice
    Fate will not hide this after he has gone.

B7:179

Fate cannot hide the deeds of the just, and in celebrating the past the poet's words make their memory "young" again, and alive in our own time. And so after this "re-creation" of those who are gone, the poet is like a lord of time, one who can pass away from his own time without regret, and who dies without dying or being forgotten:

When this renowned book comes to an end
    The face of the land will be filled with talk of me
From that moment on I shall not die, I am alive,
    For I have scattered the seeds of speech
Whoever has intelligence, understanding, and faith
    Will praise me after my death
Since they threw to the winds my efforts
    These thirty-five (years) brought me no recompense
Now my life has almost reached eighty (years)
    My hope is gone in a moment on the wind

B9:382

These are the last lines of the poem, in which the poet, for all that he had hoped for "greatness, cash, and a crown" in his old age, boasts about himself and says: "Speech will remain as my memorial / Do not compare wealth and knowledge" (B8:283). In the Shahnameh, both history and "history's observer" know sadness in the end, but it is not a sadness without hope; Ferdowsi knows that from now on "he is not black earth / that the wind scatters on the wind." Something—and not a trivial thing—remains, something that is not only greater than wealth but greater than death. He puts this thought into words many times, that by reaching the end of his book and making the justice of the just live again, "From this moment on I shall not die I am alive, for I have scattered the seeds of speech," and speech endures, and this is our memorial.

How can someone preoccupied with the shortness of life and the incompleteness of his work hope to survive and not die? Without concerning ourselves with the concepts of finite and infinite time, it is as though Ferdowsi ends in two dimensions of time, the horizontal and the vertical, time that flows in the body and time that flows in the soul. His body is impermanent, his soul remains, and it is in speech that it does so. Perhaps this is the reason that he constructs it like a castle, so that he can live there as in a home:

Buildings fall into ruin
From rain and from the heat of the sun
With verse I have founded a high castle
That will not be harmed by wind or by rain
Lives will pass while this book remains
Whoever has wisdom will read it.

V4:173

This "architectural" metaphor for speech, and thinking of it as a place that is safe from the evils of fate, and this as a metaphor referring to the poet's language by which he has given himself life—what does this indicate? It is as if Ferdowsi has made a refuge for his soul within this "castle." Speech is the house of the poet's being; a house that is safe from the wind that passes like time, and the rain that pours down from heaven like destiny. The wind's harm and the rain's destructiveness bring oblivion, but after a thousand years the house of poetry has not been destroyed, nor has the house of God been forgotten. It is a house that stands firm against time and fate.

Notes

Time

1. Arthur Christensen, *Karnameh-ye Shahan dar ravayat-e iran bastan*, translated by Baqer Mirkhani and Bahman Sarkarati (Tabriz: Danehsgah-e, 1350 / 1971), 4.

2. Avesta, Yasht 19, verses 35–37.

3. Zend Avesta, the Second Fargard. Mehrdad Bahar, *Pazhuheshi dar Asatir-e Iran* [An inquiry into the mythology of Iran] (Tehran: Agah Publishing House, 1376 / 1997), 223. Also, Mahshid Mirfakhai, *Ravayet-e Pahlavi* [Pahlavi narratives] (Tehran: The Institute of Cultural Studies, 1367 / 1988), 43.

4. Vendidad, Fargard 11, 666.

5. Jalil Dustkhah, *Avesta, kohantarin sorudha va matnha-ye irani—gozaresh o pazuhesh* [Avesta, the oldest Iranian verses and texts—interpretations and investigations] (Tehran: Morvarid Publishing House, 1370 / 1991), 2:665–66. For the symbols of sovereignty, see Bahar, *Pazhuheshi dar Asatir-e Iran*, 228.

6. See Ebrahim Pourdavoud's translation of Yasht-ha (Tehran: 2nd printing, 1347 / 1968), 2:41. See also Mehrdad Bahar's translation of the Bondahesh (Tehran: Tus Publishing, 1369 / 1990), 81. In the chapter on Creation we shall return to this subject in more detail.

7. There can be no doubt that the cultures of Iran and India originally saw Yima (Jamshid) as the first man. Evidence of this is to be found in Yasht-ha 13–130 where Yima's name is placed at the head of the list of kings and heroes revered for their glory. The mythology of the Vedas, in which Yima is known as the first man, confirms this. Both peoples knew him as the first immortal human being and elevated him to virtual godhead. In Iran, where Yima was the first man, he also became the first king and ruled over a paradise free from all wants, and where sickness and death were unknown. In India Yima became the first man who dies, and so became the first man to enter the realm of the dead, where he became the king of the dead and the gatherer of their souls. Ehsan Yarshater, *The History of*

Iran from the Seleucids to the Fall of the Sasanids, translated by Hasan Anousheh (Tehran: Amir Kabir Publishing House, 1372 / 1993), 534.

8. Avesta Yasht-ha, translated by Jalil Dustkhah (Tehran: Morvarid, 1370 / 1991), 407.

9. Naturally other conceptions and narratives concerning this subject also exist in Iranian mythology. I have introduced this one here so that it may perhaps be useful in interpreting Jamshid's and Hallaj's claims to divinity, and Mowlana's "My Shams and My God." In the same way, I didn't want to go beyond the limits of our own myths and narratives to, for example, Hindu scriptures and figures like Arjuna in particular, which would involve going very far afield.

10. For the concept of "Iran" in the ancient world, see Gerhard Gnoli, *The Idea of Iran* (Rome: Roma Instituto Iran o Per Il Medio e Estremo Oriente, 1989).

11. Shahrokh Meskoob, *Soug-e Seyavash* (Tehran: Kharazmi, 1971), 33.

12. I have suggested a solution to this problem of two completely different interpretations of a single person in *Dar Moqadameh-i bar Rostam o Esfandyar*. Shahrokh Meskoob, *Moqadameh bar Rostam o Esfandyar* [Introduction to Rostam and Esfandyar] (Tehran: Entesharat-e Amir Kabir, 1342 / 1963).

13. Finally "for fifty seven years he is the ruler and chief priest." *Menoy i Khrad* [Divine wisdom], translated by Ahmad Tafazoli (Tehran: Tus Publishing House, 2nd printing, 1364 / 1985), 45, 73, and 94.

14. Bahar, Bondahesh, 35.

15. V5:420; see also Meskoob, *Moqadameh bar Rostam o Esfandyar*, 65.

16. R. C. Zaehner, *Zurvan, a Zoroastrian Dilemma*, translated by Teimur Qaderi as *Zurvan, Mo'ama-ye Zartoshtigari* (Tehran: Entesharat-e Fekr-e Ruz, 2nd printing, 1375 / 1996), 182.

17. Bahar, Bondahesh, 35.

18. See also Shahrokh Meskoob, *Chand goftar dar farhang-e iran* (Tehran: 1371 / 1992), 138.

19. Or as in two lines from the story of Rostam and Sohrab, V2:237, relegated to a footnote in the Khaleghi Motlaq edition:

Whenever you are thirsty for blood
  You stain that shining dagger
Fate will become thirsty for your blood
  The hairs on your body will become daggers.

20. In *Iran Nameh* 16, No. 4 (Fall 1998), I have written a little about ethics in the article "From the Avesta to the Shahnameh," which I shall not repeat here.

21. On this quality in these two figures, see *Soug-e seyavash*.

22. For a discussion of "name" and "shame," see Shahrokh Meskoob, *Ruz-ha dar rah* [Days on the journey] (Paris: Kavran, 1379 / 2000), entry for 25/12/92, or

Meskoob, "zeh madar hameh-ra zadeh-im" [We are all born from our mothers for death], *Iran Nameh* 7, No. 2 (Spring 1999).

23. "Espandarmaz (the earth) received some of Kayumars's seed, which remained in the earth for forty years. When forty years had passed a robust stalk like a column with fifteen leaves sprang up from the soil . . . Hormozd said to Mashi and Mashianeh, 'You are human beings, the father and mother of mortals; I have created you with the highest and clearest intelligence . . . think good thoughts, say good sayings, do good deeds, and do not follow the ways of demons.'" Bahar, Bondahesh, 81. Earth is the acceptor and nourisher of mankind; at fifteen (the fifteen leaves) puberty comes, and at forty a man reaches clear judgment.

24. The *Masnavi-ye Ma'navi* is also a narrative work that tells anecdotes and stories of various kinds, but in the case of mysticism (*'erfan*) "time" is in a completely different category; it takes place in another region and any discussion of it needs a separate inquiry. But where Mowlana in his *Masnavi-ye Ma'navi* says,

Heaven in its turning is the prisoner of our intelligence
Wine in its fermentation is the beggar of our enthusiasm
Wine becomes drunk from us, not we from it
The mold takes its being from us, not we from it
Time is not a foreign matter, but a personal truth with a separate origin.

25. For the lines from Sa'di, see the complete works compiled by the late Mohammad Ali Foroughi. Mohammad Ali Foroughi, *Kolliyat-e Sa'di* [The complete works of Sa'di], edited by Baha-aldin Khoramshahi (Tehran: Nahid Publishing House, 1375 / 1996).

Creation

1. In the same way, in this text, "world" and "universe" are equivalent to "the earth," with the meaning of "physical existence."

2. In the mythology of "Zurvan," because he intends to abandon sovereignty over the world to his first-born, a conception of both infinite space and infinite time (Zurvan) exists before the appearance of the world.

3. It seems that this "good-speech" of the Bondahesh should have a wider application, and not be confined simply to "good-speech" but also to the righteous ordering and customs of creation, as we have already seen. For the circumstances of the creation of Ahura Mazda, see Yasna, 16 and 31, section 11.

4. (1) Vahman, (2) Asha, (3) Shahrivar, (4) Armiti, (5) Haurvatat, (6) Amurdad.

5. (1) Good thought, (2) justice (the ordering of the world), (3) sovereignty (strength), (4) fortitude, (5) health, (6) immortality.

6. "Oh Mazda! When in the beginning you created our body and our belief, and bestowed on us wisdom from your own nature. . . ." Dustkhah, Avesta, Yasna 31, 11.

7. Bahar, Bondahesh, 36; this is an example of the interpolation of Zurvanite conceptions into the Bondahesh, which is a Mazdean text.

8. For the influence of Islamic philosophy and Esmaili beliefs on this opening section of the Shahnameh, see Abbas Zaryab Khoi, "A new look at the introduction to the Shahnameh," *Iran Nameh*, Special Issue on the Shahnameh, 10, No. 1, (Winter 1992). See also Jalal Khaleghi Motlagh, "A Commentary on the prologue to the *Shahnameh*," in *Notes on the Shahnameh* (New York: Bibliotheca Persica Press, 1380/ 2001.

9. The first number refers to the chapter, the second to the verse.

10. In the traditions of Mazdaism, many Zurvanite concepts found their way into the official religion of Iran under the Sasanids; an example of this can be seen in the *Menoy i Khrad*; see Qaderi's translation of the Zurvan in *Mo'ama-ye Zartoshtigari*.

11. It has the breath of a dragon, the claws of a lion
It gnaws at the person it brings down
Its voice is thunder, its strength is a rhinoceros's
In one hand it bears pain, in the other death
It makes the lovely cypress bow down,
The petals of jasmine turn yellow as amber
It turns the red-bud's blossom to saffron
It subjects saffron to innumerable pains
It is closed up with no chains, and swiftly
Its precious substance is ground to powder
How easily it captures our splendor
And brings the tall cypress low . . .
The happy heart that knew no sorrow becomes filled with pain
And so our days have lost their chivalry

B8:52

12. Ahura Mazda's other attributes include being "mighty, beyond the reach of enemies, invulnerable, the giver of rewards, guardian and healer," as well as much else. Dustkhah, Avesta, Hormozd Yasht, section 7 and sections 11, 12, 13, vol. 1, p. 272. Also Pourdavoud, Yasht-ha, 1:51.

13. V3:77. See also the splendid opening of "The Tale of Kamus-e Kashani" on the attributes of God; V3:105.

14. In the previous chapter, and in this speech by the astrologers:

Thus it appears from the stars' justice
That this bright water will flow

From this daughter of Mehrab and from this son of Sam
Say that a mighty and famous (son) shall be born
His life shall be long
It shall be all vigor, all strength and glory . . .
The eagle will not fly above his helmet
He will consider the world's great ones as contemptible
He will be stronger than all others
He will catch lions in the loop of his lariat
He will roast an onager over fire
He will make the air weep with his sword
He will be girt to help princes
A horseman that will be Iran's refuge.

V1:246

15. Seyavash says:

He who holds the world has written thus on the heavens
It is by His command that whatever happens is so

V2:308

Although I am innocent the turning heavens
Will have me destroyed at the hands of evil men
Manliness will give me no strength of purpose
There is no fighting with the Creator of the world.

But immediately the Creator's will becomes one with the "evil star" that has arisen from the heavens' turning, and he adds:

What did that most intelligent wise man say
"Do not strive manfully against an evil star."

V2:349

History

1. See Shahrokh Meskoob, *Hoviyat-e iran o zaban-e farsi* [Iranian identity and the Persian language] (Tehran: Farzan Ruz, 2nd printing, 1379 / 2001), 38 et seq., for a slightly more detailed account of the relationship between the Shahnameh and the Persian language and the connections between history and language.

2. G. Widengren, *Les Religions de l'Iran* (Paris: Payot, 1968), 174, 314.

3. Bahar, Bondahesh, 80–81. Lead, silver, iron, brass, glass, steel, and gold, like the head, blood, brain, legs, bone, fat, arms, and the soul, appeared with the passing of Kayumars.

4. Tafazoli, *Menoy i Khrad*, 42–43.

5. Zhaleh Amuzegar and Ahmad Tafazoli, *Astureh-ye zandegi-e zardosht* [Myths concerning the life of Zoroaster] (Tehran: Ketab-e sara-ye Babol, 1370 / 1991), 37–38.

6. Beside the classic work of Noldeke, and the mass of other works on this subject, two thoughtful and perceptive articles, one by Ehsan Yarshater and the other by Bahman Sarkarati, should be referred to, the former asking "Why are the Median and Achaemenid kings not mentioned in the Shahnameh?" and the latter discussing the mythical foundations of the national epic of Iran. See Ehsan Yarshater, "The Absence of Median and Chaemenian Kings in Iran's Traditional History," *Iran Nameh* 3, No. 2 (Winter 1985), 191–213; Bahman Sarkarati, "The Mythological Foundations of the National Persian Epics," in *Understanding the Shahnamehh: Collected Speeches of the First Scientific Conference of Shahnamehh* (Tehran: Shanameh Institute, 1978), 70–120. Yarshater distinguishes three kinds of heroic narrative in the compilation of the "Iranian national epic": the Kayanid, the champions belonging to the family of Zal and Rostam, and finally epics from the Ashkanian period. After explaining the political and cultural necessity during the Sasanian period for bringing together and arranging these three kinds of stories—mythical, heroic and historical—he demonstrates why there is no mention of the Median and Achaemenid kings in the Shahnameh. Foundation for the Shahnameh of Ferdowsi, *Shahnameh Shenasi* (1357 / 1978), 268 et seq.

After reviewing the informed opinions of various scholars involved in Iranian Studies concerning the fictional or reality-based history of the royal and heroic dynasties of Iran's national epic, Bahman Sarkarati reached the conclusion that "The national epic of Iran has been deliberately constructed in a specifically mythical manner . . . so that a particular meaning emerges . . . we see there a grouping together of concepts and notions taken from Iranian religions, and in the mythical section of the Shahnameh we encounter this same world-view expressed in another manner, that of epic narrative." Sarkarati sees this specific mythical structure from the beginning of the epic until the end of the reign of Kay Khosrow; see Sarkarati, "The Mythological Foundations of the National Persian Epics," 70 et seq.

7. Concerning the portrait of the youngest son in the mythologies of India and Europe, according to Georges Dumézil, and the interpretation of the three sons of Feraydun according to this view, refer to the article by Shahrokh Meskoob, "Feraydun-e Farrokh," *Chand Goftar dar Farhang-e Iran* [Observations on the culture of Iran] (Tehran: Zendehrud), 1371 / 1992).

8. For a clear and comprehensive discussion of the subject, see Dick Davis, *Epic and Sedition* (Washington, DC: Mage Publishers, 1992).

9. For a further account, see Meskoob, *Hoviyat-e irani o zaban-e farsi*, 5 et seq.

10. In order to understand the importance of combatants' ethical principles, reference should be made to, among other examples, the deeds and words of the twelve champions when they are engaged in single combat.

In only one place, the introduction to the story of Rostam and the seven warriors in Afrasyab's hunting grounds (V2:103), does Ferdowsi exhibit another view of the matter, when he says that for a hero seeking fame the way of wisdom and faith is separate from that of war, and that in battle one cannot avoid evil since "If you fight according to wisdom / you will not be considered a brave warrior."

11. Zabihollah Safa, *Hemaseh Sarai dar Iran* [Epic composition in Iran] (Tehran: Sepehri Publishing House, 3rd printing, 1352 / 1973), 44; see also Mojtaba Minovi, *Dastan-e Rostam o Sohrab*, edited by Mehdi Qarib and Mehdi Hedayat, *Mo'asesheh-ye motalle'at o tahqiqat-e farhangi* (Tehran: 1369), introduction on page "d."

12. Mohammad Amin Riahi, *Sarchashmeh-ha-ye ferdowsi shenasi* [Sources for Ferdowsi studies] (Tehran: Institute for Cultural Study and Research, 1372 / 1993), 173–74.

13. For a more extensive account of commentators' accounts of history, see, among others, Meskoob, *Hoviyat-e Iran o zaban-e farsi*, 71 et seq.

14. Concerning Kavus's journey into the heavens:

I have heard that Kavus went into the sky
    he ascended till he reached the angels
Another said that he went into the heavens
    to do battle with bow and arrow
All kinds of reports exist about this
    only one filled with wisdom knows its secret.

V2:97

In Khaleghi's commentary these lines are relegated to a footnote as being of doubtful authenticity. If this is the case it is clear that neither the poet—nor perhaps his copyist, in his place—considered his readers to be wise.

15. Since I have already discussed this subject elsewhere, in *Hoviyat-e Iran va zaban-e farsi*, I shall not repeat the same discussion here.

16. Shahrokh Meskoob, *Moqadamehi bar rostam o esfandyar* [An introduction to Rostam and Esfandyar] (Tehran: Amir Kabir Publishing House, 1st printing, 1342 / 1963), 6.

17. *Fars Nameh-ye Ebn Balkhi*, edited by Guy LeStrange and Reynold Nicholson (Cambridge: E. J. W. Gibb Memorial Trust, 2016), 41 and 45. In the same book, the battles between Esfandyar and Arjasp and between Rostam and Esfandyar are not recounted since their stories are well-known.

18. *Eskandar Nameh*, edited by Iraj Afshar (Tehran: 1964), 129, 201, 249.

19. Mohammad Hashem Asef, *Ketabha-ye jibi* (Tehran: 1352 / 1973).

20. Safa, *Hemaseh-sarai dar Iran.*

21. Ahmad Nezami 'Aruzi Samarqandi, *Chahar Maqaleh,* edited by Mohammad Qazvini (Tehran: 1368 / 1989).

22. *Tarikh-e Sistan* [The history of Sistan] edited by Malek al-Sho'ara Bahar (Tehran: Khavar, 1314 / 1935), 7.

Sovereignty

1. Ahura Mazda, Vahman, Asha, Shahrivar, Armiti, and Haurvatat.

2. For further information, and the naming of countries, refer to Pourdavoud, Yasht-ha, 1:431. See also Mehrdad Bahar, "Mythical Geography of the World in Pahlavi Literature." In *Az ostureh ta tarikh* [From mythology to history], edited by AbulQasem Esmailpour (Tehran: Cheshmeh Publishing House, 1377 / 1998), 13 et seq. Also, Henri Corbin, *Corps Spirituel et terre de résurrection* (Paris: Buchet-Chastel, 1979). Corbin suggests that the name of each country is related to the name of the leader that will hasten from that country to the aid of Saoshyant at the end of time. Also, Darmesteter, *Le Zend-Avesta* (Paris: Adrien-Maisonneuve, 1960), 2:547.

3. Tafazoli, *Menoy i Khrad*, 65. The stars "in charge of water," etc., are stars in which the origins of waters, vegetation, and animals are stored. Indications of the connections between the earth and the heavens are not rare, especially in the Yasht-ha, but there is not space to mention this other than briefly here.

4. Mohammad Amin Riahi, *Sarchashmeh-ha-ye ferdowsi shenasi* [Sources for Ferdowsi studies] (Tehran: Institute for Cultural Study and Research, 1372 / 1993), 175.

5. Mirfendereski, quoted in Zabiholla Safa, *Tarikh-e adabiyat dar iran* [The history of literature in Iran], vol. 5, part 1 (Tehran: 1362 / 1983), 312.

6. Mohammad Mehdi Malayeri, *Tarikh o farhang-e iran*, vol. 2, *Del-e iranshahr,* part 1 (Tehran: Tus Publishing House, 1375/1996), 44. Also, Seyed Hosein Nasr, *Nezar-e motafekran-e eslami dar barehiye tabi'at* (Tehran: Tehran University, 1342 / 1963), 205–6; for the views of the Akhvan-e Sales on the seven climes, see Nasr 122.

7. Pourdavoud Yasht-ha, 303.

8. Dustkhah, Avesta, Vendidad, Fargard 19, verse 13.

9. Dustkhah, Avesta, 1:7.

10. A god who is the defender of the world of animals. In the Avesta he is the guardian of flocks and herds. Bahar, *Pazhuheshi dar asatir-e iran*, 77.

11. For the various meanings of "Asha," see Widengren, *Les Religions de l'Iran*, and Dustkhah, Avesta, 2:919.

12. Dustkhah, Avesta, Yasna 29, section 1 et seq.

13. Pourdavoud, Yasht-ha, 2:315. See also Dustkhah, Avesta, 2:1017, and Bahar, *Pazhuheshi dar Asatir-e.*

14. Dustkhah, Avesta, Yasna 48, verse 5.

15. Is it not likely that this kind of introduction, that mentions the creation of the world and man, that refers to Daqiqi and the assembly of the book's materials, and that praises a dead unimportant ruler before the name of a powerful king like Sultan Mahmud, was one of the causes for Mahmud's being angry with the poet?

16. Bahram Gur's letter to Shangal, the king of India, begins as follows:

The letter began with calling down God's blessings
 On him who sought for blessing
For those things that He gives to his slave
 To servants and to crowned kings
There is no greater thing in the world than wisdom
 Illuminating both the common people and their rulers
Whoever rejoices in wisdom
 Will not give the world up to evil deeds

B7:412

17. Bahar, Bondahesh, 121.

18. Mirfakhai, *Ravayet-e Pahlavi*, 63.

19. This version of history is also present in the old introduction to the Shahnameh.

20. The absence of information about the Ashkanians in the Shahnameh and in histories of the era is considered to be a result of the Sasanids' enmity towards them. It is debatable whether this enmity is simply a matter of politics and the difference between ruler and ruled as is claimed, or has deeper roots that reach further back into history, to the Achaemenids and the struggle which perhaps went on between eastern and western Iran. According to the Avesta's culture and worldview, Mazdaism and Zoroaster came from one area, and the observances of Zurvanism and the rituals of Zoroastrian priests came from another. The sovereignty and government of the country's peripheral regions (Kiani/Parthian), according to the examples given in the Shahnameh—Jamshid and Feraydun—were derived from one area, while the Achaemenid empire, and the central sovereignty of the Sasanids, came from a different area.

The enmity between the "outer" Arians (eastern and north eastern) and those that were internal—that is, the enmity between Turan and central Iran—belongs to the heroic-epic section of the Shahnameh. During Bahram Chubin's revolt against Khosrow Parviz and their flyting when they meet face to face on the battlefield (B9:29), Bahram sees himself as a descendant of the Ashkanian and says, "Greatness belongs to the Ashkanians," while Khosrow considers that it belongs to the Sasanids since they are descended from the Kiani royal line. According to him the Ashkanians allied with Eskandar and the Greeks in order to seize Iran, until Ardeshir finally defeated them. The battle between Bahram and Khosrow seems to be an example of the enmity between Rey and Pars. It is also possible that in the Sasanid official history (the Khoda-i nameh) the image of both the Parthians and Medes was of peoples who came from further north than the Sasanids (and Achaemenids) so that the two were confused with one another, and that the Ashkanians, like the Medes, considered themselves as descendants of the people of Rey (B9:32).

21. This deceptive and ominous union of religion and government was also repeated during the Safavid era. The rule of a completely clerical government led to an expansion of Iran equivalent to that of the Sasanids, and in the end to the same old oppression and corruption.

22. See Mojtaba Minovi, *Nameh-ye Tansar* (Tehran, 1311 / 1932).

23. The first musician said to the king of kings
O Khosrow whose face is like the moon
You are as the moon in the heavens
Filling your royal chambers with joy
Lucky is she who sees your face at night
Lucky is she who inhales your hair's scent
Your narrow waist is like a lion's, your arm is sturdy,
The glory of your crown reaches to the clouds
Your face resembles pomegranate blossom
The heart rejoices at your kindness
Your heart is just like the sea, your counsel like a cloud
When you hunt, I see you hunt only lions
You split a hair with an arrow head
From your justice water turns to milk
The army that sees your bow
And your strong arm
The hearts and brains of its warriors split open
No matter how mighty an army it is

B7:344

24. After the coming of Islam a large part of this advice found its way into, for example, *Kalileh o Demneh*, the *Qabus nameh*, the *Siasat nameh*, *Kimia-ye Sa'adat*, the *Golestan* and the *Bustan*, and other Persian didactic works, as well as literary works in Arabic. For further information, see Ahmad Tafazoli, "Pahlavi Advice Literature in Texts from the Islamic Period." *In Tarikh-e adabiyat-e iran pish az islam*, edited by Zhaleh Amuzegar (Tehran: University of Tehran, 1376 / 1997), 202.

25. *Sowg-e Seyavash*, 177.

26. *Astva* = manifest, *Artah* = Asha, justice. Yasht-ha, Farvardin Yasht, section 142; also Widengren, *Les Religions de l'Iran*, 128. *Astut Arteh*, a word meaning a person who is the manifestation of divine justice. Also, Ebrahim Pourdavoud, *Soshyans, the Promise of Mazdeanism* (Bombay, 1967) 15.

27. See also Meskoob, *Moqadameh bar Rostam o Esfandyar*, first printing, 86.

28. V8:207. A similar incident occurs with the sealed casket from the emperor of Rome, the contents of which Bozorgmehr instinctively intuits and announces, so that the Romans are obliged to send tribute. V8:260.

29. *Dastanha-ye Bidpai*, translated by Mohammad ebn Abdollah Al-Bakhari, edited by Parviz Natal Khanlari and Mohammad Roshan (Tehran: Khavarazmi, 1361 / 1982), 48.

Speech

1. This creative word was named (as Dabhar) in Hebrew before the religions of Egypt and Mesopotamia knew of it; the Alexandrian translators of the Hellenistic period translated it as Logos. Jacques Duschesne-Guillemin, "Iran and Greece: Mythology of the Creation of the World in Ancient Times," translated by Mehdi Samsar, *Iranshenasi* 15, No. 1 (Spring 1382 / 2003).

2. New Testament, The Revelations of St. John the Divine, 21:5, 6.

3. The words of Naser Khosrow, a contemplative poet educated in the tradition of Irano-Islamic thought, may be cited as one example out of a thousand: "The existence of the world and all that is in it came into being by means of God's creation, which occurred when He spoke a word consisting of the two letters that make the word "Be" ("k-n"), which means that intellect first came into existence from this command, since the command is one with it, and it is through language, through these two letters, that the world and all that is in it came into being." *Jame' al Hekmatin*, edited and with an introduction in French and Persian by Henri Corbin, *Ganjineh-ye neveshteh-ha-ye irani*, (Tehran: Ketabkhaneh-ye Tahuri, 2nd printing, 1363 / 1984), 77.

4. Dustkhah, Avesta, 1:173. "Yata ahu vairyo" is the most important prayer of the Zoroastrian faith and is possessed of miraculous properties. Dustkhah, Avesta, 1:174.

5. Naser Khosrow, in another passage in which he is considering man as the summit of Creation, says: "If you imagine man as separated from the world, it becomes necessary that the world turns to nothing." *Vajeh-ye Din*, edited by Gholam Reza A'vani (Tehran: Anjoman-e Shahanshahi Falsafeh, 1356) / 1977), 66.

6. For further information on this, see Dustkhah, Avesta, Gathas Yasna, 46, 1 and 2; 33, 4 and 8; 31, 3; 33, 7 and 12.

7. Kay Khosrow sat and like Jamshid
    Lifted the world-revealing cup before the sun
He looked and saw all the seven climes
    And from there the course of the seven stars
Nothing good or bad remained hidden from him
    Everything was represented in the world-revealing cup
He looked and searched within the cup
    In one moment he saw all the world together.

Farid ud-Din Attar, *Elahi Nameh*, edited by Helmut Ritter (Tehran: Tus Publishing, 2nd printing, 1368 / 1989), 184. Kay Khosrow's world-revealing cup is also associated with Jamshid in Persian literature, as we shall see, and the two references are considered to refer to the same cup.

8. In Esmaili belief God's qualities are negative, and according to some, for example the late Zaryab Khoi [*Iran-nameh*, 10, No. 1, (Winter 1370 / 1991)], Ferdowsi was an Esmaili. We should also remember that Ferdowsi was from Khorasan and that Khorasan was an Esmaili center. But whether we are talking about seven or twelve imams, in Ferdowsi's thought God is such that He cannot be known.

9. O high heaven lifted above us
    What do you hold in store for my unhappy old age?
When I was young you exalted me
    Why in my old age have you made me wretched?
The lovely rose (of my face) turns yellow
    From their suffering the petals become thorns
In the garden the sweet cypress is bent double
    The loved lamp has become dark
The black mountain top is covered in snow
    The army sees its king as being at fault
Till now you were as a mother (to me)
    But blood must flow from the suffering you inflict
You have neither loyalty nor wisdom
    I am filled with suffering because of your black intentions
Would that you had never reared me
    Or that having reared me you did not torment me
When I pass from this darkness
    I shall tell my Judge of your cruelty.

B7:111

10. Like Satan! And this is the unforgiveable sin. Jamshid and Kavus in our own epic narratives, Prometheus and Faust in Western culture, and Mansur—who considered himself to be a mystical savior—are examples of this.

11. Although it is not a part of this comparison, one can also perhaps say that, despite all their differences, Mowlana is in the same sense a "lyric" poet in his *Divan-e Shams*, and in his *Masnavi* an "epic" poet.

12. When the turning of days is shortened (for them)
 speech remains a memory of those great men
(Saying) this one's nature was such and such, that one's was not
 there is blame for one, and for the other praise

B7:337

The great Feraydun was praised
 He died and his eternal name did not die
Speech stayed in the world as (his) memorial
 Speech is better than royal jewels

B7:114

13. I ask from the just sole God
 that I stay here in the world for a while
So that I may compose this book
 of the former kings in fine language
After this the body belongs to the earth
 the soul of the speaker is a mine of purity

V5:71

Or as he says elsewhere:

I ask from the shining Creator
 That I find some respite from passing time
So that I may leave behind in the world
 A narrative drawn from this account of the former kings
So that anyone who speaks justly
 Will remember me only with approbation

V2:380

14. Ahmad Nezami 'Aruzi Samarqandi, *Chahar Maqaleh*, edited by Mohammad Qazvini (Tehran: 1368 / 1989), 85.

15. Abul-Fazl Bayhaqi, *Tarikh-e Bayhaqi* [Bayhaqi's history]. From the 11th century CE.

16. I have referred elsewhere to the unity of form and content in the Shahnameh.

17. Unless this happens in weak lines, about which Ferdowsi himself says

If you come across a bad line / there are less than five hundred of them

B9:210

18. I am a lover, a libertine, a flirt, and I say so openly
so that you will know how many skills I am adorned with
I am ashamed of the stains on my Sufi cloak
that I have patched with a hundred kinds of trickery

19. Here only a few examples of the poetic images of dawn breaking have been given. Throughout the whole book there are many such images, and each time the break of dawn is presented in a different way. For various images of the sun and morning, as evidence of the brilliance of the poet's creative imagination, among other sources reference can be made to the Shahnameh edited by Khaleghi-Motlagh; in the 240 opening pages of volume 3 alone, the following instances can be found: 6, 7, 67, 99, 108–10, 123, 138, 140, 148, 156, 161, 165, 170, 176, and 189.

And as for night:

When the sun drew its dagger
dark night drew its skirts back from it
When the golden sun lifted its shield
dark night acknowledged its authority
It threw off its musk-colored cloak
the sun's face glowed like a ruby
V5:179 AND V5:209

20. Attar's *Tazkirat al-Auliya* [Memorials of the saints] begins by memorializing Imam Ja'far Sadeq, "That lord of the realm of the Prophet's family, that demonstrable proof of prophecy, that true agent, that world of inquiry, that fruit of saints' hearts, that beloved of the prophets, that transmitter of the words of Ali, that heir of the Prophet, that gnostic of love, al-Sadeq," and ends by memorializing Imam Mohammad Baqer, "That proof of the pious, that verification of the lords of martyrdom, that imam of the Prophet's companions, that chosen one of the grandchild of Ali, that lord of the inner and outer, Abu Ja'far Mohammad Baqer." It is worth noting that after recording the name of Imam Sadeq, Attar says that this book is concerned with "Auliya" (those who follow the mystic way), not prophets or the learned or members of the Prophet's family, " . . . but as a blessing we shall begin with Ja'far Sadeq . . . who was a member of the Prophet's family, about whose religious path much has been said, and there are many stories about him, and about whom we shall say a word or two, for they are all one, and if there is a description of one it applies to all of them; can you not see that they are all of his faith, which is the faith of the twelve Emams, since one is twelve and the twelve are one?"

Sheikh Fariduddin Attar, *Tazkirat al-Auliya* [Memorials of the saints], edited by Mirza Mohammad Khan Qazvini (Tehran: Markazi, 4th printing), 20.

We can also adduce as examples the beginning of the second and third entries: "That qebleh of the Prophet's companions, that strength of mourning for the righteous, that hidden sun, that breath of the divine, that sign of Canopus, Avis Qarni . . . That man nourished by prophecy, brought up to generosity, that ka'beh of deeds and knowledge, that compendium of chastity and forbearance, that surpassing excellence, that throne of religious tradition, Hasan Basri . . ." and so on throughout the *Auliya* until the end of the book. Attar, *Tazkirat al-Auliya,* 34 and 36.

21. These same incidents, abbreviated and in simple prose, are elegantly and forcefully set out in the *Tarikh-e Bal'ami* (Muhammad Bal'ami's translation of Tabari). A comparison of the two accounts of the narrative shows Ferdowsi's capability as a storyteller to great advantage.

22. In the fourth trial Rostam describes his cares as follows:

Rostam took up his lute
    He struck it and sang
Rostam is a wanderer, an unfortunate man,
    His share of happy days is small
Every site of warfare is his arena
    Deserts and mountains are his orchards
He fights with lions and dragons
    He finds no escape from demons and deserts
Wine and wine-cups, sweet-smelling flowers and convivial gatherings,
    Fate has not bestowed these things on him
He is always fighting with some sea-monster
    Or fighting with leopards.

V2:30

Like Rostam, in his fourth trial before he kills the sorceress, Esfandyar sings as follows:

He took up his lute and struck it
    And began to sing what was in his heart
He sang: Ill-fated Esfandyar
    Never sees wine and convivial gatherings
He sees nothing but lions and male dragons
    He finds no escape from the claws of misfortune.

V5:237

23. According to the customs associated with wine-drinking (as in Rudaki's "khomrieh" (a poem celebrating wine) and also in the *Tarikh-e Bayhaqi*), musicians sang, while the drinkers crowned themselves with chaplets of roses and little by

little began to drink and continued to do so until they were "happy and cheerful" (*Tarikh-e Bayhaqi* 378).

In another place, when Bahram asks how the world and the poor are getting on, the answer is that, throughout the earth

The poor rail against the king
    for their misfortunes
Since when powerful men drink
    they crown themselves with chaplets of roses
And drink wine to the sound of musicians' songs
    And don't consider us as of any account
The poor drink wine without music and roses
    And the powerful are ignorant of this

TARIKH-E BAYHAQI 451

24. This father's open-mindedness, and the daughter's freedom—like that of the character and behavior of other women in the Shahnameh—is not at all compatible with the manners and customs of Khorasan in the fourth century Hejri (tenth century CE). I think the reason for this must be sought first of all in the poet's opinions concerning women and their relationships with men, perhaps as a remnant of previous sociocultural traditions, or at the urging of some other stimulus that is unknown to me. And if this were not the case, during that same period, and in the same greater Khorasan, though a little beyond Tus, the brother of Rabe'eh Qozdari would not have killed his sister simply on suspicion of the "crime" of being in love [see Zabihollah Safa, *Tarikh-e adabiyat dar iran* (Tehran: Amir Kabir), 1:449]. The battle between Gord-Afarid and Sohrab, and their behavior towards one another, presents a similar case.

On the other hand, centuries after the Shahnameh was written, when the most transgressively open woman we know of in the Qajar era, Tahereh Qorat al-ayn, spoke at the Babi Conference in Badasht to men from behind a veil and the veil fell, an uproar ensued and many of her friends and male co-religionists fled so that they should not glimpse a woman whom they were not in religious terms supposed to observe (*Loqatnameh-yeh Dehkhoda*, under "Tahereh").

25. Do not let ambition rule over wisdom.
    Honorable men will not call you wise
Although I am a woman and much younger
    Than my brother I give a man's advice
Do not throw the deeds of our ancestors to the winds
    God forbid that you should recall my advice (when it's too late)
All the company was astonished at her
    The general bit his lip

He knew that what she said was true
    She followed none but the right course . . .
He said, This noble woman
    Who is eloquent, pure-hearted, and sagacious
You would say that her words are from a book
    And that she is greater in her knowledge than Jamasp.

B8:415

26. You left and took my heart and gave me over to grief
    Night and day I imagine you and don't know where you are
I said when you come I shall tell you of my heart's grief
    What shall I say, since my heart's grief will leave when you come

Kolliyat-e Sa'di, edited by Mohammad Ali Forughi, revised by Baha'al-din Khorramshahi (Tehran: Nahid Publishing, 1375 / 1996), 497, 546–47.

27. He shouted, O warrior tried in battle
    Your opponent has come, don't retreat
Kashani laughed, and was astonished
    He grasped his reins tightly and called out to him
Laughing, he said to him, What is your name?
    Who will weep over your bodiless head?
Rostam answered thus, Why do you ask
    For my name? You will never see what you hope for
My mother named me as "Your Death"
    Fate made me the hammer to smash your helmet
Kashani said to him, You've no horse
    You're heading for death in an instant
This was Rostam's answer to him
    O useless belligerent man,
Haven't you seen a fighter on foot
    Drag the heads of stubborn men beneath the stones?
In your land, do lions and leopards and crocodiles,
    All three of them, ride to war?

V3:183

28. When Bahram saw the king of king's face
    The color of his own face grew pale with anger
Then he said to his haughty companions
    This ugly son of a whore
Has risen from baseness and stupidity to be a man
    He's become powerful, and is ready for war.

B9:19

29. Piran said in his heart, This is an evil business
    To go from Turan to that prince
Besides, it would be a sinful act
    And it would not mitigate revenge for Seyavash
The nobles and Afrasyab's family
    Who have wealth and thrones, dignity and honor . . .
All of them would see it this way, this is not possible
    There is no course in the world in which this water can flow
I must work out my own solution
    I must take the dry road that lies ahead

V3:210

30. Sa'di's *qasideh* in praise of Shams al-din Mohammad Jovayni, *Saheb-e Divan*, is another clear example of this. The poem opens with the line, "Do not give your mind to any friend or to any country / for lands and seas are wide, and people are many . . ." but one cannot recall the forceful, inventive lines of the rest of the *qasideh* or the beautiful inner form of the poem and still conclude that the poet is saying one should not give one's heart to any friend or country.

31. From beginning to end, the Shahnameh, and especially Ferdowsi's regret at the victory of the Arabs, the fall of the Sasanids and the ruin of Iran, has never been welcome to the closed minds of the religiously prejudiced, and it still isn't. Hojat al-Islam Imam Mohammad Ghazali, the author of *Ahia-ye Olum-e Din* and a fellow townsman of Ferdowsi, declared Now-Ruz to be a Zoroastrian, heathen relic, and forbade the buying and selling of materials for its celebration, never mind stories about the leadership and rule of these "Zoroastrian heathens" and the history of their sovereignty and empire. In the Safavid era and subsequently, people were harping on this same old theme. In the early years of the most recent period we ourselves have been witness to this same opposition to Now-Ruz and the celebrations associated with it, like "Chahar-shanbeh suri." There has always been some kind of negative propaganda directed against the civilization and history of ancient Iran by a group of clerics, and the Shahnameh more than anything else has been the focus of their disgust, or at the least has been ignored and discounted by them. Despite the valuable research of the past one hundred years, some people have bestowed on the poet the honor of being an army general, and even today some others are trying to turn Hakim AbolQasem Ferdowsi into the cleric "Sheikh AbolQasem" or as the height of ignorance and spite to make him into "Mirza AbolQasem."

32. Similarly, there is another account of Bahram Gur becoming separated from a hunt and seeing Borzin and his daughters, Mah Afarid, Faranak, and Shambalid, a dancer, a musician, and other singers with beautiful voices who sing a charming song in praise of Bahram (B7:343).

33. In a meeting at Anushirvan's court, Bozorgmehr says:

To give to a knowledgeable man a mindful ear
The body must have provisions, thoughtfulness and awareness in the heart
Do not forget the speech you have heard
Since speech is a crown and a royal throne
Choose silence when you are among others
If you wish everyone to congratulate you
When you speak, say what you have learned
Learned so that you are burned within your vitals

B8:129, B8:140

34. In the Shahnameh the hero who is a man of action remains "alive" through his "fame," as the poet does through his language. I have referred to the hero in this sense before in "Shahnameh dar Tarikh," *Iran Nameh*, 20, No. 4 (Fall 2002), 397.

35. For clear, appropriate information on the nature of paper, the thickness of the handwriting, the bulkiness of the script, the exorbitant expense of producing a manuscript like the Shahnameh, see Riahi, *Sar chashmeh-ha-ye ferdowsi shenasi*, 53.

36. For twenty years I kept back my language
Seeking (to know) who was worthy of this trouble

V5:177

I was composing this book for some time
It remained hidden from the sun and Saturn and the moon
When the crown of language became the name of Mahmoud
His praise spread to the horizons

B8:275

I put together this book of ancient times
Chosen from the books of the truthful
So that in the days of my old age it would produce for me
Greatness, money and a crown
I did not see a generous king
Under an auspicious star, benevolent and shining
I was waiting to see who would appear
A generous man whose open-handedness needed no key

V4:171

37. Zabiholla Safa, *Tarikh-e adabiyat dar iran*, 1:471; see also Riahi, *Sarchashmeh-ha-ye ferdowsi shenasi*, 26–57.

38. For further information, see Riahi, *Sarchashmeh-ha-ye ferdowsi shenasi*, 33.

39. Or elsewhere:

If I remain alive in this fleeting world
  My soul and wisdom will be my guide
I shall bring this book of ancient matters to an end
  I myself shall remain in the world as a story

V5:439

Shahrokh Meskoob (1924–2005) was a translator, writer, scholar, and one of the most influential public intellectuals in Iran. He published translations of Sophocles's *Antigone* and *Oedipus Rex*, and Steinbeck's *Grapes of Wrath*. He is the author of *In the Alley of the Friend: On the Poetry of Hafez.*

Dick Davis is emeritus professor of Persian at Ohio State University.

LANGUAGE AND LITERACY SERIES

Teaching Beyond Spoken Words: Communicating With Bilingual Nonspeaking Children in the Classroom
LILLY PADÍA

Amplifying the Curriculum: Designing Quality Learning Opportunities for Multilingual Learners, 2nd Ed.
AIDA WALQUI, GEORGE C. BUNCH, & PEGGY MUELLER, EDS.

Reading, Writing, and Talk: Teaching for Equity and Justice in the Early Grades, 2nd Ed.
MARIANA SOUTO-MANNING, JESSICA MARTELL, & BENELLY ÁLVAREZ

When Teaching Writing Gets Tough: Challenges and Possibilities in Secondary Writing Instruction
ANNAMARY CONSALVO & ANN D. DAVID, EDS.

Equitable Literacy Instruction for Students in Poverty
DORIS WALKER-DALHOUSE & VICTORIA J. RISKO

Reading and Relevance, Reimagined: Celebrating the Literacy Lives of Young Men of Color
KATIE SCIURBA

Teaching With Arts-Infused Writing Pedagogies: Freedom Dreaming for Educational Justice
KELLY K. WISSMAN, ED.

A Cyclical Model of Literacy Learning: Expanding the Gradual Release of Responsibility
ADRIENNE MINNERY & ANTONY T. SMITH

Educating African Immigrant Youth: Schooling and Civic Engagement in K–12 Schools
VAUGHN W. M. WATSON, MICHELLE G. KNIGHT-MANUEL, & PATRIANN SMITH, EDS.

Pose, Wobble, Flow: A Liberatory Approach to Literacy Learning in All Classrooms, 2nd Ed.
ANTERO GARCIA & CINDY O'DONNELL-ALLEN

Teaching Climate Change to Children: Literacy Pedagogy That Cultivates Sustainable Futures
REBECCA WOODARD & KRISTINE M. SCHUTZ

Widening the Lens: Integrating Multiple Approaches to Support Adolescent Literacy
DEBORAH VRIEND VAN DUINEN & ERICA R. HAMILTON

Connecting Equity, Literacy, and Language: Pathways Toward Advocacy-Focused Teaching
ALTHIER M. LAZAR, KAITLIN K. MORAN, & SHOSHANNA EDWARDS-ALEXANDER

Writing Instruction for Success in College and in the Workplace
CHARLES A. MACARTHUR & ZOI A. PHILIPPAKOS

Black Immigrant Literacies: Intersections of Race, Language, and Culture in the Classroom
PATRIANN SMITH

Teens Choosing to Read: Fostering Social, Emotional, and Intellectual Growth Through Books
GAY IVEY & PETER JOHNSTON

Critical Encounters in Secondary English: Teaching Literary Theory to Adolescents, 4th Ed.
DEBORAH APPLEMAN

Reading With Purpose: Selecting and Using Children's Literature for Inquiry and Engagement
ERIKA THULIN DAWES, KATIE EGAN CUNNINGHAM, GRACE ENRIQUEZ, & MARY ANN CAPPIELLO

Core Practices for Teaching Multilingual Students: Humanizing Pedagogies for Equity
MEGAN MADIGAN PEERCY, JOHANNA M. TIGERT, & DAISY E. FREDRICKS

Bringing Sports Culture to the English Classroom: An Interest-Driven Approach to Literacy Instruction
LUKE RODESILER

Culturally Sustaining Literacy Pedagogies: Honoring Students' Heritages, Literacies, and Languages
SUSAN CHAMBERS CANTRELL, DORIS WALKER-DALHOUSE, & ALTHIER M. LAZAR, EDS.

Curating a Literacy Life: Student-Centered Learning With Digital Media
WILLIAM KIST

Understanding the Transnational Lives and Literacies of Immigrant Children
JUNGMIN KWON

The Administration and Supervision of Literacy Programs, 6th Ed.
SHELLEY B. WEPNER & DIANA J. QUATROCHE, EDS.

Writing the School House Blues: Literacy, Equity, and Belonging in a Child's Early Schooling
ANNE HAAS DYSON

Playing With Language: Improving Elementary Reading Through Metalinguistic Awareness
MARCY ZIPKE

Restorative Literacies: Creating a Community of Care in Schools
DEBORAH L. WOLTER

Compose Our World: Project-Based Learning in Secondary English Language Arts
ALISON G. BOARDMAN, ANTERO GARCIA, BRIDGET DALTON, & JOSEPH L. POLMAN

Digitally Supported Disciplinary Literacy for Diverse K–5 Classrooms
JAMIE COLWELL, AMY HUTCHISON, & LINDSAY WOODWARD

The Reading Turn-Around with Emergent Bilinguals: A Five-Part Framework for Powerful Teaching and Learning (Grades K–6)
AMANDA CLAUDIA WAGER, LANE W. CLARKE, & GRACE ENRIQUEZ

Race, Justice, and Activism in Literacy Instruction
VALERIE KINLOCH, TANJA BURKHARD, & CARLOTTA PENN, EDS.

continued

For volumes in the NCRLL Collection (edited by JoBeth Allen and Donna E. Alvermann), the Practitioners Bookshelf Series (edited by Celia Genishi and Donna E. Alvermann), and other titles in this series, please visit www.tcpress.com

Language and Literacy Series, *continued*

Letting Go of Literary Whiteness
CARLIN BORSHEIM-BLACK
& SOPHIA TATIANA SARIGIANIDES

The Vulnerable Heart of Literacy
ELIZABETH DUTRO

Arts Integration in Diverse K–5 Classrooms
LIANE BROUILLETTE

Translanguaging for Emergent Bilinguals
DANLING FU, XENIA HADJIOANNOU, & XIAODI ZHOU

Before Words
JUDITH T. LYSAKER

Seeing the Spectrum
ROBERT ROZEMA

A Think-Aloud Approach to Writing Assessment
SARAH W. BECK

"We've Been Doing It Your Way Long Enough"
JANICE BAINES, CARMEN TISDALE, & SUSI LONG

Summer Reading, 2nd Ed.
RICHARD L. ALLINGTON & ANNE MCGILL-FRANZEN, EDS.

Educating for Empathy
NICOLE MIRRA

Preparing English Learners for College and Career
MARÍA SANTOS ET AL.

Reading the Rainbow
CAITLIN L. RYAN & JILL M. HERMANN-WILMARTH

Social Justice Literacies in the English Classroom
ASHLEY S. BOYD

Remixing Multiliteracies
FRANK SERAFINI & ELISABETH GEE, EDS.

Culturally Sustaining Pedagogies
DJANGO PARIS & H. SAMY ALIM, EDS.

Assessing Writing, Teaching Writers
MARY ANN SMITH & SHERRY SEALE SWAIN

The Teacher-Writer
CHRISTINE M. DAWSON

Every Young Child a Reader
SHARAN A. GIBSON & BARBARA MOSS

"You Gotta BE the Book," 3rd Ed.
JEFFREY D. WILHELM

Personal Narrative, Revised
BRONWYN CLARE LAMAY

The Vocabulary Book, 2nd Ed.
MICHAEL F. GRAVES

Go Be a Writer!
CANDACE R. KUBY & TARA GUTSHALL RUCKER

Partnering with Immigrant Communities
GERALD CAMPANO ET AL.

Teaching Outside the Box but Inside the Standards
BOB FECHO ET AL., EDS.

Literacy Leadership in Changing Schools
SHELLEY B. WEPNER ET AL.

Literacy Theory as Practice
LARA J. HANDSFIELD

Teaching Transnational Youth
ALLISON SKERRETT

Uncommonly Good Ideas
SANDRA MURPHY & MARY ANN SMITH

WHAM! Teaching with Graphic Novels Across the Curriculum
WILLIAM G. BROZO ET AL.

Critical Literacy in the Early Childhood Classroom
CANDACE R. KUBY

Inspiring Dialogue
MARY M. JUZWIK ET AL.

Reading the Visual
FRANK SERAFINI

ReWRITING the Basics
ANNE HAAS DYSON

Writing Instruction That Works
ARTHUR N. APPLEBEE ET AL.

Critical Media Pedagogy
ERNEST MORRELL ET AL.

A Search Past Silence
DAVID E. KIRKLAND

Reading in a Participatory Culture
HENRY JENKINS ET AL., EDS.

Teaching Vocabulary to English Language Learners
MICHAEL F. GRAVES ET AL.

Bridging Literacy and Equity
ALTHIER M. LAZAR ET AL.

Reading Time
CATHERINE COMPTON-LILLY

Interrupting Hate
MOLLIE V. BLACKBURN

Playing Their Way into Literacies
KAREN E. WOHLWEND

Teaching Literacy for Love and Wisdom
JEFFREY D. WILHELM & BRUCE NOVAK

Urban Literacies
VALERIE KINLOCH, ED.

Envisioning Knowledge
JUDITH A. LANGER

Envisioning Literature, 2nd Ed.
JUDITH A. LANGER

Artifactual Literacies
KATE PAHL & JENNIFER ROWSELL

Change Is Gonna Come
PATRICIA A. EDWARDS ET AL.

Harlem on Our Minds
VALERIE KINLOCH

Children, Language, and Literacy
CELIA GENISHI & ANNE HAAS DYSON

Children's Language
JUDITH WELLS LINDFORS

Storytime
LAWRENCE R. SIPE